SUPER COOKERY

Potatoes &
Vegetables

p

This is a Parragon Publishing Book
This edition published in 2002

Parragon Publishing
Queen Street House
4 Queen Street
Bath BA1 1HE, UK

Copyright © Parragon 2000

ISBN: 0-75257-561-9

A copy of the CIP data for this book is available from the British Library, upon request.

Printed in China

Note
Cup measurements used in this book are for American cups. Tablespoons are assumed to be 15 ml. Unless otherwise stated, milk is assumed to be full fat, eggs are medium and pepper is freshly ground black pepper.

Contents

Introduction

Everybody, whether meat-eating, vegetarian, or vegan, should eat a good balance of nutritious and flavorsome foods in their diet. This book features 246 recipes, all of which show just how versatile and healthy cooking with vegetables can be.

Potatoes are one of the world's most popular vegetables and they have enormous nutritional value. They lend themselves to most culinary styles and are perhaps the most versatile staple food available in the world today. It is one of the most important crops cultivated for human consumption, with Russia, Poland, and Germany being the highest consumers, closely followed by Holland, Cyprus, and Ireland.

On average we eat 242 lb per head per annum, which is good news when you consider the nutritional properties of this best-loved tuber. The average 8 oz potato, containing 180 calories, has protein, starch for energy and fiber, as well as being a good source of vitamin C. Most of the vitamins are found just beneath the skin, so it is often suggested they are cooked in their skins and then peeled. If not cooked with fat, the potato even has a great role to play in the slimming diet.

However, the potato has not always been held in such high regard. It originated in South America and is thought to date back to as far as 3000 BC. First known as the *papa* and eaten by the Incas, the potato was unknown to the rest of the world until the sixteenth century, when Spanish conquistador Francisco Pizarro captured Peru, which was famed for its richness in minerals. The mineral trade brought many people to Peru, who, in turn, carried the potato to the rest of the world. The potato was known by many names, which reflected the different cooking methods used by the Indians. Even this far back in its history, the potato was eaten fresh in season, and dried by the Incas for use in the winter. Nowadays the storage life of potatoes and the different methods of preservation have increased its popularity in the food market.

The potato first arrived in Europe via Spain, and its name gradually changed from *papa* to *battata*. It became famous for both its nutritional and healing properties—the Italians believed it could heal a wound if the cooked flesh was rubbed into the infected area. One person who believed this was Pope Pious IV, who grew his own crop in Italy. It spread to Belgium, Germany, Switzerland, and France, but did not reach the British Isles until Frances Drake stopped in the New World and shared his cargo of potatoes with English colonists.

Later repatriated by Sir Walter Raleigh, the colonists brought the potato to Britain, where Raleigh grew the crop on his land. He was also responsible for taking the potato to Ireland, discovering that Irish soil was perfect for growing it. The Irish soon adopted the potato and it became a mainstay of their diet.

Today there are many varieties of potato, each being suitable for different cooking methods, be it roasting, boiling, steaming, baking, mashing, or frying. What makes it particularly versatile is the fact that it absorbs other flavours very readily and it has a consistency which lends itself to many uses.

CHOOSING AND USING POTATOES

Look for a firm, regular-shaped potato, either red or yellow in color, with a smooth, tight skin. Avoid potatoes which are turning green or sprouting, as the flavor will be bitter and they will have higher levels of natural toxicants called glycoalkaloids. Store potatoes in a cool, dark, dry place, as too much light turns them green.

The recipes that follow in this book open up a world of delightful dishes, from light salads and snacks to hearty main meals and beautiful bakes, many potato-based. In addition, there are many tempting recipes, from nourishing soups to healthy snacks, which make skilfull use of myriad other vegetables—all of these vegetable-based dishes are suitable for vegetarian cooking.

TYPES OF POTATO

There are about 3,000 known varieties of potato, but only about 100 of these are regularly grown. Of these, about 20 are found with ease on our greengrocers' and supermarket shelves. The following is a brief description of the most popular varieties and their uses, as a guide for the recipes in this book.

Charlotte New Potatoes

Craig Royal Red: *a main crop potato, ready in July, it is non-mealy and has a pink or red skin. A waxy potato, it is best for frying and boiling or using in salads.*

New Potatoes: *these generally have a white flesh and grow quickly. They are dug up in early summer and are best scraped and boiled to use in salads or eaten with melted butter.*

Cyprus New Potato: *found in late winter and spring, it is best simply scrubbed and boiled. Not a good mashing potato.*

Pentland Crown: *a thin-skinned, creamy white potato which is at its best in late winter. It has a mealy texture, making it ideal for mashing and baking.*

Francine

Desiree: *a high quality, pink-skinned mealy potato, good for baking, frying, boiling, and mashing.*

Pentland Hawk: *a firm, pale potato with pale yellow flesh, it is a general, all-purpose potato.*

Home Guard: *generally the first of the new potatoes. It blackens easily and collapses on cooking, so it is best boiled lightly in its skin.*

Pentland Squire: *a firm, white-fleshed potato, which is suitable for all methods of cooking.*

Jersey Royal: *a delicious new potato. It appears from May to October, but is at its peak in August. It has a flaky skin and firm yellow flesh.*

Pink Fir Apple: *this long, knobbly potato has pink flesh and a firm, waxy texture. Good in salads.*

Anya

King Edward: *a large potato which is creamy white, or sometimes yellow in color. Ideal for all cooking methods, it is a very popular variety.*

White Sweet Potato: *smaller than the yam, although interchangeable, it is yellow-fleshed with a drier texture. Best fried, boiled, or casseroled, it is ideal with spices.*

Maris Piper: *a medium-firm potato with creamy white flesh. It is good for boiling and frying.*

Yam: *a red sweet potato which is orange-fleshed. It is best mashed in cakes and soufflés or roasted.*

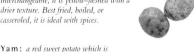

Pentland Squire

Many of the recipes in this book are designed to appeal to vegetarians and vegans, and they dispel the myth that all vegetarian food is brown, stodgy, and bland. When browsing through the recipes you will discover just how versatile, and flavorsome, cooking with vegetables can be.

Fresh produce is now brought from all over the world to give us a whole array of fresh fruit and vegetables with which to work. In addition, the use of spices, fresh herbs, and garlic makes for a very exciting and healthy diet.

Eating a balanced, nutritional diet is very important, and can be easily achieved by combining the recipes in this book when planning your meal to include protein, carbohydrate, vitamins, minerals, and some fats.

It is very important in any diet, and especially a vegetarian diet, that a good balance is achieved and sufficient protein is eaten.

The recipes in this book come from all over the world, but there are also traditional recipes such as Vegetable Toad-in-the-Hole, a family dish in which it is guaranteed you won't miss the meat. As a number of the potato-based dishes include meat, there is something for everyone here. It is the perfect way to introduce your family to a healthy and delicious diet.

When cooking the following recipes, feel free to substitute some ingredients to suit your specific diets, for example, use soya milk in place of cow's milk. Cooking with vegetables has progressed from nut cutlets to a colorful and imaginative way of eating. Go ahead and enjoy!

THE STORE-CUPBOARD

Flour

You will need to keep a selection of flour: selfraising and whole wheat are the most useful. You may also like to keep some rice flour and cornstarch for thickening sauces and to add to cakes, biscuits, and puddings. Buckwheat, garbanzo bean, and soya flours can also be bought. These are useful for combining with other flours to add different flavors and textures.

Grains

A good variety of grains is essential. For rice, choose from long-grain, basmati, Italian arborio, short-grain, and wild rice. Look out for fragrant Thai rice, jasmine rice, and combinations of different varieties to add color and texture to your dishes. When choosing your rice, remember that brown rice is a better source of vitamin B1 and fiber.

Other grains add variety to the diet. Try to include some barley millet, bulgur wheat, polenta, oats, semolina, sago, and tapioca.

Pasta

Pasta is so popular nowadays, and there are many types and shapes to choose from. Keep a good selection, such as basic lasagne sheets, tagliatelle, or fettuccine (flat ribbons) and spaghetti. For a change, sample some of the many fresh pastas now available. Better still, make your own—handrolling pasta can be very satisfying, and you can buy a special machine for rolling the dough and cutting certain shapes.

Legumes

Legumes are a valuable source of protein, vitamins, and minerals. Stock up on soya beans, navy beans, red kidney beans, cannellini beans, garbanzo beans, lentils, split peas, and butter beans. Buy dried legumes for soaking and cooking yourself, or canned varieties for speed and convenience.

Spices and herbs

A good selection of spices and herbs is important for adding variety to your cooking. There are some good spice mixtures available —try Cajun, Chinese five-spice, Indonesian piri-piri, and the different curry blends. Although spices will keep well, don't leave them in the cupboard for too long, as they may lose some of their strength. Buy small amounts as you need them. Fresh herbs are preferable to dried ones, but it is essential to have dried ones in stock as a useful back-up.

Chiles

These come both fresh and dried and in many colors. The "hotness" varies so use with caution. The seeds are hottest and are usually discarded. Chili powder should also be used sparingly. Check whether the powder is pure chili, or a chili seasoning, or blend, which should be milder.

Nuts and seeds

As well as adding protein, vitamins, and useful fats to the diet, nuts and seeds add important flavor and texture to vegetarian meals. Make sure that you keep a good supply of nuts, such as hazelnuts, pine nuts, and walnuts. Coconut is useful too.

For your seed collection, have sesame, sunflower, pumpkin, and poppy. Pumpkin seeds in particular are a good source of zinc.

Dried fruits

Currants, raisins, golden raisins, dates, apples, apricots, figs, pears, peaches, prunes, papayas, mangoes, figs, bananas, and pineapples can all be purchased dried and can be used in lots of different recipes. When buying dried fruits, look for untreated varieties: for example, buy figs that have not been rolled in sugar, and choose unsulfured apricots if they are available.

Oils and fats

Oils are useful for adding subtle flavorings to foods, so it is a good idea to have a selection in your cupboard. Use a light olive oil for cooking and extra-virgin olive oil for salad dressings. Use sunflower oil as a good general-purpose oil. Sesame oil is wonderful in stir-fries; hazelnut and walnut oils are superb in salad dressings. Oils and fats add flavor to foods, and contain the important fat-soluble vitamins A, D, E, and K. Remember that all fats and oils are high in calories, and that oils are higher in calories than butter or margarine.

Vinegars

Choose three or four vinegars—red or white wine, cider, light malt, tarragon, sherry, or balsamic vinegar, to name just a few. Each will add its own character to your recipes.

Mustards

Mustards are made from black, brown, or white mustard seeds which are ground and mixed with spices. Meaux mustard is made from mixed mustard seeds and has a grainy texture with a warm taste. Dijon mustard, made from husked and ground mustard seeds, has a sharp flavour. Its versatility in salads and with barbecues makes it ideal for the vegetarian. German mustard is mild and is best used in Scandinavian and German dishes.

Bottled sauces

Soy sauce is widely used in Eastern cookery and is made from fermented yellow soya beans mixed with wheat, salt, yeast, and sugar. Light soy sauce tends to be rather salty, whereas dark soy sauce tends to be sweeter. Teriyaki sauce gives an authentic Japanese flavoring to stir-fries. Black bean and yellow bean sauces add an instant authentic Chinese flavor to stir-fries.

Soups
& Salads

Potatoes form the basis of many delicious and easy-to-prepare home-made soups, as they are the perfect thickening ingredient while adding a subtle flavor. With the addition of just a few ingredients such as vegetables, you have a whole selection of inexpensive soups at your fingertips. Add herbs, onion, garlic, meat, or fish, top with herbs or croutons and vegetables, or serve with crusty bread.

Also featured in this chapter are salads based on potatoes and vegetables. In addition to the creamy potato salads with herbs that are so popular, there are many other recipes to tempt your palate. Starters should be colorful and flavorsome but should complement the remainder of the meal. Avoid repeating ingredients in following courses. In this chapter are well-known classics as well as innovative alternatives. There are salads suitable for light lunches as well as hearty main-course salads. Many are also ideal for barbecues and picnics.

Sweet Potato & Onion Soup

Serves 4

INGREDIENTS

2 tbsp vegetable oil	2¹/₂ cups vegetable stock	TO GARNISH:
2 pounds sweet potatoes, diced	1¹/₄ cups unsweetened orange juice	cilantro sprigs
1 carrot, diced	1 cup unsweetened yogurt	orange rind
2 onions, sliced	2 tbsp chopped fresh cilantro	
2 garlic cloves, crushed	salt and pepper	

1 Heat the vegetable oil in a large saucepan and add the diced sweet potatoes and carrot, sliced onions, and garlic. Sauté gently for 5 minutes, stirring constantly.

2 Add the vegetable stock and orange juice and bring to a boil.

3 Reduce the heat to a simmer, cover the saucepan, and cook the vegetables for 20 minutes or until the sweet potato and carrot cubes are tender.

4 Transfer the mixture to a food processor or blender in batches and process for 1 minute until puréed. Return the purée to the rinsed-out saucepan.

5 Stir in the unsweetened yogurt and chopped cilantro and season to taste. Serve the soup garnished with cilantro sprigs and orange rind.

COOK'S TIP

This soup can be chilled before serving, if preferred. If chilling it, stir the yogurt into the dish just before serving. Serve in chilled bowls.

Potato, Apple, & Arugula Soup

Serves 4

INGREDIENTS

4 tbsp butter
2 pounds waxy potatoes, diced
1 red onion, quartered
1 tbsp lemon juice
4¹/₂ cups chicken stock

1 pound eating apples, peeled and
diced
pinch of ground allspice
1³/₄ ounces arugula leaves
salt and pepper

TO GARNISH:
slices of red apple
chopped scallions

1 Melt the butter in a large saucepan and add the diced potatoes and sliced red onion. Sauté gently for 5 minutes, stirring constantly.

2 Add the lemon juice, chicken stock, diced apples, and the ground allspice.

3 Bring to a boil, then reduce the heat to a simmer, cover the pan, and cook for 15 minutes.

4 Add the arugula to the soup and cook for a further 10 minutes, until the potatoes are cooked through.

5 Transfer half the soup to a food processor or blender and process for 1 minute. Return to the pan and stir the purée into the remaining soup.

6 Season to taste with salt and pepper. Ladle into hot soup bowls and garnish with the apple slices and chopped scallions. Serve at once with warm crusty bread.

COOK'S TIP

If arugula is unavailable, use baby spinach instead for a similar flavor.

Indian Potato & Pea Soup

Serves 4

INGREDIENTS

2 tbsp vegetable oil

8 ounces mealy potatoes, diced

1 large onion, chopped

2 garlic cloves, crushed

1 tsp garam masala

1 tsp ground coriander

1 tsp ground cumin

3¾ cups vegetable stock

1 red chili, chopped

1 cup frozen peas

4 tbsp unsweetened yogurt

salt and pepper

chopped fresh cilantro, to garnish

1 Heat the vegetable oil in a large saucepan and add the diced potatoes, onion, and garlic. Sauté gently for about 5 minutes, stirring constantly.

2 Add the ground spices and cook for 1 minute, stirring all the time.

3 Stir in the vegetable stock and chopped red chili and bring the mixture to a boil. Reduce the heat, cover the pan, and simmer for 20 minutes, until the potatoes begin to break down.

4 Add the peas and cook for a further 5 minutes. Stir in the yogurt and season to taste.

5 Pour into warm soup bowls, garnish with chopped fresh cilantro, and serve hot with warm bread.

COOK'S TIP

Potatoes blend perfectly with spices, this soup being no exception. For an authentic Indian dish, serve this soup with warm naan bread.

VARIATION

For slightly less heat, seed the chili before adding it to the soup. Always wash your hands after handling chiles as they contain volatile oils that can irritate the skin and make your eyes burn if you touch your face.

Broccoli & Potato Soup

Serves 4

INGREDIENTS

2 tbsp olive oil	8 ounces broccoli florets	$^2/_3$ cup heavy cream
2 potatoes, diced	2 cups crumbled blue cheese,	pinch of paprika
1 onion, diced	$4^1/_2$ cups vegetable stock	salt and pepper

1 Heat the oil in a large saucepan and add the diced potatoes and onion. Sauté gently for 5 minutes, stirring constantly.

2 Reserve a few broccoli florets for the garnish and add the remaining broccoli to the pan. Add the cheese and stock.

3 Bring to a boil, then reduce the heat, cover the pan, and simmer for 25 minutes, until the potatoes are tender.

4 Transfer the soup to a food processor or blender in 2 batches and process until the mixture is a smooth purée.

5 Return the purée to a clean saucepan and stir in the cream and a pinch of paprika. Season to taste with salt and pepper.

6 Blanch the reserved broccoli florets in a little boiling water for about 2 minutes, then drain with a slotted spoon.

7 Pour the soup into warm bowls and garnish with the broccoli florets and a sprinkling of paprika. Serve at once.

COOK'S TIP

This soup freezes very successfully. Follow the method described here up to step 4, and freeze the soup after it has been puréed. Add the cream and paprika just before serving. Garnish and serve.

Potato & Dried Mushroom Soup

Serves 4

INGREDIENTS

2 tbsp vegetable oil

2 large mealy potatoes, sliced

1 onion, sliced

2 garlic cloves, crushed

4 1/2 cups beef stock

1 ounce dried mushrooms

2 celery stalks, sliced

2 tbsp brandy

salt and pepper

TOPPING:

3 tbsp butter

2 thick slices white bread,
    crusts removed

3 tbsp grated Parmesan cheese

TO GARNISH:

rehydrated dried mushrooms

parsley sprigs

1 Heat the vegetable oil in a large skillet and add the potato and onion slices and the garlic. Sauté gently for 5 minutes, stirring constantly.

2 Add the beef stock, dried mushrooms, and the sliced celery. Bring to a boil, then reduce the heat to a simmer, cover the saucepan, and cook the soup for 20 minutes, until the potatoes are tender.

3 Meanwhile, melt the butter for the topping in the skillet. Sprinkle the bread slices with the grated cheese and fry the slices in the butter for 1 minute on each side, until crisp. Cut each slice into triangles.

4 Stir the brandy into the soup, season with salt and pepper, pour into warm bowls, and top with the triangles. Serve garnished with mushrooms and parsley.

COOK'S TIP

Probably the most popular dried mushroom is the cep, but any variety will add a lovely flavor to this soup. If you do not wish to use dried mushrooms, add 1 3/4 cups sliced fresh mushrooms of your choice to the soup.

Potato, Split Pea, & Cheese Soup

Serves 4

INGREDIENTS

2 tbsp vegetable oil

2 mealy potatoes, diced with skins left on

2 onions, diced

1/3 cup split green peas

4¹/₂ cups vegetable stock

5 tbsp grated Swiss cheese

salt and pepper

CROUTONS:

3 tbsp butter

1 garlic clove, crushed

1 tbsp chopped fresh parsley

1 thick slice white bread, cubed

1 Heat the vegetable oil in a large saucepan and add the diced potatoes and onions. Sauté gently for about 5 minutes, stirring constantly.

2 Add the split green peas to the pan and stir to mix together well.

3 Pour the vegetable stock into the pan and bring to a boil. Reduce the heat to a simmer and cook for 35 minutes, until the potatoes are tender and the split peas cooked.

4 Meanwhile, make the croutons. Melt the butter in a skillet. Add the garlic, chopped parsley, and bread cubes and cook for about 2 minutes, turning frequently until the bread cubes are golden brown on all sides.

5 Stir the grated cheese into the soup and season to taste with salt and pepper.

6 Pour the soup into warm bowls and sprinkle the croûtons on top. Serve the soup at once.

VARIATION

Red lentils could be used instead of split green peas if preferred, for a richly colored soup. Add a large pinch of brown sugar to the recipe for sweetness if red lentils are used.

Leek, Potato, & Bacon Soup

Serves 4

INGREDIENTS

2 tbsp butter	3³/₄ cups vegetable stock	TO GARNISH:
²/₃ cup diced potatoes	1 cup heavy cream	vegetable oil
4 leeks, shredded	2 tbsp chopped fresh parsley	1 leek, shredded
2 garlic cloves, crushed	salt and pepper	
¹/₂ cup smoked bacon, diced		

1 Melt the butter in a large saucepan and add the diced potatoes, shredded leeks, garlic, and diced bacon. Sauté gently for 5 minutes, stirring constantly.

2 Add the vegetable stock and bring to a boil. Reduce the heat, cover the saucepan, and simmer for 20 minutes, until the potatoes are cooked. Stir in the heavy cream.

3 Meanwhile, make the garnish. Half-fill a pan with oil and heat to 350°F–375°F or until a cube of bread browns in 30 seconds. Add the shredded leek and deep-fry for 1 minute until browned and crisp, taking care as the leek contains water. Drain the leek thoroughly on paper towels and reserve.

4 Reserve a few pieces of potato, leek, and bacon, and set aside. Put the rest of the soup in a food processor or blender in batches and process each batch for 30 seconds. Return the puréed soup to a clean saucepan and heat through.

5 Stir in the reserved vegetables, bacon, and parsley and season to taste. Pour into warm bowls and garnish with the fried leeks.

VARIATION

For a lighter soup, omit the cream and stir yogurt or crème fraîche into the soup at the end of the cooking time.

Potato, Cabbage, & Chorizo Soup

Serves 4

INGREDIENTS

2 tbsp olive oil	1 garlic clove, crushed	$^1/_2$ cup sliced chorizo sausage
3 large potatoes, cubed	$4^1/_2$ cups pork or vegetable stock	salt and pepper
2 red onions, quartered	$1^1/_2$ cups shredded Savoy cabbage	paprika, to garnish

1 Heat the olive oil in a large saucepan and add the cubed potatoes, quartered red onions, and garlic. Sauté gently for 5 minutes, stirring constantly.

2 Add the pork or vegetable stock and bring to a boil. Reduce the heat and cover the saucepan. Simmer the vegetables for about 20 minutes, until the potatoes are tender.

3 Process the soup in a food processor or blender in 2 batches for 1 minute each. Pour the puréed soup into a clean pan.

4 Add the shredded Savoy cabbage and sliced chorizo sausage to the pan and cook for a further 7 minutes. Season to taste.

5 Ladle the soup into warm soup bowls, garnish with a sprinkling of paprika, and serve.

VARIATION

If chorizo sausage is not available, you could use any other spicy sausage or even salami in its place.

COOK'S TIP

Chorizo sausage requires no pre-cooking. In this recipe, it is added toward the end of the cooking time so that it does not to overpower the other flavors in the soup.

Chinese Potato & Pork Broth

Serves 4

INGREDIENTS

4¹/₂ cups chicken stock
2 large potatoes, diced
2 tbsp rice wine vinegar
4¹/₂ ounces pork tenderloin, sliced
2 tbsp cornstarch

4 tbsp water
1 tbsp light soy sauce
1 tsp sesame oil
1 carrot, cut into very thin strips
1 tsp fresh ginger root, chopped

3 scallions, sliced thinly
1 red bell pepper, sliced
8 ounce can bamboo shoots, drained

1 Add the stock, diced potatoes, and 1 tbsp of the rice wine vinegar to a saucepan and bring to a boil. Reduce the heat until the stock is just simmering.

2 In a small bowl, mix the cornstarch with the water. Stir the cornstarch mixture into the hot stock.

3 Bring the stock back to a boil, stirring until thickened, then reduce the heat until it is just simmering again.

4 Place the pork slices in a shallow dish and season with the remaining rice wine vinegar, soy sauce, and sesame oil.

5 Add the pork slices, carrot strips, and chopped ginger to the stock and cook for 10 minutes. Stir in the sliced scallions, red bell pepper, and bamboo shoots. Cook for a further 5 minutes.

6 Pour the soup into warm bowls and serve immediately.

COOK'S TIP

Sesame oil is very strongly flavored and is, therefore, only used in small quantities.

VARIATION

For extra heat, add 1 chopped red chili or 1 tsp chili powder to the soup in step 5.

Chunky Potato & Beef Soup

Serves 4

INGREDIENTS

2 tbsp vegetable oil	2 celery stalks, sliced	1 bouquet garni
8 ounces braising or frying steak, cut into strips	2 leeks, sliced	2 tbsp dry sherry
	3¾ cups beef stock	salt and pepper
8 ounces new potatoes, halved	8 baby corn cobs, sliced	chopped fresh parsley, to garnish
1 carrot, diced		

1 Heat the vegetable oil in a large saucepan. Add the strips of meat and cook for 3 minutes, turning constantly.

2 Add the halved potatoes, diced carrot, and sliced celery and leeks. Cook for a further 5 minutes, stirring.

3 Pour the beef stock into the saucepan and bring to a boil. Reduce the heat until the liquid is simmering, then add the sliced baby corn cobs and the bouquet garni.

4 Cook the soup for a further 20 minutes, or until the meat strips and all the vegetables are cooked through.

5 Remove the bouquet garni from the saucepan and discard. Stir the dry sherry into the soup and then season to taste with salt and pepper.

6 Pour the soup into warm bowls and garnish with the chopped fresh parsley. Serve at once, accompanied by chunks of fresh, crusty bread.

COOK'S TIP

Make double the quantity of soup and freeze the remainder in a rigid container for later use. When ready to use, leave in the refrigerator to defrost thoroughly, then heat until piping hot.

Potato & Mixed Fish Soup

Serves 4

INGREDIENTS

2 tbsp vegetable oil
1 pound small new potatoes, halved
1 bunch scallions, sliced
1 yellow bell pepper, sliced
2 garlic cloves, crushed
1 cup dry white wine

$2^{1}/_{2}$ cups fish stock
8 ounces white fish fillet, skinned and cubed
8 ounces smoked cod fillet, skinned and cubed

2 tomatoes, peeled, seeded, and chopped
$3^{1}/_{2}$ ounces peeled cooked shrimp
$^{2}/_{3}$ cup heavy cream
2 tbsp shredded fresh basil

1 Heat the vegetable oil in a large saucepan and add the halved potatoes, sliced scallions, bell pepper, and the garlic. Sauté gently for 3 minutes, stirring constantly.

2 Add the white wine and fish stock and bring to a boil. Reduce the heat and simmer for 10–15 minutes.

3 Add the cubed fish fillets and the tomatoes to the soup and continue to cook for 10 minutes, or until the fish is cooked through.

4 Stir in the shrimp, cream, and shredded basil and cook for 2–3 minutes. Pour the soup into warm bowls and serve.

COOK'S TIP

The basil is added at the end of the cooking time as the flavor is destroyed by heat.

VARIATION

For a soup which is slightly less rich, omit the wine and stir unsweetened yogurt into the soup instead of the heavy cream.

Mixed Bean Soup

Serves 4

INGREDIENTS

1 tablespoon vegetable oil
1 red onion, halved and sliced
²/₃ cup diced potato
1 carrot, diced
1 leek, sliced

1 green chili, sliced
3 garlic cloves, crushed
1 teaspoon ground coriander
1 teaspoon chili powder
4 cups vegetable stock

1 pound mixed canned beans,
    such as red kidney, borlotti,
    or flageolet, drained
salt and pepper
2 tablespoons chopped cilantro,
    to garnish

1 Heat the vegetable oil in a large saucepan and add the prepared onion, potato, carrot, and leek. Sauté for about 2 minutes, stirring, until the vegetables are slightly softened.

2 Add the sliced chili and crushed garlic and cook for a further 1 minute.

3 Stir in the ground coriander, chili powder, and the vegetable stock.

4 Bring the soup to a boil, reduce the heat, and cook for 20 minutes, or until the vegetables are tender.

5 Stir in the beans, season to taste with salt and pepper, and cook for a further 10 minutes, stirring occasionally.

6 Transfer the soup to a warm tureen or individual bowls, garnish with chopped cilantro, and serve at once.

COOK'S TIP

Serve this soup with slices of warm corn bread or a cheese loaf.

Vegetable & Corn Chowder

Serves 4

INGREDIENTS

1 tablespoon vegetable oil	2½ cups milk	salt and pepper
1 red onion, diced	1¼ cups vegetable stock	1 tablespoon chopped fresh
1 red bell pepper, diced	1¾ ounces broccoli florets	cilantro, to garnish
3 garlic cloves, crushed	3 cups canned corn, drained	
1 large potato, diced	¾ cup grated vegetarian	
2 tablespoons all-purpose flour	Cheddar cheese	

1 Heat the oil in a large saucepan and sauté the onion, bell pepper, garlic, and potato for 2–3 minutes, stirring.

2 Stir in the flour and cook for 30 seconds. Stir in the milk and stock.

3 Add the broccoli florets and corn. Bring the mixture to a boil, stirring, then reduce the heat and simmer for about 20 minutes, or until the vegetables are tender.

4 Stir in ½ cup of the grated cheese until it melts.

5 Season and spoon the chowder into a warm soup tureen. Garnish with the remaining cheese and the cilantro and serve.

COOK'S TIP

Vegetarian cheeses are made with rennets of non-animal origin, using microbial or fungal enzymes.

COOK'S TIP

Add a little heavy cream to the soup after adding the milk for a really creamy flavor.

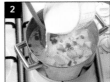
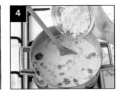

Cauliflower & Broccoli Soup with Gruyère

Serves 4

INGREDIENTS

3 tablespoons vegetable oil
1 red onion, chopped
2 garlic cloves, crushed
10 1/2 ounces cauliflower florets
10 1/2 ounces broccoli florets

1 tablespoon all-purpose flour
2 1/2 cups milk
1 1/4 cups vegetable stock
3/4 cup grated vegetarian
Swiss cheese

pinch of paprika
2/3 cup light cream
paprika and vegetarian Swiss
cheese shavings, to garnish

1 Heat the oil in a large saucepan and sauté the onion, garlic, cauliflower, and broccoli for 3–4 minutes, stirring constantly. Add the flour and cook for a further 1 minute, stirring.

2 Stir in the milk and stock and bring to a boil. Reduce the heat and simmer for 20 minutes.

3 Remove about a quarter of the vegetables and set aside.

4 Put the remaining soup in a food processor and process for 30 seconds, until smooth. Transfer the soup to a clean saucepan.

5 Return the reserved vegetable pieces to the soup.

6 Stir in the grated cheese, paprika, and light cream and heat gently for 2–3 minutes without boiling, or until the cheese starts to melt.

7 Transfer to warm soup bowls, garnish with shavings of Swiss cheese and dust with paprika.

COOK'S TIP

The soup must not start to boil after the cream has been added, otherwise it will curdle. Use unsweetened yogurt instead of the cream if desired, but again do not allow to boil.

Celery, Stilton, & Walnut Soup

Serves 4

INGREDIENTS

4 tablespoons butter	2¹⁄₂ cups vegetable stock	2 tablespoons walnut halves,
2 shallots, chopped	1¹⁄₄ cups milk	roughly chopped
3 celery stalks, chopped	1¹⁄₂ cups crumbled blue Stilton	²⁄₃ cup unsweetened yogurt
1 garlic clove, crushed	cheese, plus extra to garnish	salt and pepper
2 tablespoons all-purpose flour		chopped celery leaves, to garnish

1 Melt the butter in a large saucepan and sauté the shallots, celery, and garlic for 2–3 minutes, stirring constantly, until softened.

2 Add the all-purpose flour and cook, stirring constantly, for 30 seconds.

3 Gradually stir in the stock and milk and bring to a boil.

4 Reduce the heat to a gentle simmer and add the crumbled blue Stilton cheese and walnut halves.

Cover and simmer for 20 minutes.

5 Stir in the unsweetened yogurt and heat for a further 2 minutes without boiling.

6 Season the soup to taste with salt and pepper, then transfer to a warm soup tureen or individual serving bowls, garnish with chopped celery leaves and extra crumbled blue Stilton cheese, and serve at once.

COOK'S TIP

As well as adding protein, vitamins, and useful fats to the diet, nuts add important flavor and texture to vegetarian meals.

VARIATION

Use an alternative blue cheese, such as Dolcelatte or Gorgonzola, if desired, or a strong vegetarian Cheddar cheese, grated.

Curried Parsnip Soup

Serves 4

INGREDIENTS

1 tablespoon vegetable oil	2 teaspoon garam masala	salt and pepper
1 tablespoon butter	$\frac{1}{2}$ teaspoon chili powder	lemon zest, to garnish
1 red onion, chopped	1 tablespoon all-purpose flour	
3 parsnips, chopped	3$\frac{3}{4}$ cups vegetable stock	
2 garlic cloves, crushed	grated rind and juice of 1 lemon	

1 Heat the oil and butter in a large saucepan until the butter has melted.

2 Add the onion, parsnips, and garlic and sauté for 5–7 minutes, stirring, until the vegetables have softened.

3 Add the garam masala and chili powder and cook for 30 seconds, stirring well.

4 Sprinkle in the flour, mixing well and cook for a further 30 seconds.

5 Stir in the stock, lemon rind, and juice and bring to a boil. Reduce the heat and simmer for 20 minutes.

6 Remove some of the vegetable pieces with a slotted spoon and reserve until required. Process the remaining soup and vegetables in a food processor for 1 minute, or until smooth.

7 Return the soup to a clean saucepan and stir in the reserved vegetables. Heat the soup through for 2 minutes.

8 Season, then transfer to soup bowls, garnish with grated lemon zest, and serve.

VARIATION

Use 1 medium orange instead of the lemon, if desired, and garnish with grated orange zest.

Jerusalem Artichoke Soup

Serves 4

INGREDIENTS

1 1/2 pounds Jerusalem artichokes
5 tablespoons orange juice
2 tablespoons butter
1 leek, chopped

1 garlic clove, crushed
1 1/4 cups vegetable stock
2/3 cup milk
2 tablespoons chopped cilantro

2/3 cup unsweetened yogurt
grated orange rind, to garnish

1 Rinse the Jerusalem artichokes and place in a large saucepan with 2 tablespoons of the orange juice and enough water to cover. Bring to a boil, reduce the heat, and cook for 20 minutes, or until the artichokes are tender.

2 Drain the artichokes, reserving 2 cups of the cooking liquid. Set the artichokes aside to cool.

3 Once cooled, peel the artichokes and place in a large bowl. Mash the flesh with a potato masher.

4 Melt the butter in a large saucepan and sauté the leek and garlic, stirring, for about 2–3 minutes, until the leek softens.

5 Stir in the artichoke flesh, the reserved cooking water, the stock, milk, and remaining orange juice. Bring the soup to a boil, reduce the heat, and simmer for 2–3 minutes.

6 Remove a few pieces of leek with a slotted spoon and reserve. Transfer remaining soup to a food processor and process for 1 minute, until smooth.

7 Return the soup to a clean saucepan and stir in the reserved leeks, cilantro, and yogurt.

8 Transfer to individual soup bowls, garnish with orange rind, and serve.

VARIATION

If Jerusalem artichokes are unavailable, you could use sweet potatoes instead.

Red Bell Pepper & Chili Soup

Serves 4

INGREDIENTS

8 oz red bell peppers, seeded and sliced	2 garlic cloves, crushed	2½ cups vegetable stock
1 onion, sliced	1 green chili, chopped	2 tablespoons chopped basil
	1½ cups sieved tomatoes	fresh basil sprigs, to garnish

1 Put the bell peppers in a large, heavy-based saucepan, together with the onion, garlic, and chili. Add the sieved tomatoes and vegetable stock and bring to a boil, stirring well.

2 Reduce the heat to a simmer and cook for 20 minutes, or until the bell peppers have softened. Drain, reserving the liquid and vegetables separately.

3 Press the vegetables through a strainer with the back of a wooden spoon. Alternatively, put them in a food processor and process until smooth.

4 Return the vegetable purée to a clean saucepan with the reserved cooking liquid. Add the basil and heat through until hot. Garnish the soup with fresh basil sprigs and serve.

COOK'S TIP

Basil is a useful herb to grow at home. It can be grown easily in a window box.

VARIATION

This soup is also delicious served chilled with ⅔ cup of unsweetened yogurt swirled into it.

Dahl Soup

Serves 4

INGREDIENTS

2 tablespoons butter

2 garlic cloves, crushed

1 onion, chopped

$^1/_2$ teaspoon turmeric

1 teaspoon garam masala

$^1/_4$ teaspoon chili powder

1 teaspoon ground cumin

$2^1/_4$ pounds canned, chopped
tomatoes, drained

1 cup red lentils

2 teaspoons lemon juice

$2^1/_2$ cups vegetable stock

$1^1/_4$ cups coconut milk

salt and pepper

chopped cilantro and lemon slices,
to garnish

naan bread, to serve

1 Melt the butter in a large saucepan and sauté the garlic and onion for 2–3 minutes, stirring. Add the spices and cook for a further 30 seconds.

2 Stir in the tomatoes, red lentils, lemon juice, vegetable stock, and coconut milk and bring to a boil.

3 Reduce the heat and simmer for 25–30 minutes, until the lentils are tender and cooked.

4 Season to taste and spoon the soup into a warm tureen. Garnish with cilantro and lemon and serve with warm naan bread.

COOK'S TIP

You can buy cans of coconut milk from supermarkets and specialty grocers. Coconut milk is also available in a lighter, reduced-fat version.

COOK'S TIP

Add small quantities of hot water to the pan while the lentils are cooking if they begin to absorb too much of the liquid.

Avocado & Vegetable Soup

Serves 4

INGREDIENTS

1 large, ripe avocado
2 tablespoons lemon juice
1 tablespoon vegetable oil
$^1/_2$ cup canned corn, drained

2 tomatoes, peeled and seeded
1 garlic clove, crushed
1 leek, chopped
1 red chili, chopped

2 cups vegetable stock
$^2/_3$ cup milk
shredded leeks, to garnish

1 Peel and mash the avocado with a fork, stir in the lemon juice, and reserve until required.

2 Heat the oil in a pan and sauté the corn, tomatoes, garlic, leek, and chili for about 2–3 minutes, or until the vegetables are softened.

3 Put half of the vegetable mixture in a food processor or blender with the avocado and process until smooth. Transfer to a clean saucepan.

4 Add the stock, milk, and reserved vegetables and cook gently for 3–4 minutes, until hot. Garnish and serve.

COOK'S TIP

To remove the pit from an avocado, first cut the avocado in half, then holding one half in your hand, rap the pit with a knife until it is embedded in the pit, then twist the knife until the pit is dislodged.

COOK'S TIP

If serving chilled, transfer from the food processor to a bowl, stir in the stock and milk, cover, and chill in the refrigerator for at least 4 hours.

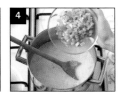

Spanish Tomato Soup with Garlic Bread Croutons

Serves 4

INGREDIENTS

4 tablespoons olive oil
1 onion, chopped
3 garlic cloves, crushed
1 green bell pepper, chopped
$^{1}/_{2}$ teaspoon chili powder

1 pound tomatoes, chopped
8 oz French or
    Italian bread, cubed
4 cups vegetable stock

GARLIC BREAD:
4 slices French or Italian bread
4 tablespoons olive oil
2 garlic cloves, crushed
$^{1}/_{4}$ cup grated vegetarian
    Cheddar cheese
chili powder, to garnish

1 Heat the olive oil in a large skillet and add the prepared onion, garlic, and bell pepper. Sauté the vegetables for 2–3 minutes or until the onion is soft and translucent.

2 Add the chili powder and tomatoes and cook over medium heat until the mixture has thickened.

3 Stir in the bread cubes and stock and cook for about 10–15 minutes, until the soup is thick.

4 To make the garlic bread, toast the bread slices under a preheated broiler. Drizzle the oil on top of the bread, rub with the garlic, sprinkle with the grated cheese, and return to the broiler for 2–3 minutes, until the cheese has melted and is bubbling. Sprinkle with chili powder and serve at once with the soup.

VARIATION

Replace the green bell pepper with red bell pepper, if you prefer.

Fava Bean & Mint Soup

Serves 4

INGREDIENTS

2 tablespoons olive oil	2 potatoes, diced	3¾ cups vegetable stock
1 red onion, chopped	3 cups fava beans,	2 tablespoons freshly chopped mint
2 garlic cloves, crushed	thawed if frozen	fresh mint sprigs and unsweetened
		yogurt, to garnish

1 Heat the olive oil in a large saucepan and sauté the onion and garlic for 2–3 minutes, until soft and translucent.

2 Add the potatoes and cook for 5 minutes, stirring well.

3 Stir in the beans and the stock, cover, and simmer for 30 minutes, or until the beans and potatoes are tender.

4 Remove a few vegetables with a slotted spoon and set aside until required. Place the remainder of the soup in a food processor or blender and process until smooth.

5 Return the soup to a clean saucepan and add the reserved vegetables and mint. Stir well and heat through gently.

6 Transfer the soup to a warm tureen or individual serving bowls. Garnish with swirls of yogurt and sprigs of fresh mint and serve immediately.

VARIATION

Use chopped fresh cilantro and ½ teaspoon ground cumin as flavorings in the soup, if desired.

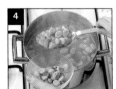

Tuscan Bean & Vegetable Soup

Serves 4

INGREDIENTS

1 medium onion, chopped	5 cups fresh vegetable stock	TO SERVE:
1 garlic clove, finely chopped	1 tsp dried oregano	low-fat pesto sauce
2 celery stalks, sliced	15 ounce can mixed beans	crusty bread
1 large carrot, diced	and legumes	
14 ounce can chopped tomatoes	2 medium zucchini, diced	
²/₃ cup Italian dry	1 tbsp tomato paste	
red wine	salt and pepper	

1 Place the prepared onion, garlic, celery, and carrot in a large saucepan. Stir in the tomatoes, red wine, vegetable stock, and oregano.

2 Bring the vegetable mixture to a boil, cover the pan, and simmer for about 15 minutes. Stir the beans and zucchini into the mixture, and continue to cook, uncovered, for a further 5 minutes.

3 Add the tomato paste and season well with salt and pepper to taste. Then heat through, stirring occasionally, for a further 2–3 minutes, but do not allow the mixture to boil again.

4 Ladle the soup into warm bowls and serve with a spoonful of low-fat pesto on each portion and accompanied with lots of fresh crusty bread.

VARIATION

For a more substantial soup, add 12 ounces diced lean cooked chicken or turkey with the tomato paste in step 3.

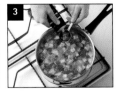

Lentil, Pasta, & Vegetable Soup

Serves 4

INGREDIENTS

1 tbsp olive oil
1 medium onion, chopped
4 garlic cloves, finely chopped
12 ounces carrots, sliced
1 celery stalk, sliced
1¼ cups red lentils

2½ cups fresh vegetable stock
3 cups boiling water
1 cup dried pasta
²⁄₃ cup natural low-fat
    unsweetened yogurt

salt and pepper
2 tbsp fresh parsley, chopped,
    to garnish

1 Heat the oil in a large saucepan and gently sauté the prepared onion, garlic, carrot, and celery, stirring gently, for about 5 minutes or until the vegetables begin to soften.

2 Add the lentils, stock, and boiling water. Season with salt and pepper to taste, stir, and bring back to a boil. Simmer, uncovered, for 15 minutes until the lentils are completely tender. Allow to cool for 10 minutes.

3 Meanwhile, bring another saucepan of water to a boil and cook the pasta according to the instructions on the packet. Drain well and set aside.

4 Place the soup in a blender and process until smooth. Return to a saucepan and add the pasta. Bring back to a simmer and heat for 2–3 minutes, until piping hot. Remove from the heat and stir in the yogurt. Adjust the seasoning if necessary.

5 Serve sprinkled with chopped parsley.

COOK'S TIP

Avoid boiling the soup once the yogurt has been added. Otherwise it will separate and become watery, spoiling the appearance of the soup.

Tomato & Red Bell Pepper Soup

Serves 4

INGREDIENTS

2 large red bell peppers
1 large onion, chopped
2 celery stalks, trimmed and
    chopped
1 garlic clove, crushed

2¹/₂ cups fresh vegetable stock
2 bay leaves
2 14 ounce cans plum tomatoes
salt and pepper
2 scallions, finely shredded,

to garnish
crusty bread, to serve

1 Preheat the broiler. Halve and seed the bell peppers, arrange them on the broiler rack and cook, turning occasionally, for 8–10 minutes until softened and charred.

2 Leave to cool slightly, then carefully peel off the charred skin. Reserving a small piece for garnish, chop the bell pepper flesh and place in a large saucepan.

3 Mix in the onion, celery, and garlic. Add the stock and the bay leaves.

Bring to a boil, cover, and simmer for 15 minutes. Remove from the heat.

4 Stir in the tomatoes and transfer to a blender. Process for a few seconds until smooth. Return to the saucepan.

5 Season with salt and pepper to taste and heat for 3–4 minutes until piping hot. Ladle the soup into warm bowls and garnish with the reserved bell pepper cut into strips and the scallion. Serve with lots of fresh crusty bread.

COOK'S TIP

If you prefer a coarser, more robust soup, lightly mash the tomatoes with a wooden spoon and omit the blending process in step 4.

Carrot, Apple, & Celery Soup

Serves 4

INGREDIENTS

2 pounds carrots, finely diced	3 medium-size eating	$^1/_2$ large lemon
1 medium onion, chopped	apples	salt and pepper
3 celery stalks, trimmed and	2 tbsp tomato paste	celery leaves, washed and
diced	1 bay leaf	shredded, to garnish
4 cups fresh vegetable stock	2 tsp superfine sugar	

1 Place the prepared carrots, onion, and celery in a large saucepan and add the fresh vegetable stock. Bring to a boil, cover and simmer for about 10 minutes.

2 Meanwhile, peel, core, and dice 2 of the apples. Add the pieces of apple, tomato paste, bay leaf, and superfine sugar to the saucepan and bring to a boil. Reduce the heat, half cover the pan, and allow to simmer for 20 minutes. Remove and discard the bay leaf.

3 Meanwhile, wash, core, and cut the remaining apple into thin slices, leaving on the skin. Place the apple slices in a small saucepan and squeeze in the lemon juice. Heat gently and simmer for 1–2 minutes, until tender. Drain and set aside.

4 Place the carrot and apple mixture in a blender or food processor and blend until smooth. Alternatively, press the mixture through a strainer with the back of a wooden spoon, until smooth.

5 Gently reheat the soup if necessary and season with salt and pepper to taste. Ladle the soup into warm bowls and serve topped with the reserved apple slices and shredded celery leaves.

COOK'S TIP

Soaking light colored fruit in lemon juice prevents it from turning brown when exposed to the air.

Potato, Mixed Bean, & Apple Salad

Serves 4

INGREDIENTS

8 ounces new potatoes, scrubbed
and quartered

1²/₃ cups mixed canned beans, such
as red kidney beans, flageolet,
and borlotti beans, drained and
rinsed

1 red eating apple, diced and tossed
in 1 tbsp lemon juice

1 small yellow bell pepper, diced

1 shallot, sliced

¹/₂ bulb fennel, sliced

oak leaf lettuce leaves

DRESSING:

1 tbsp red wine vinegar

2 tbsp olive oil

¹/₂ tbsp American mustard

1 garlic clove, crushed

2 tsp chopped fresh thyme

1 Cook the quartered
potatoes in a saucepan
of boiling water for 15
minutes, until tender.
Drain and transfer to
a mixing bowl.

2 Add the mixed beans
to the potatoes with
the diced apple and yellow
bell pepper, and the sliced
shallots and fennel. Mix
well, taking care not to break
up the cooked potatoes.

3 In a bowl, beat all the
dressing ingredients
together, then pour it on
the potato salad.

4 Line a plate or salad
bowl with the oak leaf
lettuce and spoon the potato
mixture into the center.
Serve immediately.

VARIATION

*Use Dijon or wholegrain
mustard in place of
American mustard for a
different flavor.*

COOK'S TIP

*Canned beans are used here
for convenience, but dried
beans may be used instead.
Soak for 8 hours or
overnight, drain, and place
in a saucepan. Cover with
water, bring to a boil, and
boil for 10 minutes, then
simmer until tender.*

Potato, Beet, & Cucumber Salad with Dill Dressing

Serves 4

INGREDIENTS

1 pound waxy potatoes, diced	DRESSING:
4 small cooked beets, sliced	1 garlic clove, crushed
1/2 small cucumber, sliced thinly	2 tbsp olive oil
2 large dill pickles, sliced	2 tbsp red wine vinegar
1 red onion, halved and sliced	2 tbsp chopped fresh dill
dill sprigs, to garnish	salt and pepper

1 Cook the diced potatoes in a saucepan of boiling water for 15 minutes, or until tender. Drain and let cool.

2 When cool, mix the potato and beet together in a bowl and set aside.

3 Line a salad platter with the slices of cucumber, dill pickles, and red onion. Spoon the potato and beet mixture into the center of the platter.

4 In a small bowl, beat all the dressing ingredients together, then pour it on the salad.

5 Serve the salad immediately, garnished with dill sprigs.

COOK'S TIP

If making the salad in advance, do not mix the beet and potatoes until just before serving, as the beet will bleed its color.

VARIATION

Line the salad platter with 2 heads of endive, separated into leaves, and arrange the cucumber, dill pickle, and red onion slices on top of the leaves.

Potato, Radish, & Cucumber Salad

Serves 4

INGREDIENTS

1 pound new potatoes, scrubbed
and halved

1/2 cucumber, sliced thinly

2 tsp salt

1 bunch radishes, sliced thinly

DRESSING:

1 tbsp Dijon mustard

2 tbsp olive oil

1 tbsp white wine vinegar

2 tbsp mixed chopped herbs

1 Cook the potatoes in a saucepan of boiling water for 10–15 minutes, or until tender. Drain and let cool.

2 Meanwhile spread out the cucumber slices on a plate and sprinkle with the salt. Let stand for 30 minutes, then rinse under cold running water, and pat dry with paper towels.

3 Arrange the cucumber and radish slices on a serving plate in a decorative pattern and pile the cooked potatoes in the center of the slices.

4 In a small bowl, mix the dressing ingredients together. Pour the dressing on the salad, tossing well to coat all the salad ingredients. Chill in the refrigerator before serving.

VARIATION

Dijon mustard has a mild clean taste, which is perfect for this salad as it does not overpower the other flavors. If unavailable, use another mild mustard— English mustard is too strong for this salad.

COOK'S TIP

The cucumber adds not only color, but a real freshness to the salad. It is salted and let stand to remove the excess water which would make the salad soggy. Wash the cucumber well to remove all the salt, before adding to the salad.

Sweet Potato & Banana Salad

Serves 4

INGREDIENTS

1 pound sweet potatoes, diced	1 green bell pepper, diced	DRESSING:
10 tsp butter	2 bananas, thickly sliced	2 tbsp clear honey
1 tbsp lemon juice	2 thick slices white bread, crusts	2 tbsp chopped fresh chives
1 garlic clove, crushed	removed, diced	2 tbsp lemon juice
1 red bell pepper, diced	salt and pepper	2 tbsp olive oil

1 Cook the sweet potatoes in a saucepan of boiling water for 10–15 minutes, until tender. Drain thoroughly and reserve.

2 Meanwhile, melt the butter in a skillet. Add the lemon juice, garlic, and bell peppers and cook for 3 minutes, turning constantly.

3 Add the banana slices to the skillet and cook for 1 minute. Remove the bananas from the pan with a slotted spoon and stir into the potatoes.

4 Add the bread cubes to the skillet and cook for 2 minutes, turning frequently until they are golden brown on all sides.

5 Mix the dressing ingredients together in a small saucepan and heat the mixture until the honey is runny.

6 Spoon the potato mixture into a serving dish and season to taste with salt and pepper. Pour the dressing on the potatoes and sprinkle the croutons over the top. Serve immediately.

COOK'S TIP

Use firm, slightly underripe bananas in this recipe as they won't turn soft and mushy when fried.

Sweet Potato & Nut Salad

Serves 4

INGREDIENTS

1 pound sweet potatoes, diced	1/2 cup chopped pecans	DRESSING:
2 celery stalks, sliced	2 heads endive, separated	4 tbsp vegetable oil
1 cup grated celery root	1 tsp lemon juice	1 tbsp garlic wine vinegar
2 scallions, sliced	thyme sprigs, to garnish	1 tsp light brown sugar
		2 tsp chopped fresh thyme

1 Cook the sweet potatoes in a saucepan of boiling water for 5 minutes, until tender. Drain thoroughly and let cool.

2 When cooled, stir in the celery, celery root, scallions and pecans.

3 Line a salad plate with the endive leaves and sprinkle them with lemon juice.

4 Spoon the potato mixture into the center of the leaves.

5 In a small bowl, beat the dressing ingredients together.

6 Pour the dressing over the salad and serve at once, garnished with thyme sprigs.

COOK'S TIP

Sweet potatoes do not store as well as ordinary potatoes. It is best to store them in a cool, dark place (not the refrigerator) and use within 1 week of purchase.

VARIATION

For variety, replace the garlic wine vinegar in the dressing with a different flavored vinegar, such as chili or herb.

Indian Potato Salad

Serves 4

INGREDIENTS

4 medium mealy potatoes, diced

2³/₄ ounces small broccoli flowerets

1 small mango, diced

4 scallions, sliced

salt and pepper

small cooked spiced poppadoms,
to serve

DRESSING:

¹/₂ tsp ground cumin

¹/₂ tsp ground coriander

1 tbsp mango chutney

²/₃ cup unsweetened yogurt

1 tsp fresh ginger root, chopped

2 tbsp chopped fresh cilantro

1 Cook the potatoes in a saucepan of boiling water for 10 minutes, or until tender. Drain and place in a mixing bowl.

2 Meanwhile, blanch the broccoli florets in a separate saucepan of boiling water for 2 minutes. Drain thoroughly and add to the potatoes in the bowl.

3 When the potatoes and broccoli have cooled, add the diced mango and sliced scallions. Season to

taste with salt and pepper and mix well to combine.

4 In a small bowl, stir all the dressing ingredients together.

5 Spoon the dressing on the potato mixture and mix together carefully, taking care not to break up the potatoes and broccoli.

6 Serve the salad at once, accompanied by small cooked spiced poppadoms.

COOK'S TIP

Mix the dressing ingredients together in advance and chill in the refrigerator for a few hours for a stronger flavor to develop.

Mexican Potato Salad

Serves 4

INGREDIENTS

4 large waxy potatoes, sliced	1 onion, chopped	salt and pepper
1 ripe avocado	2 large tomatoes, sliced	lemon wedges, to garnish
1 tsp olive oil	1 green chili, chopped	
1 tsp lemon juice	1 yellow bell pepper, sliced	
1 garlic clove, crushed	2 tbsp chopped fresh cilantro	

1 Cook the potato slices in a saucepan of boiling water for 10–15 minutes, or until tender. Drain and let cool.

2 Meanwhile, cut the avocado in half and remove the pit. Using a spoon, scoop the avocado flesh from the 2 halves and place in a mixing bowl.

3 Mash the avocado flesh with a fork and stir in the olive oil, lemon juice, garlic, and chopped onion. Cover the bowl with plastic wrap and set aside.

4 Mix the tomatoes, chili, and yellow bell pepper together and transfer to a salad bowl with the potato slices.

5 Spoon the avocado mixture on top and sprinkle with the cilantro. Season to taste and serve garnished with lemon wedges.

COOK'S TIP

Mixing the avocado flesh with lemon juice prevents it from turning brown once exposed to the air.

VARIATION

Omit the green chili from this salad if you do not like hot dishes.

Potato Nests of Chinese Salad

Serves 4

INGREDIENTS

POTATO NESTS:
1 pound mealy potatoes, grated
1 cup cornstarch
vegetable oil, for frying
fresh chives, to garnish

SALAD:
4¹⁄₂ ounces pineapple, cubed
1 green bell pepper, cut into strips
1 carrot, cut into thin strips
1³⁄₄ ounces snowpeas, thickly sliced
4 baby corn cobs, halved lengthwise
1 ounce bean sprouts
2 scallions, sliced

DRESSING:
1 tbsp clear honey
1 tsp light soy sauce
1 garlic clove, crushed
1 tsp lemon juice

1 To make the nests, rinse the potatoes several times in cold water. Drain well on paper towels and place them in a mixing bowl. Add the cornstarch, mixing well to coat the potatoes.

2 Half fill a wok with vegetable oil and heat until smoking. Line a 6-inch diameter wire strainer with a quarter of the potato mixture and press another strainer of the same size on top.

3 Lower the strainers into the oil and cook for 2 minutes, until the potato nest is golden and crisp. Remove from the wok, allowing the excess oil to drain off.

4 Repeat 3 more times to use up all the mixture and make a total of 4 nests. Let cool.

5 Mix the salad ingredients together in a bowl, then spoon into the potato nests.

6 Mix the dressing ingredients together in a bowl. Pour the dressing over the salad, garnish with chives, and serve.

COOK'S TIP

For this recipe, the potatoes must be washed well before use to remove excess starch. Make sure the potatoes are completely dry before cooking in the oil to prevent spitting.

Potato, Arugula, & Apple Salad

Serves 4

INGREDIENTS

2 large potatoes, unpeeled and
    sliced
2 green eating apples, diced
1 tsp lemon juice
¹/₄ cup walnut pieces
¹/₂ cup cubed goat cheese

5¹/₂ ounces arugula leaves
salt and pepper

DRESSING:
2 tbsp olive oil
1 tbsp red wine vinegar

1 tsp clear honey
1 tsp fennel seeds

1 Cook the potatoes in a pan of boiling water for 15 minutes, until tender. Drain and let cool. Transfer the cooled potatoes to a serving bowl.

2 Toss the diced apples in the lemon juice, drain, and stir into the cold potatoes.

3 Add the walnut pieces, cheese cubes, and arugula leaves, then toss the salad to mix.

4 In a small bowl, beat the dressing ingredients together and pour the dressing on the salad. Serve immediately.

VARIATION

Use smoked or blue cheese instead of goat cheese, if you prefer. In addition, if arugula is unavailable use baby spinach instead.

COOK'S TIP

Serve this salad immediately to prevent the apple from discoloring. Alternatively, prepare all the other ingredients in advance and add the apple at the last minute.

Potato & Mixed Vegetable Salad with Lemon Mayonnaise

Serves 4

INGREDIENTS

1 pound waxy new potatoes, scrubbed

1 carrot, cut into matchsticks

8 ounces cauliflower florets

8 ounces baby corn cobs, halved lengthwise

6 ounces green beans

1 cup diced ham,

²/₃ cup sliced mushrooms

salt and pepper

DRESSING:

2 tbsp chopped fresh parsley

²/₃ cup mayonnaise

²/₃ cup unsweetened yogurt

4 tsp lemon juice

rind of 1 lemon

2 tsp fennel seeds

1 Cook the potatoes in a pan of boiling water for 15 minutes, or until tender. Drain and let cool. When the potatoes are cold, slice them thinly.

2 Meanwhile, cook the carrot matchsticks, cauliflower florets, baby corn cobs, and green beans in a pan of boiling water for 5 minutes. Drain well and let cool.

3 Reserve 1 tsp of the chopped parsley for the garnish. In a bowl, mix the remaining dressing ingredients together.

4 Arrange the vegetables on a salad platter and top with the ham strips and sliced mushrooms.

5 Spoon the dressing over the the salad and garnish with the reserved parsley. Serve at once.

COOK'S TIP

For a really quick salad, use a frozen packet of mixed vegetables, thawed, instead of fresh vegetables.

Indonesian Potato & Chicken Salad

Serves 4

INGREDIENTS

4 large waxy potatoes, diced	3 celery stalks, cut into matchsticks	DRESSING:
10¹/₂ ounces fresh pineapple, diced	1 cup unsalted peanuts	6 tbsp crunchy peanut butter
2 carrots, grated	2 cooked chicken breast fillets,	6 tbsp olive oil
6 ounces bean sprouts	about 4¹/₂ ounces each, sliced	2 tbsp light soy sauce
1 bunch scallions, sliced		1 red chili, chopped
1 large zucchini, cut into		2 tsp sesame oil
matchsticks		4 tsp lime juice

1 Cook the diced potatoes in a saucepan of boiling water for 10 minutes, or until tender. Drain and let cool.

2 Transfer the cooled potatoes to a salad bowl.

3 Add the pineapple, carrots, bean sprouts, scallions, zucchini, celery, peanuts, and sliced chicken to the potatoes. Toss well to mix all the salad ingredients together.

4 To make the dressing, put the peanut butter in a small bowl and gradually beat in the olive oil and light soy sauce.

5 Stir in the chopped red chili, sesame oil, and lime juice. Mix until well combined.

6 Pour the spicy dressing on the salad and toss lightly to coat all the ingredients. Serve the salad immediately, garnished with the lime wedges.

COOK'S TIP

Unsweetened canned pineapple may be used in place of the fresh pineapple for convenience. If only sweetened canned pineapple is available, drain it and rinse under cold running water before using.

Potato & Spicy Chicken Salad

Serves 4

INGREDIENTS

2 skinless chicken breast fillets,
  about 4^1/$_2$ ounces each
2 tbsp butter
1 red chili, chopped
1 tbsp clear honey
^{1}/$_2$ tsp ground cumin

2 tbsp chopped fresh cilantro
2 large potatoes, diced
^{1}/$_3$ cup thin green beans, halved
1 red bell pepper, cut into thin strips
2 tomatoes, seeded and diced

DRESSING:
2 tbsp olive oil
pinch of chili powder
1 tbsp garlic wine vinegar
pinch of superfine sugar
1 tbsp chopped fresh cilantro

1 Cut the chicken into thin strips. Melt the butter in a pan over a medium heat and add the chicken, chili, honey and cumin. Cook for 10 minutes, turning until cooked through.

2 Transfer the mixture to a bowl, let cool, then stir in the cilantro.

3 Meanwhile, cook the diced potatoes in a saucepan of boiling water for 10 minutes, until tender. Drain and let cool.

4 Blanch the green beans in boiling water for 3 minutes, drain, and let cool. Mix the green beans and potatoes together in a salad bowl.

5 Add the bell pepper strips and diced tomatoes to the potatoes and beans. Stir in the spicy chicken mixture.

6 In a small bowl, beat the dressing ingredients together and pour the dressing on the salad, tossing well. Serve at once.

VARIATION

If you prefer, use lean turkey meat instead of the chicken for a slightly stronger flavor. Use the white meat for the best appearance and flavor.

Broiled New Potato Salad

Serves 4

INGREDIENTS

1 1/2 pounds new potatoes, scrubbed	salt and pepper	DRESSING:
3 tbsp olive oil	parsley sprig, to garnish	4 tbsp mayonnaise
2 tbsp chopped fresh thyme		1 tbsp garlic wine vinegar
1 tsp paprika		2 garlic cloves, crushed
4 slices smoked bacon		1 tbsp chopped fresh parsley

1 Cook the new potatoes in a saucepan of boiling water for 10 minutes. Drain thoroughly.

2 Mix the olive oil, chopped thyme, and paprika together and pour the mixture over the warm potatoes.

3 Place the bacon under a preheated broiler and cook for 5 minutes, turning once, until crisp. When thoroughly cooked, roughly chop the bacon and keep warm.

4 Transfer the potatoes to the broiler pan and cook for 10 minutes, turning once.

5 Mix the dressing ingredients in a small serving bowl. Transfer the potatoes and bacon to a large serving bowl. Season with salt and pepper and mix together.

6 Spoon over the dressing, garnish with a parsley sprig, and serve immediately for a warm salad. Alternatively, let cool and serve chilled.

VARIATION

Add spicy sausage to the salad in place of bacon— you do not need to cook it under the broiler before adding to the salad.

Potato & Italian Sausage Salad

Serves 4

INGREDIENTS

1 pound waxy potatoes
1 radicchio or lollo rosso lettuce
1 green bell pepper, sliced
6 ounces Italian sausage, sliced

1 red onion, halved and sliced
4 1/2 cups sun-dried tomatoes, sliced
2 tbsp shredded fresh basil

DRESSING:
1 tbsp balsamic vinegar
1 tsp tomato paste
2 tbsp olive oil
salt and pepper

1 Cook the potatoes in a saucepan of boiling water for 20 minutes, or until cooked through. Drain and let cool.

2 Line a large serving platter with the radicchio or lollo rosso lettuce leaves.

3 Slice the cooled potatoes and arrange them in layers on the lettuce-lined serving platter, together with the sliced green bell pepper, sliced Italian sausage, red onion, sun-dried tomatoes, and shredded fresh basil.

4 In a small bowl, beat the balsamic vinegar, tomato paste, and olive oil together and season to taste with salt and pepper. Pour the dressing on the potato salad and serve immediately.

COOK'S TIP

You can use either packets of sun-dried tomatoes or jars of sun-dried tomatoes in oil. If using tomatoes packed in oil, simply rinse the oil from the tomatoes and pat them dry on paper towels before using.

VARIATION

Any sliced Italian sausage or salami can be used in this salad. Italy is the home of the salami and there are numerous varieties to choose from—those from the south tend to be more highly spiced than those from the north of the country.

Potato & Lobster Salad with Lime Dressing

Serves 4

INGREDIENTS

1 pound waxy potatoes, scrubbed
and sliced

8 ounces cooked lobster meat

²/₃ cup mayonnaise

2 tbsp lime juice

finely grated rind of 1 lime

1 tbsp chopped fresh parsley

2 tbsp olive oil

2 tomatoes, seeded and diced

2 hard-cooked eggs, quartered

1 tbsp quartered pitted green olives

salt and pepper

1 Cook the potatoes in a saucepan of boiling water for 10–15 minutes, or until cooked through. Drain and reserve.

2 Remove the lobster meat from the shell and separate it into large pieces.

3 In a bowl, mix together the mayonnaise, 1 tbsp of the lime juice, half the grated lime rind, and half the chopped parsley, then set aside.

4 In a separate bowl, beat the remaining lime juice with the olive oil and pour the dressing on the potatoes. Arrange the potatoes on a serving plate.

5 Top with the lobster meat, tomatoes, eggs, and olives. Season with salt and pepper and sprinkle with the reserved parsley.

6 Spoon the mayonnaise onto the center of the salad, top with the reserved rind, and serve.

COOK'S TIP

As shellfish is used in this salad, serve it immediately, or keep covered and chilled for up to 1 hour before serving.

VARIATION

Crab meat or shrimp may be used instead of the lobster, if you prefer.

Potato & Tuna Salad

Serves 4

INGREDIENTS

1 pound new potatoes, scrubbed and quartered	10^1/$_2$ ounces canned tuna in brine, drained and flaked	DRESSING:
1 green bell pepper, sliced	2 tbsp chopped pitted black olives	2 tbsp mayonnaise
^{1}/$_3$ cup canned corn, drained	salt and pepper	2 tbsp sour cream
1 red onion, sliced	lime wedges, to garnish	1 tbsp lime juice
		2 garlic cloves, crushed
		finely grated rind of 1 lime

1 Cook the potatoes in a saucepan of boiling water for 15 minutes, until tender. Drain and let cool in a mixing bowl.

2 Gently stir in the sliced green bell pepper, corn and sliced red onion.

3 Spoon the potato mixture into a large serving bowl and arrange the flaked tuna and chopped black olives over the top. Season the salad generously with salt and pepper.

4 To make the dressing, mix together the mayonnaise, sour cream, lime juice, garlic, and lime rind in a bowl.

5 Spoon the dressing onto the tuna and olives, garnish with lime wedges, and serve.

COOK'S TIP

Served with a crisp white wine, this salad makes the perfect light lunch for summer or winter.

VARIATION

Green beans and hard-cooked egg slices can be added to the salad for a more traditional Salade Niçoise.

Eggplant Salad

Serves 4

INGREDIENTS

1 large eggplant
3 tablespoons sesame seed paste
juice and rind of 1 lemon
1 garlic clove, crushed
pinch of paprika

1 tablespoon chopped cilantro
salt and pepper
lettuce leaves

garnish:
strips of pimiento
lemon wedges
toasted sesame seeds

---

1 Cut the eggplant in half, place in a colander, and sprinkle with salt. Set aside for 30 minutes to allow the bitter juices to drain. Rinse thoroughly under cold running water and drain well. Pat thoroughly dry with paper towels.

2 Place the eggplant halves, skin side uppermost, on an oiled cookie sheet. Bake in a preheated oven at 450°F for 10–15 minutes. Remove from the oven and set aside to cool.

3 Cut the eggplant into cubes and set aside until required. Mix the sesame seed paste, lemon juice and rind, garlic, paprika, and cilantro together. Season to taste with salt and pepper and stir in the eggplant.

4 Line a serving dish with lettuce leaves and spoon the eggplant mixture into the center. Garnish the salad with slices of pimiento, lemon wedges, and toasted sesame seeds and serve at once.

COOK'S TIP

Sesame seed paste, also called tahini, is a nutty-flavored sauce available from most health food shops. It is good served with many Middle-Eastern dishes.

Salad with Garlic & Yogurt Dressing

Serves 4

INGREDIENTS

2³/₄ ounces cucumber,
    cut into batons
6 scallions, halved
2 tomatoes, seeded
    and cut into eight
1 yellow bell pepper, cut into strips

2 celery stalks, cut into strips
4 radishes, quartered
2³/₄ ounces arugula
1 tablespoon chopped mint, to
    serve

dressing:
2 tablespoons lemon juice
1 garlic clove, crushed
²/₃ cup plain yogurt
2 tablespoons olive oil
salt and pepper

1 Mix the cucumber, scallions, tomatoes, bell pepper, celery, radishes, and arugula together in a large serving bowl.

2 To make the dressing, stir the lemon juice, garlic, plain yogurt, and olive oil together. Season well with salt and pepper to taste.

3 Spoon the dressing over the salad and toss well to coat thoroughly.

4 Sprinkle the salad with chopped mint and serve.

COOK'S TIP

Do not toss the dressing into the salad until just before serving, otherwise it will turn soggy.

COOK'S TIP

Arugula has a distinct warm, peppery flavor which is ideal in salads. Once you have grown it in your garden or greenhouse, you will always have plenty as it re-seeds all over the place! If arugula is unavailable, spinach makes a good substitute.

Zucchini, Yogurt, & Mint Salad

Serves 4

INGREDIENTS

2 zucchini, cut into sticks
3¹/₂ ounces green beans,
    cut into three
1 green bell pepper, cut into strips

2 celery stalks, sliced
1 bunch watercress

DRESSING:
³/₄ cup plain yogurt
1 garlic clove, crushed
2 tablespoons chopped mint
pepper

1 Cook the zucchini and green beans in a saucepan of salted boiling water for 7–8 minutes. Drain well and set aside to cool completely.

2 Mix the zucchini and green beans with the bell pepper, celery, and watercress in a large serving bowl.

3 To make the dressing, mix together the plain yogurt, garlic, and chopped mint in a bowl until thoroughly combined. Season with pepper to taste.

4 Spoon the dressing onto the salad and serve at once.

COOK'S TIP

Watercress is available all year around. Its fresh peppery flavor makes it a delicious addition to many salads.

COOK'S TIP

The salad must be served as soon as the yogurt dressing has been added—the dressing will start to separate if kept for any length of time.

Bean, Avocado, & Tomato Salad

Serves 4

INGREDIENTS

red butter lettuce
2 ripe avocados
2 teaspoons lemon juice
4 medium tomatoes

1 onion
2 cups mixed canned beans, drained

DRESSING:
4 tablespoons olive oil

dash of chili oil
2 tablespoons garlic wine vinegar
pinch of sugar
pinch of chili powder
1 tablespoon chopped parsley

1 Line a serving bowl with the lettuce.

2 Using a sharp knife, thinly slice the avocados and sprinkle with the lemon juice.

3 Thinly slice the tomatoes and onion. Arrange the avocado, tomatoes, and onion around the salad bowl, leaving a space in the center.

4 Spoon the beans into the center of the salad and whisk the dressing ingredients together. Pour the dressing over the salad and serve.

COOK'S TIP

Instead of whisking the dressing, place all the ingredients in a screw-top jar and shake vigorously. Any leftover dressing can then be kept and stored in the same jar.

COOK'S TIP

The lemon juice is sprinkled onto the avocados to prevent discoloration when in contact with the air. For this reason the salad should be prepared, assembled, and served quite quickly.

Gado Gado

Serves 4

INGREDIENTS

1 cup white cabbage, shredded
3 ¹/₂ ounces green beans,
    cut into 3
3 ¹/₂ ounces carrots,
    cut into matchsticks
3 ¹/₂ ounces cauliflower florets

3 ¹/₂ ounces bean sprouts
dressing:
¹/₂ cup vegetable oil
1 cup unsalted peanuts
2 garlic cloves, crushed
1 small onion, finely chopped

¹/₂ teaspoon chili powder
¹/₃ teaspoon light brown sugar
2 cups water
juice of ¹/₂ lemon
salt
sliced scallions, to garnish

1 Cook the vegetables separately in saucepans of salted boiling water for 4–5 minutes, drain well, and chill in the refrigerator.

2 To make the dressing, heat the oil in a skillet and fry the peanuts for 3–4 minutes, turning.

3 Remove from the skillet with a slotted spoon and drain on absorbent paper towels.

Grind the peanuts in a blender or crush with the end of a rolling pin until a fine mixture is formed.

4 Pour all but 1 tablespoon of the oil from the skillet and fry the garlic and onion for 1 minute. Add the chili powder, sugar, a pinch of salt, and the water and bring to a boil.

5 Stir in the peanuts. Reduce the heat and simmer for 4–5 minutes, until thickened. Add the lemon juice and let cool.

6 Arrange the vegetables in a serving dish and spoon the peanut dressing into the center. Garnish and serve.

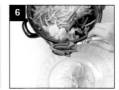

Broiled Vegetable Salad with Mustard Dressing

Serves 4

INGREDIENTS

1 zucchini, sliced	3 tablespoons olive oil	2 tablespoons balsamic vinegar
1 yellow bell pepper, sliced	1 garlic clove, crushed	2 teaspoons chopped rosemary
1 eggplant, sliced	fresh rosemary sprigs, to garnish	1 teaspoon Dijon mustard
1 fennel bulb, cut into eight		1 teaspoon clear honey
1 red onion, cut into eight	DRESSING:	2 teaspoons lemon juice
16 cherry tomatoes	4 tablespoons olive oil	

1 Put all of the vegetables, except for the cherry tomatoes, onto a cookie sheet.

2 Mix together the olive oil and garlic and brush the mixture over the vegetables. Cook under a preheated broiler for 10 minutes, until tender and just beginning to char and blister. Set aside to cool. Spoon the vegetables into a serving bowl.

3 Mix the dressing ingredients and pour it over the vegetables. Cover and chill for 1 hour. Garnish and serve.

COOK'S TIP

This dish could also be served warm—heat the dressing in a pan and then toss into the vegetables.

COOK'S TIP

Balsamic vinegar is made in and around Modena in Italy. It is dark and mellow with a sweet-sour flavor. Although it is rather expensive, you need only a small amount to give a wonderful taste to the dressing. If it is unavailable, use sherry vinegar or white wine vinegar instead.

Red Cabbage & Pear Salad

Serves 4

INGREDIENTS

4 cups finely shredded
    red cabbage
2 bosc pears, thinly sliced
4 scallions, sliced
1 carrot, grated

fresh chives, to garnish
lettuce leaves, to serve

DRESSING:
4 tablespoons pear juice

1 teaspoon wholegrain mustard
3 tablespoons olive oil
1 tablespoon garlic wine vinegar
1 tablespoon chopped chives

1 Put the cabbage, pears, and scallions in a bowl and mix thoroughly together.

2 Line a serving dish with lettuce leaves and spoon the cabbage and pear mixture into the center.

3 Sprinkle the carrot into the center of the cabbage to form a domed pile.

4 To make the dressing, mix together the pear juice, wholegrain mustard, olive oil, garlic wine vinegar, and chives.

5 Pour the dressing over the salad, toss to mix, garnish, and serve at once.

COOK'S TIP

Mix the salad just before serving to prevent the color from the red cabbage bleeding into the other ingredients.

VARIATION

Experiment with different types of salad greens. The slightly bitter flavor of endive or radicchio would work well with the sweetness of the pears.

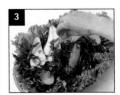

Alfalfa, Beet, & Spinach Salad

Serves 4

INGREDIENTS

3 1/2 ounces baby spinach
2 3/4 ounces alfalfa sprouts
2 celery stalks, sliced
4 cooked beet, cut into eight

DRESSING:
4 tablespoons olive oil
6 teaspoons garlic wine vinegar
1 garlic clove, crushed

2 teaspoons honey
1 tablespoon chopped chives

1 Place the spinach and alfalfa sprouts in a large bowl and mix together.

2 Add the celery and mix well.

3 Toss in the beet and mix well.

4 To make the dressing, mix the oil, wine vinegar, garlic, honey, and chopped chives.

5 Pour the dressing over the salad, toss thoroughly, and serve at once.

COOK'S TIP

If the spinach leaves are too large, tear them up, rather than cutting them, because cutting bruises the leaves.

COOK'S TIP

Alfalfa sprouts should be available from most supermarkets, if not, use bean sprouts instead.

VARIATION

Add the segments of 1 large orange to the salad to make it even more colorful and refreshing. Replace the garlic wine vinegar with a different flavored oil such as chili or herb, if desired.

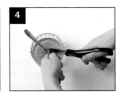

Snacks & Light Meals

Sometimes we may not feel like eating a full-scale meal but still want something appetizing and satisfying. Potatoes and vegetables are so versatile that they can be used as a base to create a whole array of tempting light meals and satisfying snacks. They are also extremely nutritious, as the carbohydrate that they contain will give a welcome energy boost.

This chapter contains a range of tempting snacks which are quick and easy to make and will satisfy those mid-morning or mid-afternoon hunger pangs! They also come in handy if an unexpected visitor drops by. The chapter also contains a range of delicious yet light meals which are ideal if you feel slightly hungry rather than ravenously. They cater to all tastes, including vegetarian, and all times of day. Many can be prepared ahead of time and will not detain you in the kitchen too long.

Potato & Bean Pâté

Serves 4

INGREDIENTS

3¹⁄₂ oz mealy potatoes, diced

1²⁄₃ cups mixed canned beans, such as borlotti, flageolet, and kidney beans, drained

1 garlic clove, crushed

2 tsp lime juice

1 tbsp chopped fresh cilantro

2 tbsp unsweetened yogurt

salt and pepper

chopped fresh cilantro, to garnish

1 Cook the potatoes in a saucepan of boiling water for 10 minutes, until tender. Drain well and mash.

2 Transfer the potato to a food processor or blender and add the beans, garlic, lime juice, and the fresh cilantro. Season the mixture and process for 1 minute to make a smooth purée. Alternatively, mix the beans with the potato, garlic, lime juice, and cilantro and mash.

3 Turn the purée into a bowl and add the yogurt. Mix well.

4 Spoon the pâté into a serving dish and garnish with the chopped cilantro. Serve at once or chill in the refrigerator.

VARIATION

If you do not have a food processor or you would prefer to make a chunkier pâté, simply mash the ingredients with a fork.

COOK'S TIP

To make Melba toast, toast ready-sliced white or brown bread lightly on both sides under a preheated broiler and remove the crusts. Holding the bread flat, slide a sharp knife between the toasted bread to split it horizontally. Cut into triangles and toast the untoasted side until the edges curl.

Smoked Fish & Potato Pâté

Serves 4

INGREDIENTS

1¹/₂ pounds mealy potatoes, diced	2 tsp lemon juice	1 tbsp chopped dill pickle
10¹/₂ ounces smoked mackerel,	2 tbsp crème fraîche	1 tbsp chopped fresh dill
skinned and flaked	1 tbsp capers	salt and pepper
³/₄ cup cooked gooseberries	1 gherkin, chopped	lemon wedges, to garnish

1 Cook the diced potatoes in a saucepan of boiling water for 10 minutes, until tender, then drain well.

2 Place the cooked potatoes in a food processor or blender.

3 Add the skinned and flaked smoked mackerel and process for 30 seconds until fairly smooth. Alternatively, mash with a fork.

4 Add the cooked gooseberries with the lemon juice and crème fraîche. Blend for a further 10 seconds or mash well.

5 Stir in the capers, gherkin, dill pickle, and chopped fresh dill. Season well with salt and pepper.

6 Turn the fish pâté into a serving dish, garnish with lemon wedges, and serve with slices of toast or warm crusty bread in chunks or slices.

COOK'S TIP

Use stewed, canned, or bottled cooked gooseberries for convenience and to save time, or when fresh gooseberries are out of season.

VARIATION

Use other tart fruits, such as stewed apples, instead of the gooseberries if they are unavailable.

Potato Kibbeh

Serves 4

INGREDIENTS

1 cup bulgur wheat	salt and pepper	1 tbsp pine nuts
12 ounces mealy potatoes, diced	oil for deep-frying	1 ounce dried apricots, chopped
2 small eggs		pinch of grated nutmeg
2 tbsp butter, melted	STUFFING:	pinch of ground cinnamon
pinch of ground cumin	6 ounces ground lamb	1 tbsp chopped fresh cilantro
pinch of ground coriander	1 small onion, chopped	2 tbsp lamb stock
pinch of grated nutmeg		

1 Put the bulgur wheat in a bowl and cover with boiling water. Soak for 30 minutes, until the water has been absorbed and the bulgur wheat has swollen.

2 Meanwhile, cook the diced potatoes in a saucepan of boiling water for 10 minutes, or until cooked through. Drain and mash until smooth.

3 Add the bulgur wheat to the mashed potato with the eggs, the melted butter, the ground cumin

and coriander, and the grated nutmeg. Season well with salt and pepper.

4 To make the stuffing, dry-fry the lamb for 5 minutes, add the onion, and cook for a further 2–3 minutes. Add the remaining stuffing ingredients and cook for 5 minutes, until the stock has been absorbed. Cool slightly, then divide into 8 portions. Roll each one into a ball.

5 Divide the potato mixture into 8 portions

and flatten each into a round. Place a portion of stuffing in the center of each round. Shape the coating around the stuffing to encase it completely.

6 In a large saucepan or deep fat fryer, heat the oil to 350°F–375°F or until a cube of bread browns in 30 seconds, and cook the kibbeh for 5–7 minutes, until golden brown. Drain well and serve at once.

Potato & Meatballs in Spicy Sauce

Serves 4

INGREDIENTS

8 ounces mealy potatoes, diced	salt and pepper	14 ounce can chopped tomatoes
8 ounces ground beef or lamb	chopped fresh cilantro,	1 green chili, chopped
1 onion, finely chopped	to garnish	1 tsp paprika
1 tbsp chopped fresh cilantro		$^2/_3$ cup vegetable stock
1 celery stalk, finely chopped	SAUCE:	2 tsp cornstarch
2 garlic cloves, crushed	1 tbsp vegetable oil	
2 tbsp butter	1 onion, finely chopped	
1 tbsp vegetable oil	2 tsp light brown sugar	

1 Cook the diced potatoes in a saucepan of boiling water for 25 minutes, until cooked through. Drain well and transfer to a large mixing bowl. Mash until smooth.

2 Add the ground beef or lamb, onion, cilantro, celery, and garlic and mix well.

3 Bring the mixture together with your hands and roll it into 20 small balls.

4 To make the sauce, heat the oil in a pan and sauté the onion for 5 minutes. Add the remaining sauce ingredients and bring to a boil, stirring. Lower the heat and simmer for 20 minutes.

5 Meanwhile, heat the butter and oil for the potato and meatballs in a skillet. Add the balls in batches and cook for 10–15 minutes, until browned, turning frequently. Keep warm while cooking the remainder. Serve the potato and meatballs in a warm shallow ovenproof dish with the sauce poured around them and garnished with cilantro.

COOK'S TIP

Make the potato and meatballs in advance and chill or freeze them for later use. Make sure you defrost them thoroughly before cooking.

Potato & Fish Balls with Tomato Sauce

Serves 4

INGREDIENTS

1 pound mealy potatoes, diced	1 tbsp chopped fresh dill	SAUCE:
2 smoked fish fillets, such as cod,	$\frac{1}{2}$ tsp cayenne pepper	$1\frac{1}{4}$ cups sieved tomatoes
about 8 ounces total weight,	oil for deep-frying	1 tbsp tomato paste
skinned	salt and pepper	2 tbsp chopped fresh dill
3 tbsp butter	dill sprigs, to garnish	$\frac{2}{3}$ cup fish stock
2 eggs, beaten		

1 Cook the diced potatoes in a saucepan of boiling water for 10 minutes, or until cooked. Drain well, then add the butter to the potato and mash until smooth. Season well with salt and pepper.

2 Meanwhile, poach the fish in boiling water for 10 minutes, turning once. Drain and mash the fish. Stir it into the potato mixture and let cool.

3 While the potato and fish mixture is cooling, make the sauce. Put the sieved tomatoes, tomato paste, dill, and stock in a pan and bring to a boil. Reduce the heat, cover the pan, and simmer for 20 minutes, until thickened.

4 Add the eggs, dill, and cayenne pepper to the potato and fish mixture and beat until well mixed.

5 In a large saucepan or deep-fryer, heat the oil to 350°F–375°F, or until a cube of bread browns in 30 seconds. Drop in spoons of the mixture and cook for 3–4 minutes, until golden brown. Drain on paper towels.

6 Garnish the potato and fish balls with dill sprigs and serve with the tomato sauce.

VARIATION

Smoked fish is used for extra flavor, but white fish fillets or ground shrimp may be used, if desired.

Thai Potato Crab Cakes

Serves 4

INGREDIENTS

1 pound mealy potatoes, diced

6 ounces white crab meat, drained
    if canned

4 scallions, chopped

1 tsp light soy sauce

1/2 tsp sesame oil

1 tsp chopped lemon grass

1 tsp lime juice

3 tbsp all-purpose flour

2 tbsp vegetable oil

salt and pepper

SAUCE:

4 tbsp finely chopped cucumber

2 tbsp clear honey

1 tbsp garlic wine vinegar

1/2 tsp light soy sauce

1 red chili, chopped

TO GARNISH:

1 red chili, sliced

cucumber slices

1 Cook the diced potatoes in a saucepan of boiling water for 10 minutes, until cooked through. Drain well and mash.

2 Mix the crab meat into the potato with the scallions, soy sauce, sesame oil, lemon grass, lime juice, and flour. Season with salt and pepper.

3 Divide the potato mixture into 8 portions of equal size and shape them into small rounds, using floured hands.

4 Heat the oil in a wok or skillet and cook the cakes, 4 at a time, for 5–7 minutes, turning once. Keep warm and repeat with the remaining mixture.

5 Meanwhile, make the sauce. In a small serving bowl, mix the cucumber, honey, vinegar, soy sauce, and chopped red chili.

6 Garnish the cakes with the sliced red chili and cucumber slices and serve with the sauce.

COOK'S TIP

Do not make the cucumber sauce too far in advance as the water from the cucumber will make the sauce runny and dilute the flavor.

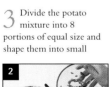

Potato & Mixed Mushroom Cakes

Serves 4

INGREDIENTS

1 pound mealy potatoes, diced	2 garlic cloves, crushed	flour, for dusting
2 tbsp butter	1 small egg, beaten	oil, for frying
6 ounces mixed mushrooms, chopped	1 tbsp chopped fresh chives, plus extra to garnish	salt and pepper

1 Cook the potatoes in a pan of boiling water for 10 minutes, or until cooked through. Drain well, mash, and set aside.

2 Meanwhile, melt the butter in a skillet and cook the mushrooms and garlic for 5 minutes, stirring. Drain well.

3 Stir the mushrooms and garlic into the potato, together with the beaten egg and chives.

4 Divide the mixture equally into 4 portions and shape them into round patties. Toss them in the flour until the outsides are completely coated.

5 Heat the oil in a skillet and cook the potato patties over a medium heat for 10 minutes, until they are golden brown, turning them over halfway through. Serve the cakes at once, with a salad.

COOK'S TIP

Prepare the cakes in advance, cover, and chill in the refrigerator for up to 24 hours, if desired.

VARIATION

If chives are unavailable, use other fresh herbs of your choice. Sage, tarragon, and cilantro all combine well with mixed mushrooms.

Potato, Cheese, & Onion Rosti

Serves 4

INGREDIENTS

2 pounds Maris Piper, or other main crop potato	2 tbsp chopped fresh parsley	TO GARNISH:
1 onion, grated	1 tbsp olive oil	shredded scallion
½ cup grated Swiss cheese	2 tbsp butter	1 small tomato, quartered
	salt and pepper	

1 Parboil the potatoes in a pan of boiling water for 10 minutes, drain, and let cool. Peel the potatoes and grate with a coarse grater. Place the grated potatoes in a large mixing bowl.

2 Stir in the onion, cheese, and parsley. Season well with salt and pepper. Divide the potato mixture into 4 portions of equal size and form them into patties.

3 Heat half of the olive oil and butter in a skillet and cook

2 of the potato patties over a high heat for 1 minute, then reduce the heat and cook for 5 minutes, until they are golden underneath. Turn them over and cook for a further 5 minutes.

4 Repeat with the other half of the oil and butter to cook the remaining 2 patties. Transfer to serving plates, garnish, and serve.

COOK'S TIP

The potato patties should be flattened as much as possible during cooking, otherwise the outside will be cooked before the center.

VARIATION

To make these rosti into a more substantial meal, add chopped cooked bacon or ham to the potato mixture.

Potato & Cauliflower Fritters

Serves 4

INGREDIENTS

8 ounces mealy potatoes, diced
8 ounces cauliflower florets
2 tbsp grated Parmesan cheese
1 egg

1 egg white for coating
oil, for frying
paprika, for dusting (optional)
salt and pepper

crispy bacon slices, chopped,
to serve

1 Cook the potatoes in a saucepan of boiling water for 10 minutes, until cooked through. Drain well and mash.

2 Cook the cauliflower florets in a separate pan of boiling water for 10 minutes.

3 Drain the cauliflower florets and mix into the mashed potato. Stir in the grated Parmesan cheese and season well with salt and pepper.

4 Separate the whole egg and beat the yolk into the potato and cauliflower, mixing well.

5 Lightly beat both the egg whites in a clean bowl, then carefully fold into the potato and cauliflower mixture.

6 Divide the potato mixture into 8 equal portions and shape them into rounds.

7 Heat the oil in a skillet and cook the fritters for

3–5 minutes, turning once halfway through cooking.

8 Dust the cooked fritters with a little paprika, if desired, and serve at once accompanied by the crispy chopped bacon.

VARIATION

Any other vegetable, such as broccoli, can be used in this recipe instead of the cauliflower florets, if desired.

Potato Fritters with Garlic Sauce

Serves 4

INGREDIENTS

1 pound waxy potatoes, cut into large cubes	SAUCE:	BATTER:
1½ cups grated Parmesan cheese	2 tbsp butter	½ cup all-purpose flour
oil, for deep-frying	1 onion, halved and sliced	1 small egg
	2 garlic cloves, crushed	⅔ cup milk
	¼ cup all-purpose flour	
	1¼ cups milk	
	1 tbsp chopped fresh parsley	

1 To make the sauce, melt the butter in a saucepan and cook the sliced onion and garlic for 2–3 minutes. Add the flour and cook for 1 minute.

2 Remove from the heat and stir in the milk and parsley. Return to the heat and bring to a boil. Keep warm.

3 Meanwhile, cook the cubed potatoes in a saucepan of boiling water for 5–10 minutes, until just firm. Do not overcook or they will fall apart.

4 Drain the potatoes and toss them in the Parmesan cheese.

5 To make the batter, place the flour in a mixing bowl and gradually beat in the egg and milk until smooth. Dip the potato cubes into the batter to coat them.

6 In a large saucepan or deep-fryer, heat the oil to 350°F–375°F, or until a cube of bread browns in 30 seconds, and cook the fritters for 3–4 minutes, or until golden. Drain the fritters with a slotted spoon and transfer them to a serving bowl. Serve with the sauce.

COOK'S TIP

Coat the potatoes in the Parmesan while still slightly wet to ensure that the cheese sticks and coats well.

Potato Croquettes with Ham & Cheese

Serves 4

INGREDIENTS

1 pound mealy potatoes, diced	COATING:	SAUCE:
1½ cups milk	2 eggs, beaten	2 tbsp butter
2 tbsp butter	2¼ cups fresh whole wheat bread	¼ cup all-purpose flour
4 scallions, chopped	crumbs	⅔ cup milk
2¾ ounces Cheddar cheese		⅔ cup vegetable stock
1¾ ounces smoked ham, chopped		⅔ cup Cheddar cheese, grated
1 celery stalk, diced		1 tsp Dijon mustard
1 egg, beaten		1 tbsp chopped cilantro
½ cup all-purpose flour		
oil, for deep frying		
salt and pepper		

---

1 Place the potatoes in a pan with the milk and bring to a boil. Reduce to a simmer until the liquid has been absorbed and the potatoes are cooked.

2 Add the butter and mash the potatoes. Stir in the scallions, cheese, ham, celery, egg, and flour. Season with salt and pepper to taste and let cool.

3 To make the coating, beat the eggs in a bowl. Put the bread crumbs in a separate bowl.

4 Shape the potato mixture into 8 balls. First dip them in the egg, then in the bread crumbs.

5 To make the sauce, melt the butter in a small pan. Add the flour and cook for

1 minute. Remove from the heat and stir in the milk, stock, cheese, mustard, and herbs. Bring to a boil, stirring until thickened. Reduce the heat and keep warm.

6 In a deep-fryer, heat the oil to 350°F–375°F and fry the croquettes for 5 minutes, until golden. Drain well and serve with the sauce.

Hash Browns with Tomato Sauce

Serves 4

INGREDIENTS

1 pound waxy potatoes	4 tbsp vegetable oil	SAUCE:
1 carrot, diced	2 tbsp butter	$1^1/_4$ cups sieved tomatoes
1 celery stalk, diced	salt and pepper	2 tbsp chopped fresh cilantro
$^3/_4$ cup diced button mushrooms		1 tbsp Worcestershire sauce
1 onion, diced		$^1/_2$ tsp chili powder
2 garlic cloves, crushed		2 tsp brown sugar
1 ounce frozen peas, thawed		2 tsp American mustard
$^2/_3$ cup grated Parmesan cheese		$^1/_3$ cup vegetable stock

1 Cook the potatoes in a saucepan of boiling water for 10 minutes. Drain and let cool. Meanwhile, cook the carrot in boiling water for 5 minutes.

2 When cool, grate the potato with a coarse grater.

3 Drain the carrot and add it to the grated potato with the celery, mushrooms, onion, peas, and cheese. Season well.

4 Place all the sauce ingredients in a pan and bring to a boil. Reduce the heat and simmer for 15 minutes.

5 Divide the potato mixture into 8 portions of equal size and shape into flattened rectangles with your hands.

6 Heat the oil and butter in a skillet and cook the hash browns over a low heat for 4–5 minutes

on each side, until crisp and golden brown.

7 Serve the hash browns with the tomato sauce.

COOK'S TIP

Use any mixture of vegetables for this recipe. For a non-vegetarian dish, add bacon pieces or diced ham for added flavor.

Potato Pancakes with Soured Cream & Salmon

Serves 4

INGREDIENTS

1 pound mealy potatoes, grated	salt and pepper	TOPPING:
2 scallions, chopped	fresh chives, to garnish	²/₃ cup sour cream
2 tbsp self-rising flour		4¹/₂ ounces smoked salmon
2 eggs, beaten		
2 tbsp vegetable oil		

1 Rinse the grated potatoes under cold running water, drain, and pat dry on paper towels. Transfer to a mixing bowl.

2 Mix the chopped scallions, flour, and eggs into the potatoes and season well with salt and pepper.

3 Heat 1 tbsp of the oil in a skillet. Drop about 4 tablespoonfuls of the mixture into the pan and spread each one with the back of a spoon to form a round (the mixture should make 16 pancakes). Cook for 5–7 minutes, turning once, until golden. Drain well.

4 Heat the remaining oil and cook the remaining mixture in batches.

5 Top the pancakes with the sour cream and smoked salmon, garnish with fresh chives, and serve hot.

COOK'S TIP

Smaller versions of this dish may be made and served as appetizers.

VARIATION

These pancakes are equally delicious topped with prosciutto or any other dry-cured ham instead of the smoked salmon.

Potato Omelet with Feta Cheese & Spinach

Serves 4

INGREDIENTS

$^1/_3$ cup butter
6 waxy potatoes, diced
3 garlic cloves, crushed
1 tsp paprika

2 tomatoes, skinned, seeded, and
    diced
12 eggs
pepper

FILLING:
8 ounces baby spinach
1 tsp fennel seeds
1 cup diced feta cheese
4 tbsp unsweetened yogurt

1 Heat 2 tbsp of the butter in a skillet and cook the potatoes over a low heat for 7–10 minutes, until golden, stirring constantly. Transfer to a bowl.

2 Add the garlic, paprika, and tomatoes and cook for a further 2 minutes.

3 Beat the eggs together and season with pepper. Pour the eggs into the potato mixture and mix well.

4 Place the spinach in boiling water for 1 minute, until just wilted. Drain, rinse the spinach under cold running water, and pat dry with paper towels. Stir in the fennel seeds, feta cheese, and yogurt.

5 Heat 1 tbsp of the butter in a 6-inch omelet pan or skillet. Ladle a quarter of the egg and potato mixture into the pan. Cook for 2 minutes, turning once, until just set.

6 Transfer the omelet to a serving plate. Spoon a quarter of the spinach mixture onto one half of the omelet, then fold the omelet in half over the filling. Repeat to make 4 omelets.

VARIATION

Use any other cheese, such as blue cheese, instead of the feta, and blanched broccoli in place of the baby spinach, if you prefer.

138

Spanish Tortilla

Serves 4

INGREDIENTS

2¼ pounds waxy potatoes,
    thinly sliced
4 tbsp vegetable oil
1 onion, sliced

2 garlic cloves, crushed
1 green bell pepper, diced
2 tomatoes, seeded and chopped
1 ounce canned corn, drained

6 large eggs, beaten
2 tbsp chopped fresh parsley
salt and pepper

1 Parboil the potatoes in a saucepan of boiling water for 5 minutes. Drain well.

2 Heat the oil in a large skillet, add the potato and onions, and sauté gently for 5 minutes, stirring constantly, until the potatoes have browned.

3 Add the garlic, diced bell pepper, chopped tomatoes, and corn, mixing well.

4 Pour in the eggs and add the chopped parsley. Season well with salt and pepper. Cook for 10–12 minutes, until the underside is cooked through.

5 Remove the skillet from the heat and continue to cook the tortilla under a preheated broiler for 5–7 minutes, or until the tortilla is set and the top is golden brown.

6 Cut the tortilla into wedges or cubes, depending on your preference, and serve with salad. In Spain tortillas are served hot, cold, or warm.

COOK'S TIP

Ensure that the handle of your skillet is heatproof before placing it under the broiler and be sure to use potholders when removing it as it will be very hot.

Paprika Crisps

Serves 4

INGREDIENTS

2 large potatoes
3 tbsp olive oil

$^1/_2$ tsp paprika pepper
salt

1 Using a sharp knife, slice the potatoes very thinly so that they are almost transparent. Drain the potato slices thoroughly and pat dry with paper towels.

2 Heat the oil in a large skillet and add the paprika, stirring constantly, to ensure that the paprika doesn't catch and burn on the bottom of the pan.

3 Add the potato slices to the skillet and cook them in a single layer for about 5 minutes, or until the potato slices just begin to brown and curl slightly at the edges.

4 Remove the potato slices from the pan using a slotted spoon. Transfer them to paper towels and pat dry to drain thoroughly.

5 Thread the potato slices on to several wooden kabob skewers.

6 Sprinkle the potato slices with a little salt and cook over a medium hot barbecue or under a preheated broiler for 10 minutes, turning frequently, until the potato slices begin to crispen. Sprinkle with a little more salt, if desired, and serve.

VARIATION

You could use curry powder or any other spice to flavor the chips instead of the paprika, if desired.

Creamy Mushrooms & Potatoes

Serves 4

INGREDIENTS

1 ounce dried porcini, or other dried wild mushrooms

8 ounces mealy potatoes, diced

2 tbsp butter, melted

4 tbsp heavy cream

2 tbsp chopped fresh chives

$^1/_4$ cup grated Swiss cheese

8 large open-capped mushrooms

$^2/_3$ cup vegetable stock

salt and pepper

fresh chives, to garnish

---

1 Place the dried porcini in a bowl, cover with boiling water, and soak for 20 minutes.

2 Meanwhile, cook the potatoes in a saucepan of boiling water for 10 minutes, until cooked. Drain well and mash.

3 Drain the soaked porcini and chop them finely. Mix them into the mashed potato.

4 Mix the butter, cream, and chives together and add to the porcini and potato mixture. Season with salt and pepper.

5 Remove the stalks from the open-capped mushrooms. Chop the stalks and stir them into the potato mixture. Spoon the mixture into the open-capped mushrooms and sprinkle the cheese over the top.

6 Place the filled mushrooms in a shallow ovenproof dish and pour in the vegetable stock.

7 Cover the dish and cook in a preheated oven at 425°F for 20 minutes. Remove the lid and cook for 5 minutes, until golden on top.

8 Garnish the mushrooms with fresh chives and serve at once.

VARIATION

Use fresh mushrooms instead of the dried porcini, if preferred, and stir a mixture of chopped nuts into the mushroom stuffing mixture for extra crunch.

Potato Noodles with Cheese, Mushrooms, & Bacon

Serves 4

INGREDIENTS

1 pound mealy potatoes, diced

2 cups all-purpose flour

1 egg, beaten

1 tbsp milk

salt and pepper

parsley sprig, to garnish

SAUCE:

1 tbsp vegetable oil

1 onion, chopped

1 garlic clove, crushed

2 cups sliced open-capped
    mushrooms

3 smoked bacon slices, chopped

^{2}/$_3$ cup grated Parmesan cheese

1^1/$_4$ cups heavy cream

2 tbsp chopped fresh parsley

1 Cook the diced potatoes in a saucepan of boiling water for 10 minutes, until cooked through. Drain well. Mash the potatoes until smooth, then beat in the flour, egg, and milk. Season with salt and pepper and bring together to form a stiff paste.

2 On a lightly floured surface, roll out the paste to form a thin sausage shape. Cut the sausage into 1-inch lengths. Bring a large

pan of salted water to a boil, drop in the dough pieces, and cook for 3–4 minutes. They will rise to the top when cooked.

3 To make the sauce, heat the oil in a pan and sauté the onion and garlic for 2 minutes. Add the mushrooms and bacon and cook for 5 minutes. Stir in the cheese, cream, and parsley and season.

4 Drain the noodles and transfer to a warm pasta bowl. Spoon the sauce over the top and toss to mix. Garnish with a parsley sprig and serve.

COOK'S TIP

Make the dough in advance, then wrap, and store the noodles in the refrigerator for up to 24 hours.

Potato & Mushroom Bake

Serves 4

INGREDIENTS

2 tbsp butter

1 pound waxy potatoes, thinly sliced

2 cups sliced mixed mushrooms

1 tbsp chopped fresh rosemary

4 tbsp chopped fresh chives

2 garlic cloves, crushed

$^2/_3$ cup heavy cream

salt and pepper

fresh chives, to garnish

1 Grease a shallow, round ovenproof dish with butter.

2 Parboil the sliced potatoes in a saucepan of boiling water for 10 minutes. Drain well. Layer a quarter of the potatoes in the base of the dish.

3 Arrange a quarter of the mushrooms on top of the potatoes and sprinkle with a quarter of the rosemary, chives, and garlic.

4 Continue layering in the same order, finishing with a layer of potatoes on top.

5 Pour the cream over the top of the potatoes. Season well.

6 Cook in a preheated oven at 375°F for 45 minutes, or until the bake is golden brown.

7 Garnish with fresh chives and serve at once.

COOK'S TIP

For a special occasion, the bake may be made in a lined cake pan and turned out to serve.

VARIATION

Use 2 ounces re-hydrated dried mushrooms instead of the fresh mixed mushrooms, for a really intense flavor.

Spicy Potato-Filled Naan Breads

Serves 4

INGREDIENTS

8 ounces waxy potatoes, scrubbed and diced	1/2 tsp chili powder	RAITA:
1 tbsp vegetable oil	1 tbsp tomato paste	2/3 cup unsweetened yogurt
1 onion, chopped	3 tbsp vegetable stock	4 tbsp diced cucumber
2 garlic cloves, crushed	2³/₄ ounces baby spinach, shredded	1 tbsp chopped mint
1 tsp ground cumin	4 small or 2 large naan breads	
1 tsp ground coriander	lime pickle, to serve	

1 Cook the diced potatoes in a saucepan of boiling water for 10 minutes. Drain thoroughly.

2 Heat the vegetable oil in a separate saucepan and cook the onion and garlic for 3 minutes, stirring. Add the spices and cook for a further 2 minutes.

3 Stir in the potatoes, tomato paste, vegetable stock, and spinach. Cook for 5 minutes, until the potatoes are tender.

4 Warm the naan breads in a preheated oven at 300°F for about 2 minutes.

5 To make the raita, mix the yogurt, cucumber, and mint together in a small bowl.

6 Remove the naan breads from the oven. Using a sharp knife, cut a pocket in the side of each naan bread. Spoon the spicy potato filling mixture into each naan bread pocket.

7 Serve the filled naan breads at once, accompanied by the raita and lime pickle.

COOK'S TIP

To give the raita a much stronger flavor, make it in advance and chill in the refrigerator until ready to serve.

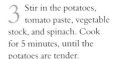

Potato & Spinach Phyllo Triangles

Serves 4

INGREDIENTS

8 ounces waxy potatoes, diced finely	½ tsp lemon juice	MAYONNAISE:
1 pound baby spinach	8 ounces packet phyllo pastry, thawed if frozen	⅔ cup mayonnaise
1 tomato, seeded and chopped	2 tbsp butter, melted	2 tsp lemon juice
¼ tsp chili powder	salt and pepper	rind of 1 lemon

1 Lightly grease a cookie sheet with a little butter.

2 Cook the potatoes in a saucepan of boiling water for 10 minutes, or until cooked through. Drain thoroughly and place in a mixing bowl.

3 Meanwhile, put the spinach in a saucepan with 2 tbsp of water, cover, and cook over a low heat for 2 minutes, until wilted. Drain the spinach thoroughly and add to the potato.

4 Stir in the chopped tomato, chili powder, and lemon juice. Season to taste with salt and pepper.

5 Lightly butter 8 sheets of phyllo pastry. Spread out 4 of the sheets and lay the other 4 on top of each. Cut them into 8 x 4-inch rectangles.

6 Spoon the potato and spinach mixture onto one end of each rectangle. Fold a corner of the pastry over the filling, fold the pointed end back over the pastry strip, then fold over the remaining pastry to form a triangle.

7 Place the triangles on the cookie sheet and bake in a preheated oven at 375°F for 20 minutes, or until a golden brown color.

8 To make the mayonnaise, mix the mayonnaise, lemon juice, and lemon rind together in a small bowl. Serve the potato and spinach phyllo triangles warm or cold with the lemon mayonnaise and crisp salad greens.

Garlic Mushrooms on Toast

Serves 4

INGREDIENTS

6 tablespoons vegetarian margarine
2 garlic cloves, crushed

4 cups sliced mixed mushrooms,
such as open-cap, button,
oyster, and shiitake

8 slices French bread
1 tablespoon chopped parsley
salt and pepper

1 Melt the margarine in a skillet over medium heat. Add the crushed garlic and cook for 30 seconds, stirring.

2 Add the mushrooms and cook for 5 minutes, turning occasionally.

3 Toast the slices of French bread under a preheated broiler for about 2–3 minutes, turning once.

4 Transfer the toasts to a serving plate.

5 Toss the parsley into the mushrooms, mixing well, and season well with salt and pepper to taste.

6 Spoon the mushroom mixture over the bread and serve at once.

COOK'S TIP

Store mushrooms for 24–36 hours in the refrigerator, in paper bags, as they sweat in plastic. Wild mushrooms should be washed but other varieties can simply be wiped with paper towels.

COOK'S TIP

Add seasonings, such as curry powder or chili powder, to the mushrooms for extra flavor, if desired.

Potato, Bell Pepper, & Mushroom Hash

Serves 4

INGREDIENTS

1½ pounds potatoes, cubed
1 tablespoon olive oil
2 garlic cloves, crushed
1 green bell pepper, cubed

1 yellow bell pepper, cubed
3 tomatoes, diced
1 cup halved button mushrooms
1 tablespoon vegetarian
   Worcestershire sauce

2 tablespoons chopped basil
salt and pepper
fresh basil sprigs, to garnish
warm, crusty bread, to serve

1 Cook the potatoes in a saucepan of boiling, salted water for 7–8 minutes. Drain well and reserve.

2 Heat the olive oil in a large, heavy-based skillet and cook the potatoes for 8–10 minutes, stirring constantly, until they are golden brown.

3 Add the garlic and bell peppers and cook for 2–3 minutes.

4 Stir in the tomatoes and mushrooms and cook, stirring, for 5–6 minutes.

5 Stir in the vegetarian Worcestershire sauce and basil and season well. Garnish and serve with crusty bread.

VARIATION

This dish can also be eaten cold as a salad.

COOK'S TIP

Most brands of Worcestershire sauce contain anchovies, so make sure you choose a vegetarian variety.

Vegetable Samosas

Makes 12

INGREDIENTS

FILLING:

2 tablespoons vegetable oil
1 onion, chopped
$^1/_2$ teaspoon ground coriander
$^1/_2$ teaspoon ground cumin
pinch of turmeric

$^1/_2$ teaspoon ground ginger
$^1/_2$ teaspoon garam masala
1 garlic clove, crushed
$1^1/_2$ cups diced potatoes
1 cup frozen peas, thawed
2 cups chopped spinach

PASTRY:

12 sheets phyllo pastry
oil, for deep-frying

1 To make the filling, heat the oil in a skillet and sauté the onion for 1–2 minutes, stirring constantly, until softened. Stir in all of the spices and garlic and cook for 1 minute.

2 Add the potatoes and cook over gentle heat for 5 minutes, stirring, until they begin to soften.

3 Stir in the peas and spinach and cook for a further 3–4 minutes.

4 Lay the phyllo pastry sheets out on a clean counter and fold each sheet in half lengthwise.

5 Place 2 tablespoons of the vegetable filling at one end of each folded pastry sheet. Fold over one corner to make a triangle. Continue folding the pastry in this way to make a triangular packet and then seal the edges by brushing with a little water.

6 Repeat with the remaining pastry and filling.

7 Heat the oil for deep-frying to 350°F or until a cube of bread browns in 30 seconds. Fry the samosas, in batches, for 1–2 minutes, until golden. Drain on absorbent paper towels and keep warm while cooking the remainder. Serve at once.

Scrambled Bean Curd
on Toasted Rolls

Serves 4

INGREDIENTS

6 tablespoons vegetarian margarine	1 red onion, chopped	2 tablespoons chopped mixed herbs
1 pound marinated,	1 red bell pepper, chopped	salt and pepper
firm bean curd	4 rolls	fresh herbs, to garnish

1 Melt the margarine in a heavy-based skillet over medium heat and crumble the bean curd into the pan.

2 Add the onion and bell pepper and cook for 3–4 minutes, stirring occasionally.

3 Meanwhile, slice the rolls in half and toast under a preheated broiler for about 2–3 minutes, turning once. Remove the toasts and transfer to a serving plate.

4 Add the herbs to the bean curd mixture, combine, and season to taste.

5 Spoon the bean curd mixture onto the toast and garnish with fresh herbs. Serve at once.

COOK'S TIP

Marinated bean curd adds extra flavor to this dish. Smoked bean curd could be used in its place.

COOK'S TIP

Rub the cut surface of a garlic clove over the toasted rolls for extra flavor.

Mixed Bean Pan-Fry

Serves 4

INGREDIENTS

4 cups mixed fresh beans, such as
    green and fava beans
2 tablespoons vegetable oil
2 garlic cloves, crushed

1 red onion, halved
    and sliced
8 ounces firm marinated
    bean curd, diced
1 tablespoon lemon juice

$^1/_2$ teaspoon turmeric
1 teaspoon pumpkin pie spice
$^2/_3$ cup vegetable stock
2 teaspoons sesame seeds

---

1 Trim and chop the
  green beans and set
aside until they are required.

2 Heat the oil in a
  skillet over medium
heat and sauté the garlic
and onion for 2 minutes,
stirring well.

3 Add the bean curd and
  cook for 2–3 minutes,
until it is just beginning to
brown.

4 Add the green beans
  and fava beans.
Stir in the lemon juice,
turmeric, pumpkin pie

spice, and vegetable stock
and bring to a boil.

5 Reduce the heat and
  simmer for 5–7 minutes,
or until the beans are tender.
Sprinkle with sesame seeds
and serve at once.

VARIATION

*Add lime juice instead of
lemon, for an alternative
citrus flavor.*

VARIATION

*Use smoked bean
curd instead of marinated
bean curd for an
alternative flavor.*

Calzone with Sun-Dried Tomatoes & Vegetables

Makes 4

INGREDIENTS

DOUGH:
3 1/2 cups all-purpose flour
2 teaspoons active yeast
1 teaspoon superfine sugar
2/3 cup vegetable stock
2/3 cup sieved tomatoes
beaten egg

FILLING:
1 tablespoon vegetable oil
1 onion, chopped
1 garlic clove, crushed
2 tablespoons chopped sun-dried tomatoes
1 cup chopped spinach

3 tablespoons canned and drained corn
1/4 cup green beans, cut into three pieces
1 tablespoon tomato paste
1 tablespoon chopped oregano
2 ounces mozzarella cheese, sliced
salt and pepper

1 Sift the flour into a bowl. Add the active dry yeast and sugar and then beat in the stock and sieved tomatoes to make a smooth dough.

2 Knead the dough on a lightly floured counter for 10 minutes, then place in a clean, lightly oiled bowl and set aside to rise in a warm place for 1 hour.

3 Heat the oil in a skillet and sauté the onion for about 2–3 minutes. Stir in the garlic, tomatoes, spinach, corn, and beans and cook for 3–4 minutes. Add the tomato paste and oregano and season well.

4 Divide the risen dough into 4 equal portions and roll each onto a floured surface to form a 7-inch round. Spoon a quarter of the filling onto one half of each round and top with cheese. Fold the dough over to encase the filling, sealing the edge with a fork. Glaze with beaten egg. Put the calzone on a lightly greased cookie sheet and cook in a preheated oven at 425°F for 25–30 minutes, until risen and golden. Transfer to warm plates and serve.

Vegetable Enchiladas

Serves 4

INGREDIENTS

4 flour tortillas
³/₄ cup grated vegetarian
    Cheddar cheese

FILLING:
2³/₄ ounces spinach
2 tablespoons olive oil
8 baby corn cobs, sliced

1 tablespoon frozen peas, thawed
1 red bell pepper, diced
1 carrot, diced
1 leek, sliced
2 garlic cloves, crushed
1 red chili, chopped
salt and pepper

SAUCE:
1¹/₄ cups sieved tomatoes
2 shallots, chopped
1 garlic clove, crushed
1¹/₄ cups vegetable stock
1 teaspoon superfine sugar
1 teaspoon chili powder

1 To make the filling, blanch the spinach in a pan of boiling water for 2 minutes, drain well, and chop.

2 Heat the oil in a heavy-based skillet and sauté the corn, peas, bell pepper, carrot, leek, garlic, and chili for 3–4 minutes, stirring briskly. Stir in the spinach and season well with salt and pepper to taste.

3 Put all of the sauce ingredients in a saucepan and bring to a boil, stirring. Cook over a high heat for 20 minutes, stirring constantly, until thickened and reduced by a third.

4 Spoon a quarter of the filling along the center of each tortilla. Roll the tortillas around the filling and place in an ovenproof dish, seam side down.

5 Pour the sauce over the tortillas and sprinkle the cheese on top. Cook in a preheated oven at 350°F for 20 minutes, or until the cheese has melted and browned. Serve at once.

Spinach Gnocchi with Tomato & Basil Sauce

Serves 4

INGREDIENTS
---

1 pound baking potatoes	³/₄ cup plain all-purpose flour	1 tablespoon tomato paste
2³/₄ ounces spinach	fresh basil sprigs, to garnish	8 ounce can chopped tomatoes
1 teaspoon water		2 tablespoons chopped basil
3 tablespoons butter or	TOMATO SAUCE:	6 tablespoons red wine
vegetarian margarine	1 tablespoon olive oil	1 teaspoon sugar
1 small egg, beaten	1 shallot, chopped	salt and pepper

---

1 Cook the potatoes in their skins in a pan of boiling salted water for 20 minutes. Drain well and press through a strainer into a bowl. Cook the spinach in 1 teaspoon water for 5 minutes, until wilted. Drain and pat dry with paper towels. Chop and stir into the potatoes.

2 Add the butter or margarine, egg, and half of the flour to the potato mixture, mixing well.

Turn out onto a floured counter, gradually kneading in the remaining flour to form a soft dough. With floured hands, roll the dough into thin ropes and cut off ¾-inch pieces. Press the center of each dumpling with your finger, drawing it toward you to curl the sides of the gnocchi. Cover and set aside to chill.

3 Heat the oil for the sauce in a pan and sauté the chopped shallots for 5 minutes. Add the tomato paste, tomatoes, basil, red wine, and sugar and season well. Bring to a boil and then simmer for 20 minutes.

4 Bring a pan of salted water to a boil and cook the gnocchi for 2–3 minutes, or until they rise to the top of the pan. Drain well and transfer to serving dishes. Spoon the tomato sauce over the top. Garnish and serve.

Vegetable Jambalaya

Serves 4

INGREDIENTS

1/2 cup brown rice	1 green bell pepper, diced	2/3 cup vegetable stock
2 tablespoons olive oil	1/2 cup baby corn cobs,	8 ounce can chopped tomatoes
2 garlic cloves, crushed	halved lengthwise	1 tablespoon tomato paste
1 red onion, cut into eight wedges	1/2 cup frozen peas	1 teaspoon Creole seasoning
1 eggplant, diced	3 1/2 ounces small broccoli florets	1/2 teaspoons chili flakes
		salt and pepper

1 Cook the rice in a saucepan of boiling water for 20 minutes, Drain and set aside.

2 Heat the oil in a heavy-based skillet. Add the garlic and onion and fry, stirring constantly, for 2–3 minutes.

3 Add the eggplant, bell pepper, corn, peas, and broccoli florets to the skillet and cook, stirring occasionally, for about 2–3 minutes.

4 Stir in the vegetable stock and canned tomatoes, tomato paste, Creole seasoning, and chili flakes.

5 Season to taste and cook over low heat for 15–20 minutes, or until the vegetables are tender.

6 Stir the brown rice into the vegetable mixture and cook, mixing well, for 3–4 minutes, or until hot. Transfer the vegetable jambalaya to warm serving dishes and serve at once.

COOK'S TIP

Use a mixture of rice, such as wild or red rice, for color and texture. Cook the rice in advance for a speedier recipe.

Stuffed Mushrooms

Serves 4

INGREDIENTS

8 open-cap mushrooms
1 tablespoon olive oil
1 small leek, chopped
1 celery stalk, chopped
3¹/₂ ounces bean
    curd, diced

1 zucchini, chopped
1 carrot, chopped
1 cup whole-wheat bread crumbs
2 tablespoons chopped basil
1 tablespoon tomato paste
2 tablespoons pine nuts

³/₄ cup grated vegetarian
    cheddar cheese
²/₃ cup vegetable stock
salt and pepper
salad greens, to serve

1 Remove the stalks from the mushrooms and chop finely. Reserve the caps.

2 Heat the oil in a heavy-based skillet. Add the chopped mushroom stalks, leek, celery, bean curd, zucchini, and carrot and cook for 3–4 minutes, stirring.

3 Stir in the bread crumbs, basil, tomato paste, and pine nuts. Season with salt and pepper to taste.

4 Spoon the mixture into the mushroom caps and top with the grated cheese.

5 Place the mushrooms in a shallow ovenproof dish and pour the vegetable stock around them.

6 Cook in a preheated oven at 425°F for 20 minutes, or until the mushroom caps and stuffing are cooked through and the cheese has melted. Remove the mushrooms from the

dish and serve at once with salad greens.

COOK'S TIP

Vary the vegetables used for flavor and color or according to those you have available.

Vegetable Crêpes

Serves 4

INGREDIENTS

CRÊPES:
$3/4$ cup all-purpose flour
pinch of salt
1 egg, beaten
$1^1/4$ cups milk
vegetable oil, for frying

FILLING:
2 tablespoons vegetable oil
1 leek, shredded
$1/2$ teaspoon chili powder
$1/2$ teaspoon ground cumin
$1^3/4$ ounces snow peas
$3^1/2$ ounces button mushrooms,
1 red bell pepper, sliced
$1/4$ cup cashew nuts, chopped

SAUCE:
2 tablespoons vegetarian margarine
3 tablespoons all-purpose flour
$2/3$ cup vegetable stock
$2/3$ cup milk
1 teaspoon Dijon mustard
$3/4$ cup grated vegetarian
    cheddar cheese,
2 tablespoons chopped cilantro

1 For the crêpes, sift the flour and salt into a bowl. Beat in the egg and milk to make a batter. For the filling, heat the oil in a skillet and sauté the leek for 2–3 minutes. Add the rest of the ingredients and cook for 5 minutes, stirring. To make the sauce, melt the margarine in a pan and add the flour. Cook for 1 minute and remove from the heat.

Stir in the stock and milk and return to the heat. Bring to a boil, stirring until thick. Add the mustard, half the cheese, and the cilantro and cook for 1 minute.

2 Heat 1 tablespoon of oil in a nonstick 6-inch skillet. Pour the oil from the pan and add an eighth of the batter, to cover the base of the skillet. Cook for

2 minutes, turn the crêpe, and cook the other side for 1 minute. Repeat with the remaining batter. Spoon a little of the filling along the center of each crêpe and roll up. Place in a heatproof dish and pour the sauce on top. Top with cheese and heat under a preheated broiler for 3–5 minutes, or until the cheese melts and turns golden. Serve at once.

Vegetable Pasta Nests

Serves 4

INGREDIENTS

6 ounces spaghetti
1 eggplant, halved and sliced
1 zucchini, diced
1 red bell pepper, seeded and
    sliced diagonally

6 tablespoons olive oil
2 garlic cloves, crushed
4 tablespoons butter or
    vegetarian margarine, melted

1 tablespoon dry white bread
    crumbs
salt and pepper
fresh parsley sprigs, to garnish

1 Bring a large saucepan of water to a boil and cook the spaghetti until "al dente," or according to the instructions on the packet. Drain well and set aside until required.

2 Place the eggplant, zucchini, and bell pepper in a single layer on a cookie sheet.

3 Mix the oil and garlic together and pour the mixture over the vegetables, tossing to coat.

4 Cook under a preheated broiler for about 10 minutes, turning frequently, until tender and lightly charred. Set aside and keep warm.

5 Divide the spaghetti among 4 lightly greased muffin pans. Using a fork, curl the spaghetti to form nests.

6 Brush the pasta nests with melted butter or margarine and sprinkle with the bread crumbs. Bake in a preheated oven, at 400°F for 15 minutes, or until lightly

golden. Remove the pasta nests from the pans and transfer to serving plates. Divide the broiled vegetables among the pasta nests, season, and garnish.

COOK'S TIP

"Al dente" means "to the bite" and describes cooked pasta that is not too soft, but still has a bite to it.

Vegetable Burgers & Fries

Serves 4

INGREDIENTS

VEGETABLE BURGERS:

3¹/₂ ounces spinach

1 tablespoon olive oil

1 leek, chopped

2 garlic cloves, crushed

1¹/₂ cups chopped mushrooms

10¹/₂ ounces firm bean
    curd, chopped

1 teaspoon chili powder

1 teaspoon curry powder

1 tablespoon chopped cilantro

1¹/₂ cups fresh whole-wheat
    bread crumbs

1 tablespoon olive oil

FRIES:

2 large potatoes

2 tablespoons all-purpose flour

1 teaspoon chili powder

2 tablespoons olive oil

hamburger bun and salad, to serve

1 To make the burgers, cook the spinach in a little water for 2 minutes. Drain thoroughly and pat dry with paper towels.

2 Heat the oil in a skillet and sauté the leek and garlic for 2–3 minutes. Add the remaining ingredients, except for the bread crumbs, and cook for about 5–7 minutes, until the vegetables have softened. Toss in the spinach and cook for 1 minute.

3 Transfer the mixture to a food processor and process for 30 seconds, until almost smooth. Stir in the bread crumbs, mixing well, and set aside until cool enough to handle. Using floured hands, form the mixture into four equal-size burgers. Chill in the refrigerator for 30 minutes.

4 To make the fries, cut the potatoes into thin wedges and cook in a pan of boiling water for 10 minutes.

Drain thoroughly and toss in the flour and chili powder. Spread out the fries on a cookie sheet and sprinkle with the oil. Cook in a preheated oven at 400°F for 30 minutes, or until cooked through and golden brown.

5 Meanwhile, heat the olive oil in a skillet and cook the burgers over medium heat for 8–10 minutes, turning once. Serve in a hamburger bun with a salad.

Vegetable Dim Sum

Serves 4

INGREDIENTS

2 scallions, chopped

1 ounce green beans, chopped

1/2 small carrot, finely chopped

1 red chili, chopped

1/3 cup bean sprouts, chopped

1/3 cup chopped button mushrooms

1/4 cup unsalted cashew nuts, chopped

1 small egg, beaten

2 tablespoons cornstarch

1 teaspoon light soy sauce

1 teaspoon hoisin sauce

1 teaspoon sesame oil

32 wonton wrappers

oil, for deep-frying

1 tablespoon sesame seeds

1 Mix all of the vegetables together in a bowl.

2 Add the nuts, egg, cornstarch, soy sauce, hoisin sauce, and sesame oil to the bowl, stirring to mix well.

3 Spread out the wonton wrappers on a chopping board and spoon small quantities of the mixture into the center of each. Gather the wrappers around the filling at the top, to make little parcels, leaving the top open.

4 Heat the oil for deep-frying in a preheated wok to 350°F or until a cube of bread browns in 30 seconds.

5 Fry the wontons, in batches, for 1–2 minutes, or until golden brown. Drain on absorbent paper towels and keep warm while frying the remaining wontons.

6 Sprinkle the sesame seeds over the wontons. Serve the vegetable dim sum with a soy or plum dipping sauce.

COOK'S TIP

If desired, arrange the wontons on a heatproof plate and then steam in a steamer for 5–7 minutes for a healthier cooking method.

Cheese & Garlic Mushroom Pizzas

Serves 4

INGREDIENTS

DOUGH:

3 1/2 cups all-purpose flour

2 teaspoons active dry yeast

2 garlic cloves, crushed

2 tablespoons chopped thyme

2 tablespoons olive oil

1 1/4 cups tepid water

TOPPING:

2 tablespoons butter or
       vegetarian margarine

5 cups sliced mixed mushrooms

2 garlic cloves, crushed

2 tablespoons chopped parsley

2 tablespoons tomato paste

6 tablespoons sieved tomatoes

3/4 cup grated mozzarella cheese

salt and pepper

chopped parsley, to garnish

1 Put the flour, yeast, garlic, and thyme in a bowl. Make a well in the center and gradually stir in the oil and water. Bring together to form a soft dough.

2 Turn the dough onto a floured counter and knead for 5 minutes, or until smooth. Roll into a 14-inch round and place on a greased cookie sheet. Set aside in a warm place for 20 minutes, or until the dough puffs up.

3 Meanwhile, make the topping. Melt the margarine or butter in a heavy-based skillet and sauté the mushrooms, garlic, and parsley over medium heat for 5 minutes, stirring occasionally.

4 Mix the tomato paste and sieved tomatoes and spoon onto the pizza base, leaving a 1/2-inch edge of dough. Spoon the mushroom mixture on top. Season well with salt and pepper and sprinkle the cheese on top. Cook the pizza in a preheated oven at 375°F for 20–25 minutes, or until the base is crisp and the cheese has melted. Garnish with chopped parsley and serve.

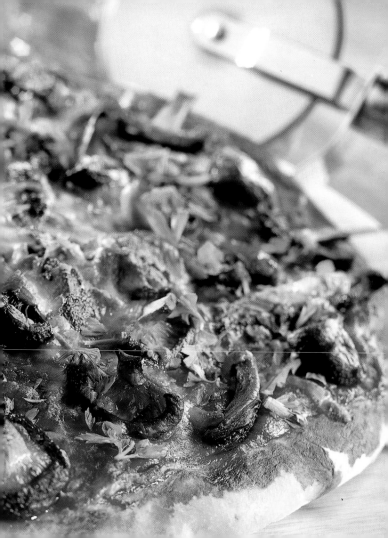

Watercress & Cheese Tartlets

Makes 4

INGREDIENTS

$3/4$ cup all-purpose flour	2 bunches watercress	4 tablespoons plain yogurt
pinch of salt	2 garlic cloves, crushed	$1/2$ teaspoons paprika
$1/2$ cup butter or	1 shallot, chopped	
vegetarian margarine	$1 1/2$ cups grated vegetarian	
2–3 tablespoons cold water	cheddar cheese,	

1 Sift the flour into a mixing bowl and add the salt. Rub $1/3$ cup of the butter or margarine into the flour until the mixture resembles bread crumbs.

2 Stir in the cold water to make a firm dough.

3 Knead the dough lightly, then roll out on a lightly floured counter and use to line four 4-inch tartlet pans. Prick the bases with a fork and set aside in the refrigerator to chill.

4 Heat the remaining butter or margarine in a skillet. Discard the stems from the watercress and add the leaves to the skillet, together with the garlic and shallot, cooking for 1–2 minutes, until the watercress is wilted.

5 Remove the skillet from the heat and stir in the cheese, yogurt, and paprika.

6 Spoon the mixture into the pastry cases and

cook in a preheated oven at 350°F for 20 minutes or until the filling is firm. Turn out the tartlets and serve hot or cold.

VARIATION

Use spinach instead of the watercress, making sure it is well drained before mixing with the remaining filling ingredients.

Vegetable-Filled Ravioli

Serves 4

INGREDIENTS

FILLING:

3 tablespoons butter or
vegetarian margarine
2 garlic cloves, crushed
1 small leek, chopped
2 celery stalks, chopped

2¹/₃ cups chopped open-
cap mushrooms
1 egg, beaten
2 tablespoons grated vegetarian
Parmesan cheese
salt and pepper

RAVIOLI:

4 sheets phyllo pastry
3 tablespoons vegetarian
margarine
oil, for deep-frying

1 To make the filling, melt the butter or margarine in a heavy-based skillet and sauté the garlic and leek for 2–3 minutes, until softened.

2 Add the celery and mushrooms and cook for a further 4–5 minutes, until all the vegetables are tender.

3 Turn off the heat and stir in the egg and grated Parmesan cheese. Season with salt and pepper to taste.

4 Lay the pastry sheets on a chopping board and cut each into nine squares.

5 Spoon a little of the filling into the center of half the squares and brush the edges of the pastry with butter or margarine. Lay another square on top and seal the edges to make a packet.

6 Heat the oil for deep-frying to 350°F or until a cube of bread browns in 30 seconds. Fry the ravioli, in batches, for about

2–3 minutes, or until golden brown. Remove from the oil with a slotted spoon and pat dry on absorbent paper towels. Transfer to a warm serving plate and serve.

COOK'S TIP

Parmesan cheese is generally non-vegetarian. However, there is an Italian Parmesan called Grano Padano, which is usually vegetarian. Alternatively you could use Pecorino.

Bulgur-Filled Eggplants

Serves 4

INGREDIENTS

4 medium eggplants
salt
$^3/_4$ cup bulgur wheat
$1^1/_4$ cups boiling water
3 tablespoons olive oil
2 garlic cloves, crushed

2 tablespoons pine nuts
$^1/_2$ teaspoons turmeric
1 teaspoon chili powder
2 celery stalks, chopped
4 scallions, chopped
1 carrot, grated

$^3/_4$ cup chopped button mushrooms
2 tablespoons raisins
2 tablespoons chopped fresh
  cilantro
salad greens, to serve

---

1 Cut the eggplants in half lengthwise and scoop out the flesh with a teaspoon without piercing the shells. Chop the flesh and set aside. Rub the insides of the eggplants with a little salt and set aside, upside down, for about 20 minutes.

2 Meanwhile, put the bulgur wheat in a mixing bowl and pour the boiling water over the top. Let stand for 20 minutes, or until the water has been absorbed.

3 Heat the oil in a skillet. Add the garlic, pine nuts, turmeric, chili powder, celery, scallions, carrot, mushrooms, and raisins and cook for 2–3 minutes.

4 Stir in the reserved eggplant flesh and cook for a further 2–3 minutes. Add the cilantro, mixing well.

5 Remove the skillet from the heat and stir in the bulgur wheat. Rinse the eggplant shells under cold water and pat dry with paper towels.

6 Spoon the bulgur filling into the eggplants and place in a roasting pan. Pour in a little boiling water and cook in a preheated oven at 350°F for 15–20 minutes.

7 Serve hot with salad greens.

Lentil Croquettes

Serves 4

INGREDIENTS

1¼ cups split red lentils
1 green bell pepper, finely chopped
1 red onion, finely chopped
2 garlic cloves, crushed
1 teaspoon garam masala
½ teaspoon chili powder
1 teaspoon ground cumin

2 teaspoons lemon juice
2 tablespoons chopped
    unsalted peanuts
2½ cups water
1 egg, beaten
3 tablespoons all-purpose flour
1 teaspoon turmeric

1 teaspoon chili powder
4 tablespoons vegetable oil
salt and pepper
salad greens and fresh herbs, to
    serve

1 Put the lentils in a large saucepan with the bell pepper, onion, garlic, garam masala, chili powder, ground cumin, lemon juice, and peanuts.

2 Add the water and bring to a boil. Reduce the heat and simmer for 30 minutes, or until the liquid has been absorbed, stirring occasionally.

3 Remove the mixture from the heat and let cool slightly. Beat in the egg and season with salt and pepper to taste. Set aside to cool completely.

4 With floured hands, form the mixture into eight oval shapes.

5 Mix the flour, turmeric, and chili powder together on a small plate. Roll the croquettes in the spiced flour mixture to coat.

6 Heat the oil in a large skillet and cook the croquettes, in batches, for 10 minutes, turning once, until they are cooked through and crisp on both sides. Serve the croquettes with salad greens and fresh herbs.

COOK'S TIP

Other lentils could be used, but they will require soaking and precooking before use. Red lentils are used for speed and convenience.

Refried Beans with Tortillas

Serves 4

INGREDIENTS

BEANS:

2 tablespoons olive oil

1 onion, finely chopped

3 garlic cloves, crushed

1 green chili, chopped

14 ounce can red kidney
    beans, drained

14 ounce can pinto beans, drained

2 tablespoons chopped cilantro

$^2/_3$ cup vegetable stock

8 wheat tortillas

$^1/_4$ cup grated vegetarian
    cheddar cheese

salt and pepper

RELISH:

4 scallions, chopped

1 red onion, chopped

1 green chili, chopped

1 tablespoon garlic wine vinegar

1 teaspoon sugar

1 tomato, chopped

1 Heat the oil for the beans in a large skillet. Add the onion and sauté for 3–5 minutes. Add the garlic and chili and cook for 1 minute.

2 Mash the beans with a potato masher and stir into the pan with the cilantro.

3 Stir in the stock and cook the beans, stirring, for 5 minutes, until soft and pulpy.

4 Place the tortillas on a cookie sheet and heat through in a warm oven for about 1–2 minutes.

5 Mix the relish ingredients together.

6 Spoon the beans into a serving dish and top with the cheese. Season well with salt and pepper. Roll the tortillas and serve with the relish and beans.

COOK'S TIP

Add a little more liquid to the beans when they are cooking if they begin to stick to the bottom of the skillet.

Brown Rice, Vegetable, & Herb Gratin

Serves 4

INGREDIENTS

1/3 cup brown rice	1 zucchini, sliced	1 cup grated mozzarella cheese
2 tablespoons butter or margarine	2³/4 ounces baby corn cobs,	2 tablespoons whole-wheat
1 red onion, chopped	halved lengthwise	bread crumbs
2 garlic cloves, crushed	2 tablespoons sunflower seeds	salt and pepper
1 carrot, cut into matchsticks	3 tablespoons chopped mixed herbs	

1 Cook the rice in a saucepan of boiling salted water for 20 minutes. Drain well.

2 Lightly grease a 3¾-cup ovenproof dish.

3 Heat the butter in a skillet. Add the onion and cook, stirring constantly, for 2 minutes, or until softened.

4 Add the garlic, carrot, zucchini, and corn cobs and cook for a further 5 minutes, stirring constantly.

5 Mix the rice with the sunflower seeds and mixed herbs and stir into the pan.

6 Stir in half of the mozzarella cheese and season with salt and pepper to taste.

7 Spoon the mixture into the greased dish and top with the bread crumbs and remaining cheese. Cook in a preheated oven at 350°F for 25–30 minutes, or until the cheese begins to turn golden. Serve at once.

VARIATION

Use an alternative rice, such as basmati, and flavor the dish with curry spices, if desired.

Green Lentil &
Mixed Vegetable Pan-Fry

Serves 4

INGREDIENTS

3³/₄ cups green lentils
4 tablespoons butter or
    vegetarian margarine
2 garlic cloves, crushed
2 tablespoons olive oil
1 tablespoon cider vinegar

1 red onion, cut into eight
1³/₄ ounces baby corn cobs,
    halved lengthwise
1 yellow bell pepper, cut into strips
1 red bell pepper, cut into strips

1³/₄ ounces green beans, halved
¹/₂ cup vegetable stock
2 tablespoons honey
salt and pepper
crusty bread, to serve

1 Soak the lentils in a large saucepan of cold water for 25 minutes. Bring to a boil, reduce the heat, and simmer for 20 minutes. Drain thoroughly.

2 Add 1 tablespoon of the butter or margarine, 1 garlic clove, 1 tablespoon of oil, and the vinegar to the lentils and mix well.

3 Melt the remaining butter, and oil in a skillet and stir-fry the garlic, onion, corn cobs, bell peppers and beans for about 3–4 minutes.

4 Add the vegetable stock and bring to a boil. Simmer for 10 minutes, or until the liquid has evaporated.

5 Add the honey and season with salt and pepper to taste. Stir in the lentil mixture and cook for 1 minute to heat through. Spoon onto warm serving plates and serve with crusty bread.

VARIATION

This pan-fry is very versatile—you can use a mixture of your favorite vegetables, if desired. Try zucchini, carrots, or snow peas.

Falafel

Serves 4

INGREDIENTS

6 cups canned garbanzo
    beans, drained
1 red onion, chopped
3 garlic cloves, crushed
3¹/₂ ounces whole-
    wheat bread

2 small red chilies
1 teaspoon ground cumin
1 teaspoon ground coriander
¹/₂ teaspoon turmeric
1 tablespoon chopped cilantro, plus
    extra to garnish

1 egg, beaten
1 cup whole-wheat bread crumbs
vegetable oil, for deep-frying
salt and pepper
tomato and cucumber salad and
    lemon wedges, to serve

1 Put the garbanzo beans, onion, garlic, bread, chilies, spices, and cilantro in a food processor and process for 30 seconds. Stir and season well.

2 Remove the mixture from the food processor and shape into walnut-size balls.

3 Place the beaten egg in a shallow bowl and place the whole-wheat bread crumbs on a plate. Dip the balls first into the egg to coat and then roll them in the bread crumbs, shaking off any excess.

4 Heat the oil for deep-frying to 350°F or until a cube of bread browns in 30 seconds. Fry the falafel, in batches, for 2–3 minutes, until crisp and browned all over. Remove from the oil with a slotted spoon and drain on absorbent paper towels. Transfer the falafel to a warm serving plate, garnish with cilantro and serve at once with a tomato and cucumber salad and lemon wedges.

COOK'S TIP

Serve the falafel with a cilantro and yogurt sauce. Thoroughly mix together ²/₃ cup plain yogurt, 2 tablespoons chopped fresh cilantro, and 1 crushed garlic clove.

Cabbage & Walnut Stir-Fry

Serves 4

INGREDIENTS

12 ounces white cabbage	2 garlic cloves, crushed	1 cup walnut halves
12 ounces red cabbage	8 scallions, trimmed	2 teaspoons Dijon mustard
4 tablespoons peanut oil	8 ounces firm bean curd, cubed	2 teaspoons poppy seeds
1 tablespoon walnut oil	2 tablespoons lemon juice	salt and pepper

1 Using a sharp knife, shred the white and red cabbages thinly and set aside until required.

2 Heat together the peanut oil and walnut oil in a preheated wok. Add the garlic, cabbage, scallions, and bean curd and cook for 5 minutes, stirring.

3 Add the lemon juice, walnuts, and mustard, season with salt and pepper, and cook for a further 5 minutes, or until the cabbage is tender.

4 Transfer the stir-fry to a warm serving bowl, sprinkle with poppy seeds, and serve.

COOK'S TIP

As well as adding protein, vitamins, and useful fats to the diet, nuts and seeds add flavor and texture to vegetarian meals. Keep a good supply of them in your cupboard, as they can be used in a great variety of dishes—salads, bakes, stir-fries, to name but a few.

VARIATION

Sesame seeds could be used instead of the poppy seeds and drizzle 1 teaspoon of sesame oil over the dish just before serving, if desired.

Spinach Frittata

Serves 4

INGREDIENTS

1 pound spinach

2 teaspoons water

4 eggs, beaten

2 tablespoons light cream

2 garlic cloves, crushed

³/₄ cup canned corn, drained

1 celery stalk, chopped

1 red chili, chopped

2 tomatoes, seeded and diced

2 tablespoons olive oil

2 tablespoons butter

¹/₄ cup pecan nut halves

2 tablespoons grated pecorino cheese

¹/₄ cup diced fontina cheese

a pinch of paprika

1 Cook the spinach in 2 teaspoons of water in a covered pan over medium heat for 5 minutes. Drain thoroughly and pat dry on absorbent paper towels.

2 Beat the eggs in a bowl and stir in the spinach, light cream, garlic, corn, celery, chili, and tomatoes until the ingredients are well mixed.

3 Heat the oil and butter in an 8-inch heavy-based skillet.

4 Spoon the egg mixture into the skillet and sprinkle with the pecans, pecorino and fontina cheeses, and paprika. Cook without stirring over medium heat for 5–7 minutes, or until the underside of the frittata is brown.

5 Put a large plate over the skillet and invert to turn out the frittata. Slide it back into the skillet and cook the other side for a further 2–3 minutes. Serve the frittata straight from the skillet or transfer to a serving plate.

Marinated Broiled Fennel

Serves 4

INGREDIENTS

2 fennel bulbs
1 red bell pepper, cut into large
    cubes
1 lime, cut into eight wedges

MARINADE:
2 tablespoons lime juice
4 tablespoons olive oil
2 garlic cloves, crushed

1 teaspoon whole-grain mustard
1 tablespoon chopped thyme
fennel fronds, to garnish
crisp salad, to serve

1 Cut each of the fennel bulbs into eight pieces and place in a shallow dish. Mix in the bell peppers.

2 To make the marinade, combine the lime juice, oil, garlic, mustard, and thyme. Pour the marinade over the fennel and bell peppers and set aside to marinate for 1 hour.

3 Thread the fennel and bell peppers onto wooden skewers with the lime wedges. Preheat a broiler to medium and broil the kebabs for 10 minutes, turning and basting frequently with the marinade.

4 Transfer to serving plates, garnish with fennel fronds and serve with a crisp salad.

VARIATION

Substitute 2 tablespoons orange juice for the lime juice and add 1 tablespoon honey, if desired.

COOK'S TIP

Soak the skewers in water for 20 minutes before using to prevent them from burning during cooking.

Ciabatta Rolls

Serves 4

INGREDIENTS

4 ciabatta rolls	FILLING:	1 yellow bell pepper
2 tablespoons olive oil	1 red bell pepper	4 radishes, sliced
1 garlic clove crushed	1 green bell pepper	1 bunch watercress
		8 tablespoons cream cheese

1 Slice the ciabatta rolls in half. Heat the olive oil and crushed garlic in a saucepan. Pour the oil mixture over the cut surfaces of the rolls and let stand while you prepare the filling.

2 Halve the bell peppers and place, skin side uppermost, on a broiler rack. Cook under a preheated broiler for about 8–10 minutes, until just beginning to char. Remove the bell peppers from the broiler, peel, and thinly slice the flesh.

3 Arrange the radish slices on one half of each roll with a few watercress leaves. Spoon the cream cheese on top. Pile the bell peppers on top of the cream cheese and top with the other half of the roll. Serve.

COOK'S TIP

To peel bell peppers, wrap them in foil after broiling. This traps the steam, loosening the skins, and making them easier to peel.

COOK'S TIP

Allow the bell peppers to cool slightly before filling the rolls, otherwise the cheese will melt.

Crispy Potato Skins

Serves 4

INGREDIENTS

4 large baking potatoes	BEAN SPROUT SALAD:	1 small garlic clove, crushed
2 tablespoons vegetable oil	$^1/_2$ cup bean sprouts	BEAN FILLING:
4 teaspoons salt	1 celery stalk, sliced	$1^1/_2$ cups canned, mixed
snipped chives, to garnish	1 orange, peeled and segmented	beans, drained
$^2/_3$ cup sour cream and	1 red eating apple, chopped	1 onion, halved and sliced
2 tablespoons chopped	$^1/_2$ red bell pepper, chopped	1 tomato, chopped
chives, to serve	1 tablespoon chopped parsley	2 scallions, chopped
	1 tablespoon light soy sauce	2 teaspoons lemon juice
	1 tablespoon clear honey	salt and pepper

1 Scrub the potatoes and place them on a cookie sheet. Prick the potatoes all over with a fork and rub the vegetable oil and salt into their skins.

2 Cook in a preheated oven at 400°F for 1 hour, or until they are soft.

3 Cut the potatoes in half lengthwise and scoop out the flesh, leaving a ½ inch thick shell. Put the shells, skin side uppermost, in the oven for 10 minutes until crisp.

4 Mix the ingredients for the bean sprout salad in a bowl, tossing in the soy sauce, honey, and garlic to coat.

5 Mix the ingredients for the bean filling in a separate bowl.

6 Mix the sour cream and chives in another bowl.

7 Serve the potato skins hot, with the two salad fillings, garnished with snipped chives, together with the sour cream and chive sauce.

Tomato, Olive, & Mozzarella Bruschetta

Serves 4

INGREDIENTS

4 muffins	8 pitted black olives, halved	DRESSING:
4 garlic cloves, crushed	1¾ oz mozzarella	1 tablespoon olive oil
2 tablespoons butter	cheese, sliced	2 teaspoons lemon juice
1 tablespoon chopped basil	salt and pepper	1 teaspoon clear honey
4 large, ripe tomatoes	fresh basil leaves, to garnish	
1 tablespoon tomato paste		

1 Cut the muffins in half to give eight thick pieces. Toast the muffin halves under a preheated broiler for 2–3 minutes, until golden.

2 Mix the garlic, butter, and basil together and spread onto each muffin half.

3 Cut a cross shape at the base of each tomato. Plunge the tomatoes in a bowl of boiling water—this will make the skin easier to peel. After a few minutes, pick each tomato up with a fork and peel away the skin. Chop the tomato flesh and mix with the tomato paste and olives. Divide the mixture between the muffins.

4 Mix the dressing ingredients and drizzle over each muffin. Arrange the mozzarella cheese on top and season to taste with salt and pepper.

5 Return the muffins to the broiler for 1–2 minutes, until the cheese melts.

6 Garnish with fresh basil leaves and serve at once.

VARIATION

Use balsamic vinegar instead of the lemon juice for an authentic Mediterranean flavor.

Lentil Pâté

Serves 4

INGREDIENTS
---

1 tablespoon vegetable oil, plus
   extra for greasing
1 onion, chopped
2 garlic cloves, crushed
1 teaspoon garam masala

$\frac{1}{2}$ teaspoon ground coriander
$1\frac{1}{4}$ cups vegetable stock
$\frac{3}{4}$ cup red lentils
1 small egg
2 tablespoons milk

2 tablespoons mango chutney
2 tablespoons chopped parsley, plus
   extra to garnish
salad greens and warm toast,
   to serve

---

1 Heat the oil in a large saucepan and sauté the onion and garlic for 2–3 minutes, stirring. Add the spices and cook for a further 30 seconds.

2 Stir in the stock and lentils and bring the mixture to a boil. Reduce the heat and simmer for 20 minutes, until the lentils are cooked and softened. Remove the pan from the heat and drain off any excess moisture.

3 Put the mixture in a food processor and add the egg, milk, mango chutney, and 2 tablespoons parsley. Process until completely smooth.

4 Grease and line the base of a 1-pound loaf pan and spoon the mixture into it, leveling and smoothing the surface. Cover and cook in a preheated oven at 400°F for 40–45 minutes, or until the pâté is firm to the touch.

5 Allow the pâté to cool in the pan for about 20 minutes, then transfer to the refrigerator to cool completely.

6 Turn out the pâté onto a serving plate, slice, and garnish with chopped parsley. Serve with salad greens and toast.

VARIATION

Use other spices, such as chili powder or Chinese five-spice powder, to flavor the pâté and add tomato relish or chili relish instead of the mango chutney, if desired.

Roasted Vegetables on Muffins

Serves 4

INGREDIENTS

1 red onion, cut into eight pieces	2 garlic cloves, crushed	1 tablespoon flour
1 eggplant, halved and sliced	1 tablespoon chopped thyme	$^2/_3$ cup milk
1 yellow bell pepper, sliced	2 teaspoons light brown sugar	$^1/_3$ cup vegetable stock
1 zucchini, sliced	4 muffins, halved	$^3/_4$ cup grated vegetarian
4 tablespoons olive oil	salt and pepper	Cheddar cheese
1 tablespoon garlic vinegar		1 teaspoon whole-grain mustard
2 tablespoons vermouth	SAUCE:	3 tablespoons chopped mixed herbs
	2 tablespoons butter	

1 Arrange the vegetables in a shallow ovenproof dish. Mix together the oil, vinegar, vermouth, garlic, thyme, and sugar and pour over the vegetables, tossing well to coat. Marinate for 1 hour.

2 Transfer the vegetables to a cookie sheet. Cook in a preheated oven at 400°F for 20–25 minutes, or until the vegetables have softened.

3 Meanwhile, make the sauce. Melt the butter in a small pan and add the flour. Cook for 1 minute and remove from the heat. Stir in the milk and stock and return the pan to the heat. Bring to a boil, stirring, until thickened. Stir in the cheese, mustard, and mixed herbs and season well.

4 Preheat the broiler. Cut the muffins in half and

broil for 2–3 minutes, until golden brown, then remove, and arrange on a warm serving plate.

5 Spoon the roasted vegetables onto the muffins and pour the sauce over the top. Serve at once.

Hummus & Garlic Toasts

Serves 4

INGREDIENTS

HUMMUS:

14 oz can garbanzo beans

juice of 1 large lemon

6 tablespoons sesame seed paste

2 tablespoons olive oil

2 garlic cloves, crushed

salt and pepper

chopped fresh cilantro and black
    olives, to garnish

TOASTS:

1 Italian loaf, sliced

2 garlic cloves, crushed

1 tablespoon chopped fresh cilantro

4 tablespoons olive oil

---

1 To make the hummus, drain the garbanzo beans, reserving a little of the liquid from the can. Put the garbanzo beans and reserved liquid in a food processor and process, gradually adding the lemon juice. Process well after each addition until the mixture is smooth.

2 Stir in the sesame seed paste and all but 1 teaspoon of the olive oil. Add the garlic, season to taste with salt and pepper and process again until smooth.

3 Spoon the hummus into a serving dish. Drizzle the remaining olive oil over the top and garnish with chopped cilantro and olives. Chill in the refrigerator while you are preparing the toasts.

4 Lay the slices of Italian bread on a broiler rack in a single layer.

5 Mix the garlic, cilantro, and olive oil together and drizzle the mixture over the bread slices. Cook under a preheated broiler for 2–3

minutes, until golden brown, turning once. Serve at once with the hummus.

COOK'S TIP

*Make the hummus
1 day in advance, and chill,
covered, in the refrigerator
until required.
Garnish and serve.*

Mixed Bean Pâté

Serves 4

INGREDIENTS

14 oz can mixed beans, drained	juice of 1 lemon	2 scallions, chopped
2 tablespoons olive oil	2 garlic cloves, crushed	salt and pepper
	1 tablespoon chopped fresh cilantro	shredded scallions, to garnish

1 Rinse the beans thoroughly under cold running water and drain well.

2 Transfer the beans to a food processor or blender and process until smooth. Alternatively, place the beans in a bowl and mash with a fork or potato masher.

3 Add the olive oil, lemon juice, crushed garlic, chopped cilantro, and scallions and process or mix thoroughly until fairly smooth. Season with salt and pepper to taste.

4 Transfer the pâté to a serving bowl and chill for at least 30 minutes. Garnish with shredded scallions and serve at once.

COOK'S TIP

Use canned beans which have no salt or sugar added and always rinse thoroughly before use.

COOK'S TIP

Serve the pâté with warm pita bread or toast.

Vegetable Fritters with Sweet & Sour Sauce

Serves 4

INGREDIENTS

³/₄ cup whole-wheat flour
pinch of salt
pinch of cayenne pepper
4 teaspoons olive oil
³/₄ cup cold water
3¹/₂ oz broccoli florets

3¹/₂ oz cauliflower florets
1³/₄ oz snow peas
1 large carrot, cut into thin sticks
1 red bell pepper, sliced
2 egg whites, beaten
oil, for deep-frying

SAUCE:
²/₃ cup pineapple juice
²/₃ cup vegetable stock
2 tablespoons wine vinegar
2 tablespoons light brown sugar
2 teaspoons cornstarch
2 scallions, chopped

1 Sift the flour and salt into a mixing bowl and add the cayenne pepper. Make a well in the center and gradually beat in the oil and cold water to make a smooth batter.

2 Cook the vegetables in boiling water for 5 minutes and drain well.

3 Whisk the egg whites until they form soft peaks and fold them into the batter.

4 Dip the vegetables into the batter, turning to coat well. Drain off any excess batter. Heat the oil for deep-frying in a deep fat fryer to 350°F or until a cube of bread browns in 30 seconds. Fry the vegetables for 1–2 minutes, in batches, until golden. Remove from the oil with a slotted spoon and drain thoroughly on paper towels.

5 Place all the sauce ingredients in a pan and bring to a boil, stirring, until thickened and clear. Serve with the fritters.

Mixed Bhajis

Serves 4

INGREDIENTS

BHAJIS:

1¼ cups besan flour*

1 teaspoon baking soda

2 teaspoons ground coriander

1 teaspoon garam masala

1½ teaspoons turmeric

1½ teaspoons chili powder

2 tablespoons chopped cilantro

1 small onion, halved and sliced

1 small leek, sliced

3½ oz cooked cauliflower

9–12 tablespoons cold water

salt and pepper

vegetable oil, for deep-frying

SAUCE:

⅔ cup unsweetened yogurt

2 tablespoons chopped mint

½ teaspoon turmeric

1 garlic clove, crushed

fresh mint sprigs, to garnish

1 Sift the flour, baking soda, and salt to taste into a large mixing bowl and add the spices and chopped fresh cilantro. Mix well until the ingredients are thoroughly combined.

2 Divide the mixture into 3 separate bowls. Stir the onion into one bowl, the leek into another, and the cauliflower into the third. Add 3–4 tablespoons of water to each bowl and mix each to form a smooth paste.

3 Heat the oil for deep-frying in a deep fat fryer to 350°F or until a cube of bread browns in 30 seconds. Using 2 dessert spoons, form the mixture into rounds and cook each in the oil for 3–4 minutes, until browned. Remove with a slotted spoon and drain on absorbent paper towels. Keep the bhajis warm in the oven while cooking the remainder.

4 Mix all of the sauce ingredients together and pour into a serving bowl. Garnish with mint sprigs and serve with the warm bhajis.

Mushroom & Garlic Soufflés

Serves 4

INGREDIENTS

4 tablespoons butter	2 garlic cloves, crushed	1 cup milk
1 cup chopped flat mushrooms	2 tablespoons chopped marjoram	salt and pepper
2 teaspoons lime juice	3 tablespoons all-purpose flour	2 eggs, separated

1 Lightly grease the inside of four ²/₃-cup individual soufflé dishes with a little butter.

2 Melt 2 tablespoons of the butter in a skillet. Add the mushrooms, lime juice, and garlic and sauté for 2–3 minutes. Remove the mushroom mixture from the skillet with a slotted spoon and transfer to a mixing bowl. Stir in the marjoram.

3 Melt the remaining butter in a pan. Add the flour and cook for 1 minute, then remove from the heat.

Stir in the milk and return to the heat. Bring to a boil, stirring until thickened.

4 Add the sauce to the mushroom mixture, mixing well, and beat in the egg yolks.

5 Whisk the egg whites until they form peaks and gently fold into the mushroom mixture until fully incorporated.

6 Divide the mixture among the prepared soufflé dishes. Place the dishes on a cookie sheet and cook in a preheated oven at

400°F for 8–10 minutes, or until the soufflés have risen and are cooked through and golden brown on top. Serve at once.

COOK'S TIP

Insert a toothpick into the center of the soufflés to test if they are cooked through—it should come out clean. If not, cook for a few minutes longer, but do not overcook.

Carrot, Fennel, & Potato Medley

Serves 4

INGREDIENTS

2 tablespoons olive oil
1 potato, cut into thin strips
1 fennel bulb, cut into thin strips
2 carrots, grated

1 red onion, cut into thin strips
chopped chives and fennel fronds,
   to garnish

DRESSING:
3 tablespoons olive oil
1 tablespoon garlic wine vinegar
1 garlic clove, crushed
1 teaspoon Dijon mustard
2 teaspoons clear honey
salt and pepper

1 Heat the olive oil in a skillet, add the potato and fennel slices, and cook for 2–3 minutes, until beginning to brown. Remove the vegetables from the skillet with a slotted spoon and drain on paper towels.

2 Arrange the carrot, red onion, potato, and fennel in separate piles on a serving platter.

3 Mix the dressing ingredients together and pour over the vegetables. Toss well and sprinkle with chopped chives and fennel fronds. Serve immediately or leave in the refrigerator until required.

COOK'S TIP

Fennel is an aromatic plant that has a delicate, aniseed flavor. It can be eaten raw in salads, or boiled, braised, sautéed, or broiled. For this salad, if fennel is unavailable, substitute 12 ounces sliced leeks.

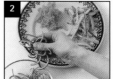

Onions à la Grecque

Serves 4

INGREDIENTS

1 pound shallots

3 tablespoons olive oil

3 tablespoons clear honey

2 tablespoons garlic wine vinegar

3 tablespoons dry white wine

1 tablespoon tomato paste

2 celery stalks, sliced

2 tomatoes, seeded and chopped

salt and pepper

chopped celery leaves, to garnish

1 Peel the shallots. Heat the oil in a large saucepan, add the shallots, and cook, stirring, for 3–5 minutes, or until they begin to brown.

2 Add the honey and cook for a further 30 seconds over a high heat, then add the garlic wine vinegar and dry white wine, stirring well.

3 Stir in the tomato paste, celery, and tomatoes and bring the mixture to a boil. Cook over a high heat for 5–6 minutes.

Season to taste and set aside to cool slightly.

4 Garnish with chopped celery leaves and serve warm or cold from the refrigerator.

COOK'S TIP

This dish, served warm, would also make an ideal accompaniment to Garbanzo Bean Roast.

VARIATION

Use button mushrooms instead of the shallots and fennel instead of the celery for another great starter.

Eggplant Timbale

Serves 4

INGREDIENTS

1 large eggplant	2 tablespoons frozen peas, thawed	SAUCE:
¹/₂ cup macaroni	3¹/₂ ounces spinach	4 tablespoons olive oil
1 tablespoon vegetable oil	¹/₄ cup grated vegetarian	2 tablespoons white wine vinegar
1 onion, chopped	Cheddar cheese	2 garlic cloves, crushed
2 garlic cloves, crushed	1 egg, beaten	3 tablespoons chopped basil
2 tablespoons drained	3 cups canned, chopped tomatoes	1 tablespoon superfine sugar
canned corn	1 tablespoon chopped basil	
	salt and pepper	

1 Cut the eggplant lengthwise into thin strips, using a swivel vegetable peeler. Place them in a bowl of salted boiling water and let stand for about 3–4 minutes. Drain well.

2 Lightly grease the base and sides of four ²/₃-cup individual ramekin dishes and use the eggplant slices to line the dishes, leaving about 1 inch of eggplant overlapping.

3 Cook the pasta in a pan of boiling water for 8–10 minutes until "al dente." Drain. Heat the oil in a pan and sauté the onion and garlic for 2–3 minutes. Stir in the corn and peas and remove from the heat.

4 Blanch the spinach, drain well, chop, and reserve. Add the pasta to the onion mixture with the cheese, egg, tomatoes, and basil. Season and mix. Half fill each ramekin with some

of the pasta. Spoon the spinach on top, and then the remaining pasta mixture. Fold the eggplant over the pasta filling to cover. Put the ramekins in a roasting pan half-filled with boiling water, cover, and cook in a preheated oven at 350°F for 20–25 minutes, or until set. Meanwhile, heat the sauce ingredients in a pan. Turn out the ramekins and serve at once with the sauce.

Puff Potato Pie

Serves 6

INGREDIENTS

1 pound 9 ounces potatoes,
    peeled and thinly sliced
2 scallions, finely chopped

1 red onion, finely chopped
²⁄₃ cup heavy cream

1 pound 2 ounces fresh
    ready-made puff pastry
2 eggs, beaten
salt and pepper

1 Lightly grease a cookie sheet. Bring a pan of water to a boil, add the sliced potatoes, bring back to a boil, and then simmer for a few minutes. Drain the potato and cool. Dry off any excess moisture with paper towels.

2 In a bowl, mix together the scallions, red onion, and the cooled potato slices. Stir in 2 tablespoons of the cream and plenty of seasoning.

3 Divide the pastry in half and roll out one piece to a 9-inch round. Roll the remaining dough to a 10-inch round.

4 Place the smaller round onto the cookie sheet and top with the potato mixture, leaving a 1-inch border all around. Brush this border with a little of the beaten egg.

5 Top with the larger round of dough, seal well, and crimp the edges of the dough. Cut a steam vent in the middle of the dough and, using the back of a knife, mark with a pattern.

Brush with the beaten egg and bake in a preheated oven at 400°F for 30 minutes.

6 Mix the remaining beaten egg with the rest of the cream and pour into the pie through the steam vent. Return the pie to the oven for 15 minutes. Serve either warm or cold.

Spinach Cheese Molds

Serves 4

INGREDIENTS

3½ ounces fresh spinach leaves
10½ ounces skim milk soft
    cheese
2 garlic cloves, crushed

sprigs of fresh parsley, tarragon,
    and chives, finely chopped
salt and pepper

TO SERVE:
salad greens and fresh herbs
pita bread

1 Trim the stalks from the spinach leaves. Rinse the leaves under running water. Pack the leaves into a saucepan while still wet, cover, and cook for 3–4 minutes until wilted–they will cook in the steam from the wet leaves (do not overcook). Drain well and pat dry with absorbent paper towels.

2 Base-line 4 small pudding basins or individual ramekin dishes with baking parchment. Line the basins or ramekins with spinach leaves so that

the leaves overhang the edges if they are large enough to do so.

3 Place the cheese in a bowl and add the garlic and herbs. Mix together thoroughly and season to taste.

4 Spoon the cheese and herb mixture into the basins or ramekins and pull over the overlapping spinach to cover the cheese, or lay extra leaves to cover the top. Place a baking paper round on top of each dish and weigh down with a 4

ounce weight. Chill in the refrigerator for 1 hour.

5 Remove the weights and peel off the paper. Loosen the molds by running a small spatula around the edges of each dish and turn them out onto individual plates.

6 Serve with a mixture of salad greens and fresh herbs, and warm pita bread.

Soufflé Omelet

Serves 4

INGREDIENTS

6 ounces cherry tomatoes
8 ounces mixed mushrooms
   (such as button, chestnut,
   shiitake, oyster)
4 tbsp fresh vegetable stock

small bunch fresh thyme
4 medium eggs, separated
4 medium egg whites
4 tsp olive oil
1 ounce arugula leaves

salt and pepper
fresh thyme sprigs, to garnish

1 Halve the tomatoes and place them in a saucepan. Wipe the mushrooms with paper towels, trim if necessary, and slice if large. Place in the saucepan.

2 Add the stock and thyme to the pan. Bring to a boil, cover, and simmer for 5–6 minutes until tender. Drain, remove the thyme and discard, and keep the mixture warm.

3 Meanwhile, whisk the egg yolks with 8 tablespoons of water until frothy. In a clean, greasefree bowl, mix the 8 egg whites until stiff and dry.

4 Spoon the egg yolk mixture into the egg whites and, using a metal spoon, fold the whites and yolks into each other until well mixed. Do not knock out too much of the air.

5 For each omelet, brush a small omelet pan with 1 tsp oil and heat until hot. Pour in a quarter of the egg mixture and cook for 4–5 minutes, until the mixture has set.

6 Preheat the broiler and finish cooking the omelet for 2–3 minutes.

7 Transfer the omelet to a warm serving plate. Fill the omelet with a few arugula leaves, and a quarter of the mushroom and tomato mixture. Flip over the top of the omelet, garnish with sprigs of thyme, and serve.

Side Dishes

If you are running short of ideas for interesting
side dishes to serve with your main meals, these
recipes will be a welcome inspiration. When the
potato is thought of as a component of a meal, it is
inevitably associated with meat and vegetables,
and is served either roasted or boiled. In fact,
the potato is so versatile in its ability to combine
with other flavorings and be cooked in so many
different ways that it is the perfect base for a
whole variety of delicious side dishes. This
chapter demonstrates that versatility with a
wide range of tantalizing recipes.

An ideal accompaniment complements the main
dish, both visually and nutritionally. Main dishes
are rich in protein so the vegetable side dishes in
this chapter have been created to be a little lighter
in texture, but still packed full of color and flavor.
They have been cooked in many different ways—
there are baked, fried, steamed, and braised
dishes, all perfect complements to main meals
for every occasion.

Colcannon

Serves 4

INGREDIENTS

2½ cups shredded green cabbage
⅓ cup milk
8 oz mealy potatoes, diced

1 large leek, chopped
pinch of grated nutmeg

1 tbsp butter, melted
salt and pepper

1 Cook the shredded cabbage in a saucepan of boiling salted water for 7–10 minutes. Drain thoroughly and set aside.

2 Meanwhile, in a separate saucepan, bring the milk to a boil and add the potatoes and leek. Reduce the heat and simmer for 15–20 minutes, or until they are cooked through.

3 Stir in the grated nutmeg and mash the potatoes and leeks together.

4 Add the drained cabbage to the potatoes and mix well.

5 Spoon the potato and cabbage mixture into a serving dish, making a hollow in the center with the back of a spoon.

6 Pour the melted butter into the hollow and serve the dish immediately.

VARIATION

Add diced cooked bacon to the recipe for extra flavor, adding it with the leeks and cabbage.

COOK'S TIP

There are many different varieties of cabbage, which produce hearts at varying times of year, so you can be sure of being able to make this delicious cabbage dish all year round.

Candied Sweet Potatoes

Serves 4

INGREDIENTS

1¹/₂ pounds sweet potatoes, sliced
3 tbsp butter
1 tbsp lime juice

¹/₂ cup dark brown sugar
1 tbsp brandy

grated rind of 1 lime
lime wedges, to garnish

---

1 Cook the sweet potatoes in a saucepan of boiling water for 5 minutes. Test the potatoes have softened by pricking with a fork. Remove the sweet potatoes with a slotted spoon and drain thoroughly.

2 Melt the butter in a large skillet. Add the lime juice and brown sugar and heat gently to dissolve the sugar.

3 Stir the sweet potatoes and the brandy into the sugar and lime juice mixture. Cook over a low heat for 10 minutes, until the potato slices are cooked through.

4 Sprinkle the lime rind over the top of the sweet potatoes and mix well.

5 Transfer the candied sweet potatoes to a serving plate. Garnish with lime wedges and serve at once.

COOK'S TIP

Sweet potatoes have a pinkish skin and either white, yellow, or orange flesh. It doesn't matter which type is used for this dish.

VARIATION

Serve this dish with spicy meats to complement the sweetness of the potatoes, if desired.

VARIATION

This dish may be prepared with waxy potatoes instead of sweet potatoes, if you prefer. Cook the potatoes for 10 minutes in step 1, instead of 5 minutes. Follow the same cooking method.

Potatoes with Onion & Herbs

Serves 4

INGREDIENTS

2 pounds waxy potatoes, cut into cubes

$\frac{1}{2}$ cup butter

1 red onion, cut into 8

2 garlic cloves, crushed

1 tsp lemon juice

2 tbsp chopped fresh thyme

salt and pepper

1 Cook the cubed potatoes in a saucepan of boiling water for 10 minutes. Drain thoroughly.

2 Melt the butter in a large, heavy-based skillet and add the red onion wedges, garlic, and lemon juice. Cook for 2–3 minutes, stirring.

3 Add the potatoes to the pan and mix well to coat in the butter mixture.

4 Reduce the heat, cover the skillet, and cook for 25–30 minutes, or until the potatoes are golden and tender.

5 Sprinkle the chopped thyme over the top of the potatoes and season with salt and pepper to taste.

6 Serve immediately as a side dish to accompany broiled meats or fish.

COOK'S TIP

Keep checking the potatoes and stirring throughout the cooking time to ensure that they do not burn or stick to the base of the skillet.

COOK'S TIP

Onions are used in a multitude of dishes to which they add their pungent flavor. The beautifully colored purple-red onions used here have a mild, slightly sweet flavor, as well as looking extremely attractive. Because of their mild taste, they are equally good eaten raw in salads .

Caramelized New Potatoes

Serves 4

INGREDIENTS

1½ pounds new potatoes, scrubbed

4 tbsp dark brown sugar

¼ cup butter

1 tbsp orange juice

1 tbsp chopped fresh parsley or cilantro

salt and pepper

orange rind curls, to garnish

1 Cook the new potatoes in a saucepan of boiling water for 10 minutes, or until almost tender. Drain thoroughly.

2 Melt the sugar in a large, heavy-based skillet over a low heat, stirring.

3 Add the butter and orange juice to the pan, stirring the mixture as the butter melts.

4 Add the potatoes to the orange and butter mixture and continue to cook, turning the potatoes frequently until they are completely coated in the caramel.

5 Sprinkle the chopped parsley or cilantro over the potatoes and season to taste with salt and pepper.

6 Transfer the caramelized new potatoes to a serving dish and garnish with the orange rind. Serve immediately.

VARIATION

Lemon or lime juices may be used instead of the orange juice, if desired. In addition, garnish the finished dish with pared lemon or lime rind, if preferred.

COOK'S TIP

Heat the sugar and butter gently, stirring constantly, to make sure that the mixture doesn't burn or stick to the base of the skillet.

Spanish Potatoes

Serves 4

INGREDIENTS

2 tbsp olive oil	1 tsp chili powder	salt and pepper
1 pound small new potatoes, halved	1 tsp prepared mustard	chopped fresh parsley, to garnish
1 onion, halved and sliced	1¼ cups sieved tomatoes	
1 green bell pepper, cut into strips	1¼ cups vegetable stock	

1 Heat the olive oil in a skillet and add the halved new potatoes and the sliced onion. Cook for 4–5 minutes, stirring frequently, until the onion slices have just softened.

2 Add the green bell pepper strips, chili powder, and mustard to the pan and cook for a further 2–3 minutes.

3 Stir the sieved tomatoes and the vegetable stock into the pan and bring to a boil. Reduce the heat and cook the mixture for about 25 minutes, or until the potatoes are tender.

4 Transfer the potatoes to a serving dish. Sprinkle the parsley over the top of the potatoes and serve hot. Alternatively, let the Spanish potatoes cool completely and serve cold.

COOK'S TIP

In Spain, tapas are traditionally served with a glass of chilled sherry or some other aperitif.

COOK'S TIP

The array of little appetizer snacks known as tapas are a traditional Spanish social custom. Spaniards often visit several bars throughout the evening eating different tapas, ranging from stuffed olives and salted almonds, to slices of ham and deep-fried squid rings.

Spicy Indian Potatoes with Spinach

Serves 4

INGREDIENTS

1/2 tsp coriander seeds	1 red chili, chopped	150 ml/1/4 pint/2/3 cup vegetable
1 tsp cumin seeds	1 onion, chopped	stock
4 tbsp vegetable oil	2 garlic cloves, crushed	4 tbsp natural yogurt
2 cardamon pods	450 g/1 lb new potatoes,	salt
1 cm/1/2 inch piece ginger	quartered	
root, grated	675 g/11/2 lb spinach, chopped	

1 Grind the coriander and cumin seeds using a pestle and mortar.

2 Heat the oil in a skillet. Add the ground coriander and cumin seeds to the pan, together with the cardamom pods and ginger and cook for about 2 minutes.

3 Add the chopped chili, onion, and garlic to the pan. Cook for a further 2 minutes, stirring frequently.

4 Add the potatoes to the pan, together with the vegetable stock. Cook gently for 30 minutes, or until the potatoes are cooked through, stirring occasionally.

5 Add the spinach to the pan and cook for a further 5 minutes.

6 Remove the pan from the heat and stir in the yogurt. Season with salt and pepper to taste. Transfer the potatoes and spinach to a serving dish and serve.

COOK'S TIP

This spicy dish is ideal served with a meat curry or alternatively, as part of a vegetarian meal.

VARIATION

Use frozen spinach instead of fresh spinach, if you prefer. Defrost the frozen spinach and drain it thoroughly before adding it to the dish, otherwise it will turn soggy.

Potatoes & Mushrooms in Red Wine

Serves 4

INGREDIENTS

¹/₂ cup butter	8 shallots, halved	salt and pepper
1 pound new potatoes, halved	2 cups oyster mushrooms	sage leaves or cilantro sprigs, to
³/₄ cup red wine	1 tbsp chopped fresh sage or	garnish
¹/₃ cup beef stock	cilantro	

1 Melt the butter in a heavy-based skillet and add the halved potatoes. Cook gently for 5 minutes, stirring constantly.

2 Add the red wine, beef stock, and halved shallots. Season to taste with salt and pepper and then simmer for 30 minutes.

3 Stir in the mushrooms and chopped sage or cilantro and cook for 5 minutes.

4 Turn the potatoes and mushrooms into a warm serving dish. Garnish with sage leaves or cilantro sprigs and serve at once.

VARIATION

If oyster mushrooms are unavailable, other mushrooms, such as large open-cap mushrooms, can be used instead.

COOK'S TIP

Oyster mushrooms may be grey, yellow, or red in color. They have a soft, melting texture and mild flavor. As they cook, they emit a lot of liquid and shrink to about half their original size. They require little cooking before they start to turn mushy, so add them at the end of the cooking time.

Gingered Potatoes

Serves 4

INGREDIENTS

1¹/₂ pounds waxy potatoes, cubed	1 green chili, chopped	3 tbsp boiling water
2 tbsp vegetable oil	1 celery stalk, chopped	¹/₄ cup butter
2-inch piece fresh ginger root, grated	¹/₄ cup cashews	celery leaves, to garnish
	few strands of saffron	

1 Cook the potatoes in a saucepan of boiling water for 10 minutes. Drain thoroughly.

2 Heat the oil in a heavy-based skillet and add the potatoes. Cook for 3-4 minutes, stirring constantly.

3 Add the grated ginger, chili, celery, and cashews and cook for 1 minute.

4 Meanwhile, place the saffron strands in a small bowl. Add a boiling water and leave to soak.

5 Add the butter to the pan and stir in the saffron mixture. Cook gently for 10 minutes, or until the potatoes are tender.

6 Garnish the gingered potatoes with the celery leaves and serve at once.

COOK'S TIP

Use a nonstick, heavy-based skillet as the potato mixture is fairly dry and may stick to an ordinary pan.

VARIATION

If you prefer a less spicy dish, seed the chopped green chili or omit the chili altogether.

Thai Potato Stir-Fry

Serves 4

INGREDIENTS

4 waxy potatoes, diced
2 tbsp vegetable oil
1 yellow bell pepper, diced
1 red bell pepper, diced
1 carrot, cut into matchstick strips

1 zucchini, cut into matchstick strips
2 garlic cloves, crushed
1 red chili, sliced
1 bunch scallions, halved lengthwise

8 tbsp coconut milk
1 tsp chopped lemon grass
2 tsp lime juice
finely grated rind of 1 lime
1 tbsp chopped fresh cilantro

1 Cook the diced potatoes in a saucepan of boiling water for 5 minutes. Drain thoroughly.

2 Heat the oil in a wok or large skillet and add the potatoes, diced bell peppers, carrot, zucchini, garlic, and chili. Stir-fry the vegetables for 2–3 minutes.

3 Stir in the scallions, coconut milk, chopped lemon grass, and lime juice and stir-fry the mixture for a further 5 minutes.

4 Add the lime rind and cilantro and stir-fry for 1 minute. Serve hot.

COOK'S TIP

Check that the potatoes are not overcooked in step 1, otherwise the potato pieces will disintegrate when they are stir-fried in the wok.

VARIATION

Almost any combination of vegetables is suitable for this dish; the yellow and red bell peppers, for example, can be replaced with crisp green beans or snow peas.

Cheese & Potato Slices

Serves 4

INGREDIENTS

3 large waxy potatoes, unpeeled and thickly sliced	½ cup grated Parmesan cheese	oil, for deep frying
1 cup fresh white bread crumbs	1½ tsp chili powder	chili powder, for dusting (optional)
	2 eggs, beaten	

1 Cook the sliced potatoes in a saucepan of boiling water for 10–15 minutes, or until the potatoes are just tender. Drain thoroughly.

2 Mix the bread crumbs, cheese, and chili powder together in a bowl then transfer to a shallow dish. Pour the beaten eggs into a separate shallow dish.

3 Dip the potato slices in egg and then roll them in the bread crumbs to coat completely.

4 Heat the oil in a large saucepan or deep-fryer to 350°F–375°F, or until a cube of bread browns in 30 seconds. Cook the cheese and potato slices, in several batches and turning occasionally, for 4–5 minutes, or until a golden brown color.

5 Remove the cheese and potato slices with a slotted spoon and leave to drain thoroughly on paper towels. Keep the cheese and potato slices warm while you cook the remaining batches.

6 Transfer the cheese and potato slices to warm serving plates. Dust with chili powder, if using, and serve immediately.

VARIATION

For a healthy alternative, use fresh whole wheat bread crumbs instead of the white ones used here, if you prefer.

COOK'S TIP

The cheese and potato slices may be coated in the breadcrumb mixture in advance and then stored in the refrigerator until ready to use.

Grilled Potatoes with Lime Mayonnaise

Serves 4

INGREDIENTS

1 pound potatoes, unpeeled and
   scrubbed
3 tbsp butter, melted
2 tbsp chopped fresh thyme
paprika, for dusting

LIME MAYONNAISE:
$^2/_3$ cup mayonnaise
2 tsp lime juice
finely grated rind of 1 lime
1 garlic clove, crushed

pinch of paprika
salt and pepper

1 Cut the potatoes into $^1/_2$-inch thick slices.

2 Cook the potatoes in a saucepan of boiling water for 5–7 minutes—they should still be quite firm. Remove the potatoes with a slotted spoon and drain thoroughly.

3 Line a broiler pan with foil. Place the potato slices on top of the foil.

4 Brush the potatoes with the melted butter and sprinkle the chopped thyme on top.

Season to taste with salt and pepper.

5 Cook the potatoes under a preheated broiler for 10 minutes, turning once.

6 Meanwhile, make the lime mayonnaise. Combine the mayonnaise, lime juice, lime rind, garlic, paprika, and salt and pepper to taste in a bowl.

7 Dust the hot potato slices with a little paprika and serve with the lime mayonnaise.

COOK'S TIP

For an impressive side dish, thread the potato slices onto skewers and cook over medium hot barbecue coals.

VARIATION

The lime mayonnaise may be spooned over the broiled potatoes to coat them just before serving, if you prefer.

Trio of Potato Purées

Serves 4

INGREDIENTS

10¹/₂ ounces mealy potatoes, chopped	1 tbsp milk	1 tbsp orange juice
4¹/₂ ounces rutabaga, chopped	1 tbsp butter	¹/₄ tsp grated nutmeg
1 carrot, chopped	¹/₄ cup all-purpose flour	salt and pepper
1 pound spinach	1 egg	carrot matchsticks, to garnish
	¹/₂ tsp ground cinnamon	

1 Lightly grease four ²/₃-cup ramekins or ovenproof mini pudding bowls.

2 Cook the potatoes in a saucepan of boiling water for 10 minutes. Meanwhile, in separate pans, cook the rutabaga and carrot in boiling water for 10 minutes. Blanch the spinach in a little boiling water for 5 minutes. Drain all the vegetables.

3 Add the milk and butter to the potatoes and mash until smooth. Stir in the flour and egg.

4 Divide the potato mixture into 3 equal portions and place in 3 separate bowls. Spoon the rutabaga into one bowl and mix well. Spoon the carrot into the second bowl and mix well. Spoon the spinach into the third bowl and mix well.

5 Add the cinnamon to the rutabaga and potato mixture and season with salt and pepper to taste. Stir the orange juice into the carrot and potato mixture. Stir the nutmeg into the spinach and potato mixture.

6 Spoon a layer of the rutabaga and potato mixture into each of the ramekins or bowls and smooth the top. Cover each with a layer of spinach and potato mixture, then top with the carrot and potato mixture. Cover the ramekins with foil and place in a roasting pan. Half fill the pan with boiling water and cook in a preheated oven at 350°F for 40 minutes, or until set.

7 Turn out onto serving plates, garnish with the carrot matchsticks, and serve at once.

Spicy Potato Fries

Serves 4

INGREDIENTS

4 large waxy potatoes	4 tbsp butter, melted	1 tsp garam masala
2 sweet potatoes	1/2 tsp chili powder	salt

1 Cut the potatoes and sweet potatoes into slices about 1/2 inch thick, then cut them into fries.

2 Place the potatoes in a large bowl of cold salted water. Soak for 20 minutes.

3 Remove the potato slices with a slotted spoon and drain thoroughly. Pat with paper towels until completely dry.

4 Pour the melted butter onto a cookie sheet. Transfer the potato slices to the cookie sheet. Sprinkle with the chili powder and garam masala, turning the potato slices to coat them thoroughly with the mixture.

5 Cook the fries in a preheated oven at 400°F for 40 minutes, turning frequently, until browned and cooked through.

6 Drain the fries on paper towels to remove the excess oil and serve at once.

COOK'S TIP

Rinsing the potatoes in cold water before cooking removes the starch, thus preventing them from sticking together. Soaking the potatoes in a bowl of cold salted water actually makes the cooked fries crisper.

VARIATION

For added flavor, sprinkle the fries with fennel seeds or cumin seeds, before serving.

Italian Potato Wedges

Serves 4

INGREDIENTS

2 large waxy potatoes, unpeeled
4 large ripe tomatoes, skinned and
seeded
$^2/_3$ cup vegetable stock

2 tbsp tomato paste
1 small yellow bell pepper, cut into
strips
$1^1/_2$ cups button mushrooms,
quartered

1 tbsp chopped fresh basil
$^1/_2$ cup grated cheese
salt and pepper

1 Cut each of the potatoes into 8 equal wedges. Parboil the potatoes in a pan of boiling water for 15 minutes. Drain well and place in a shallow ovenproof dish.

2 Chop the tomatoes and add to the dish. Mix together the vegetable stock and tomato paste, then pour the mixture on top of the potatoes and tomatoes.

3 Add the yellow bell pepper strips, quartered mushrooms, and chopped basil. Season well with salt and pepper.

4 Sprinkle the grated cheese over the top and cook in a preheated oven at 375°F for 15–20 minutes, until the topping is golden brown. Serve at once.

COOK'S TIP

For the topping, use any cheese that melts well, such as Mozzarella, the traditional pizza cheese. Alternatively, you could use Swiss cheese, if you prefer.

VARIATION

These potato wedges can also be served as a light supper dish, accompanied by chunks of crusty, fresh brown or white bread.

Saffron-Flavored Potatoes with Mustard

Serves 4

INGREDIENTS

1 tsp saffron strands	2 garlic cloves, crushed	5 tbsp dry white wine
6 tbsp boiling water	1 tbsp white wine vinegar	2 tsp chopped fresh rosemary
1½ pound waxy potatoes, unpeeled and cut into wedges	2 tbsp olive oil	salt and pepper
1 red onion, cut into 8 wedges	1 tbsp wholegrain mustard	
	5 tbsp vegetable stock	

1 Place the saffron strands in a small bowl and pour over the boiling water. Soak for about 10 minutes.

2 Place the potatoes in a roasting pan, together with the red onion wedges and crushed garlic.

3 Add the vinegar, oil, mustard, vegetable stock, white wine, rosemary, and saffron water to the potatoes and onion in the pan. Season to taste with salt and pepper.

4 Cover the roasting pan with foil and bake in a preheated oven at 400°F for 30 minutes.

5 Remove the foil and cook the potatoes for a further 10 minutes, until crisp, browned, and cooked through. Serve hot.

VARIATION

If preferred, use only wine to flavor the potatoes, rather than a mixture of wine and stock.

COOK'S TIP

Turmeric may be used instead of saffron to provide the yellow color in this recipe. However, it is worth using saffron, if possible, for the lovely nutty flavor it gives a dish.

Chili Roast Potatoes

Serves 4

INGREDIENTS

1 pound small new potatoes, scrubbed
²/₃ cup vegetable oil
1 tsp chili powder
¹/₂ tsp caraway seeds

1 tsp salt
1 tbsp chopped fresh basil

1 Cook the potatoes in a saucepan of boiling water for 10 minutes. Drain the potatoes thoroughly.

2 Pour a sufficient quantity of the oil into a shallow roasting pan to coat the base. Heat the oil in a preheated oven at 400°F for 10 minutes. Add the potatoes to the pan and brush them with the hot oil.

3 In a small bowl, mix together the chili powder, caraway seeds, and salt. Sprinkle the mixture over the potatoes, turning to coat them all over.

4 Add the remaining oil to the pan and roast in the oven for about 15 minutes, or until the potatoes are cooked through.

5 Using a slotted spoon, remove the potatoes from the the oil, and transfer them to a warm serving dish. Sprinkle the chopped basil over the top and serve immediately.

COOK'S TIP

Theses spicy potatoes are ideal for serving with plain meat dishes, such as roasted or broiled lamb, pork, or chicken.

VARIATION

Use any other spice of your choice, such as curry powder or paprika, for a variation in flavor.

Parmesan Potatoes

Serves 4

INGREDIENTS

6 potatoes
2/3 cup grated Parmesan cheese
pinch of grated nutmeg

1 tbsp chopped fresh parsley
4 smoked bacon slices, cut into
strips

oil, for roasting
salt

1 Cut the potatoes in half lengthwise and cook them in a saucepan of boiling salted water for 10 minutes. Drain thoroughly.

2 Mix the grated Parmesan cheese, nutmeg, and parsley together in a shallow bowl.

3 Roll the potato pieces in the cheese mixture to coat them completely. Shake off any excess.

4 Pour a little oil into a roasting pan and heat it in a preheated oven at 400°F for 10 minutes.

Remove from the oven and place the potatoes into the pan. Return the pan to the oven and cook for 30 minutes, turning once.

5 Remove from the oven and sprinkle the bacon on top of the potatoes. Return to the oven for 15 minutes, or until the potatoes and bacon are cooked. Drain off any excess fat and serve.

COOK'S TIP

Parmesan cheese has been used for its distinctive flavor, but any finely grated hard cheese would be suitable for this dish.

VARIATION

If you prefer, use slices of salami or prosciutto instead of the bacon, adding it to the dish 5 minutes before the end of the cooking time.

Potatoes Dauphinois

Serves 4

INGREDIENTS

1 tbsp butter	1 red onion, sliced	1¹/₄ cups heavy cream
1¹/₂ pounds waxy potatoes, sliced	³/₄ cup grated Swiss cheese	salt and pepper
2 garlic cloves, crushed		

1 Lightly grease a 4-cup shallow ovenproof dish with a little butter.

2 Arrange a single layer of potato slices in the base of the prepared dish.

3 Top the potato slices with a little of the garlic, sliced red onion, and grated Swiss cheese. Season to taste with a little salt and pepper.

4 Repeat the layers in exactly the same order, finishing with a layer of potatoes topped with cheese.

5 Pour the cream over the top of the potatoes and cook in a preheated oven at 350°F for 1¹/₂ hours, or until the potatoes are cooked through, browned, and crisp. Serve at once.

COOK'S TIP

The different versions of this classic potato dish always contain heavy cream, making it a rich side dish. Cook in a shallow dish to ensure plenty of crispy topping.

VARIATION

For meat-lovers a layer of chopped bacon or favorite ham can be added to this dish, if desired, and serve with a crispy green salad for a light supper. Alternatively this makes an excellent accompaniment to roast meat and vegetables, making a hearty winter's meal.

Pommes Anna

Serves 4

INGREDIENTS

1/4 cup butter, melted	4 tbsp chopped mixed fresh herbs	chopped fresh herbs, to garnish
1 1/2 pounds waxy potatoes	salt and pepper	

1 Brush a shallow 4-cup ovenproof dish with a little of the melted butter.

2 Slice the potatoes thinly and pat dry with paper towels.

3 Arrange a layer of potato slices in the prepared dish until the base is covered. Brush with a little butter and sprinkle with a quarter of the chopped mixed herbs. Season to taste.

4 Continue layering the potato slices, brushing each layer with melted butter and sprinkling with herbs, until all the potato slices are used up.

5 Brush the top layer of potato slices with butter, cover the dish, and cook in a preheated oven at 375°F for 1 1/2 hours.

6 Turn out onto a warm ovenproof platter and return to the oven for a further 25–30 minutes, until golden brown. Serve at once, garnished with herbs.

COOK'S TIP

Make sure that the potatoes are sliced very thinly until they are almost transparent, in order that they cook thoroughly.

COOK'S TIP

The butter holds the potato slices together so that the cooked dish can be turned out. Therefore, it is important that the potato slices are dried thoroughly with paper towels before layering them in the dish, otherwise the butter will not be able to stick to them.

Potatoes with Almonds & Cream

Serves 4

INGREDIENTS

2 large potatoes, unpeeled and
    sliced
1 tbsp vegetable oil
1 red onion, halved and sliced

1 garlic clove, crushed
$^{1}/_{2}$ cup flaked almond
$^{1}/_{2}$ tsp turmeric
$1^{1}/_{4}$ cups heavy cream

$4^{1}/_{2}$ ounces arugula
salt and pepper

1 Cook the sliced potatoes
in a saucepan of boiling
water for 10 minutes.
Drain thoroughly.

2 Heat the vegetable oil
in a skillet and cook the
onion and garlic for 3–4
minutes, stirring frequently.

3 Add the almonds,
turmeric, and potato
slices to the skillet and
cook for 2–3 minutes,
stirring constantly.
Stir in the arugula.

4 Transfer the potato and
almond mixture to a
shallow ovenproof dish.

Pour the heavy cream over
the top and season with salt
and pepper.

5 Cook in a preheated
oven at 375°F for 20
minutes, or until the potatoes
are cooked through. Serve
as an accompaniment to
broiled meat or fish dishes.

VARIATION

*You could use other
nuts, such as unsalted
peanuts or cashews, instead
of the almond flakes,
if desired.*

VARIATION

*If arugula is unavailable,
use the same quantity
of trimmed baby
spinach instead.*

Casseroled Potatoes

Serves 4

INGREDIENTS

1½ pounds waxy potatoes, cut
    into chunks
1 tbsp butter
2 leeks, sliced
⅔ cup dry white wine
⅔ cup vegetable stock

1 tbsp lemon juice
2 tbsp chopped mixed fresh herbs
salt and pepper

TO GARNISH:
grated lemon rind
mixed fresh herbs (optional)

1 Cook the potato chunks in a saucepan of boiling water for 5 minutes. Drain thoroughly.

2 Meanwhile, melt the butter in a skillet and sauté the leeks for 5 minutes, or until they have softened.

3 Spoon the partly cooked potatoes and leeks into the base of an ovenproof dish.

4 Mix together the wine, vegetable stock, lemon juice, and chopped mixed herbs. Season to taste with salt and pepper, then pour the mixture over the potatoes.

5 Cook in a preheated oven at 375°F for 35 minutes, or until the potatoes are tender—to test, insert a sharp knife or skewer.

6 Garnish the potato casserole with lemon rind and fresh herbs, if using, and serve as an accompaniment to meat casseroles or roast meat.

COOK'S TIP

Cover the ovenproof dish halfway through cooking if the leeks start to brown on the top.

Cheese Crumble-Topped Mash

Serves 4

INGREDIENTS

2 pounds mealy potatoes, diced
2 tbsp butter
2 tbsp milk
1/2 cup grated sharp cheese or blue
   cheese

CRUMBLE TOPPING:
3 tbsp butter
1 onion, cut into chunks
1 garlic clove, crushed
1 tbsp wholegrain mustard

3 cups fresh whole wheat
   bread crumbs
2 tbsp chopped fresh parsley
salt and pepper

1 Cook the potatoes in a pan of boiling water for 10 minutes, or until cooked through.

2 Meanwhile, make the crumble topping. Melt the butter in a skillet. Add the onion, garlic, and mustard and fry gently for 5 minutes, until the onion chunks have softened, stirring constantly.

3 Put the bread crumbs in a mixing bowl and stir in the fried onion. Season to taste with salt and pepper.

4 Drain the potatoes thoroughly and place them in a mixing bowl. Add the butter and milk, then mash until smooth. Stir in the grated cheese while the potato is still hot.

5 Spoon the mashed potato into a shallow ovenproof dish and sprinkle with the crumble topping.

6 Cook in a preheated oven at 400°F for 10–15 minutes, until the crumble topping is golden brown and crunchy. Serve immediately.

COOK'S TIP

For extra crunch, add freshly cooked vegetables, such as celery and bell peppers, to the mashed potato in step 4.

Carrot & Potato Soufflé

Serves 4

INGREDIENTS

2 tbsp butter, melted

4 tbsp fresh whole wheat
    bread crumbs

1 1/2 pounds mealy potatoes, baked
    in their skins

2 carrots, grated

2 eggs, separated

2 tbsp orange juice

1/4 tsp grated nutmeg

salt and pepper

carrot curls, to garnish

1 Brush the inside of a 3 3/4-cup soufflé dish with butter. Sprinkle three-quarters of the bread crumbs over the base and sides of the dish.

2 Cut the baked potatoes in half and scoop the flesh into a mixing bowl.

3 Add the carrot, egg yolks, orange juice, and nutmeg to the potato flesh. Season to taste with salt and pepper.

4 In a separate bowl, beat the egg whites until they stand in soft peaks, then gently fold into the potato mixture with a metal spoon until well incorporated.

5 Gently spoon the potato and carrot mixture into the prepared soufflé dish. Sprinkle the remaining bread crumbs over the top of the mixture.

6 Cook in a preheated oven at 400°F/ for 40 minutes, until risen and golden. Do not open the oven door during the cooking time, otherwise the soufflé will sink. Serve at once, garnished with carrot curls.

COOK'S TIP

To bake the potatoes, prick the skins and cook in a preheated oven at 375°F for about 1 hour.

Steamed Potatoes en Papillotes

Serves 4

INGREDIENTS

16 small new potatoes	1 cup green beans	4 rosemary sprigs
1 carrot, cut into matchstick strips	1 yellow bell pepper, cut into strips	salt and pepper
1 fennel bulb, sliced	16 tbsp dry white wine	rosemary sprigs, to garnish

1 Cut 4 squares of waxed paper measuring about 10 inches in size.

2 Divide the vegetables equally between the 4 paper squares, placing them in the center.

3 Bring the edges of the paper together and scrunch them together to encase the vegetables, leaving the top open.

4 Place the parcels in a shallow roasting pan and spoon 4 tbsp of white wine into each packet. Add a rosemary sprig and season with salt and pepper.

5 Fold the top of each packet over to seal it. Cook in a preheated oven at 375°F for 30–35 minutes, or until the vegetables are tender.

6 Transfer the sealed packets to 4 individual serving plates and garnish with rosemary sprigs. The packets should be opened at the table in order for the full aroma of the vegetables to be appreciated.

COOK'S TIP

These packets may be cooked in a steamer, if preferred.

VARIATION

If small new potatoes are unavailable, use larger potatoes which have been halved or quartered to ensure that they cook through in the specified cooking time.

Cheese & Potato Layer Bake

Serves 4

INGREDIENTS

1 pound potatoes

1 leek, sliced

3 garlic cloves, crushed

¹/₂ cup grated vegetarian
cheddar, cheese

¹/₂ cup grated mozzarella cheese

¹/₄ cup grated Parmesan cheese

2 tablespoons chopped parsley

²/₃ cup light cream

²/₃ cup milk

salt and pepper

freshly chopped flat leaf parsley,
to garnish

1 Cook the potatoes in a saucepan of boiling salted water for 10 minutes. Drain well.

2 Cut the potatoes into thin slices. Arrange a layer of potatoes in the base of an ovenproof dish. Layer with a little of the leek, garlic, cheeses, and parsley. Season well.

3 Repeat the layers until all of the ingredients have been used, finishing with a layer of cheese on top.

4 Mix the cream and milk together, season with salt and pepper to taste, and pour the mixture over the potato layers.

5 Cook in a preheated oven at 325°F for about 1–1¼ hours, or until the cheese is golden brown and bubbling and the potatoes are cooked through and tender.

6 Garnish with freshly chopped flat leaf parsley and serve at once straight from the dish.

COOK'S TIP

There is an Italian Parmesan called Grano Padano which is usually vegetarian. As Parmesan quickly loses its "bite", it is best to buy it in small quantities and grate only as much as you need. Wrap the rest in foil and store in the refrigerator.

Cauliflower & Broccoli with Herb Sauce

Serves 4

INGREDIENTS

2 baby cauliflowers	SAUCE:	2 teaspoons grated ginger root
8 ounces broccoli	8 tablespoons olive oil	juice and rind of 2 lemons
salt and pepper	4 tablespoons butter or	5 tablespoons chopped cilantro
	vegetarian margarine	5 tablespoons grated cheddar

1 Using a sharp knife, cut the cauliflowers in half and the broccoli into very large florets.

2 Cook the cauliflower and broccoli in a saucepan of boiling salted water for about 10 minutes. Drain well, transfer to a shallow ovenproof dish, and keep warm until required.

3 To make the sauce, put the oil and butter or vegetarian margarine in a pan and heat gently until the butter melts. Add the grated ginger root, lemon juice, lemon rind, and chopped cilantro and simmer for 2–3 minutes, stirring occasionally.

4 Season the sauce with salt and pepper to taste, then pour it over the vegetables in the dish and sprinkle the cheese on top.

5 Cook under a preheated broiler for 2–3 minutes, or until the cheese is bubbling and golden. Let cool for 1–2 minutes and then serve.

VARIATION

Lime or orange could be used instead of the lemon for a fruity and refreshing sauce.

Steamed Vegetables with Vermouth

Serves 4

INGREDIENTS

1 carrot, cut into batons	4 small onions, halved	pinch of paprika
1 fennel bulb, sliced	8 tablespoons vermouth	4 sprigs tarragon
3¹/₂ ounces zucchini, sliced	4 tablespoons lime juice	salt and pepper
1 red bell pepper, sliced	zest of 1 lime	fresh tarragon sprigs, to garnish

1 Place all of the vegetables in a large bowl and mix well.

2 Cut 4 large squares of baking parchment and place a quarter of the vegetables in the center of each. Bring the sides of the parchment up and pinch together to make an open packet.

3 Mix together the vermouth, lime juice, lime zest, and paprika and pour a quarter of the mixture into each packet. Season with salt and pepper and add a tarragon sprig to each. Pinch the tops of the packets together to seal.

4 Place in a steamer, cover, and cook for 15–20 minutes, or until the vegetables are tender. Garnish and serve.

COOK'S TIP

Seal the packets well to prevent them from opening during cooking and causing the juices to evaporate.

COOKS TIP

Vermouth is a fortified white wine flavored with various herbs and spices. It its available in both sweet and dry forms.

Spicy Peas & Spinach

Serves 4

INGREDIENTS

1¼ cups green split peas	1 teaspoon grated ginger root	2 garlic cloves, crushed
2 pounds spinach	1 teaspoon ground cumin	1¼ cups vegetable stock
4 tablespoons vegetable oil	½ teaspoon chili powder	salt and pepper
1 onion, halved and sliced	½ teaspoon ground coriander	fresh cilantro sprigs and lime wedges, to garnish

1 Rinse the peas under cold running water. Transfer to a mixing bowl, cover with cold water, and set aside to soak for 2 hours. Drain well.

2 Meanwhile, cook the spinach in a large saucepan for 5 minutes, until wilted. Drain well and roughly chop.

3 Heat the oil in a large saucepan and add the onion, spices, and garlic. Sauté for 2–3 minutes, stirring well.

4 Add the peas and spinach and stir in the stock. Cover and simmer for 10–15 minutes, or until the peas are cooked and the liquid has been absorbed. Season with salt and pepper to taste, garnish, and serve.

VARIATION

If you do not have time to soak the green peas, canned lentils are a good substitute, but remember to drain and rinse them first.

COOK'S TIP

Once the peas have been added, stir occasionally to prevent them from sticking to the pan.

Beans in Lemon & Herb Sauce

Serves 4

INGREDIENTS

2 pounds mixed green beans, such as fava beans, green beans, string beans	4 teaspoons all-purpose flour	2 tablespoons lemon juice
	1¼ cups vegetable stock	rind of 1 lemon
½ cup butter or vegetarian margarine	6 tablespoons dry white wine	salt and pepper
	6 tablespoons light cream	
	3 tablespoons chopped mixed herbs	

1 Cook the beans in a saucepan of boiling salted water for 10 minutes, or until tender. Drain and place in a warm serving dish.

2 Meanwhile, melt the butter in a saucepan. Add the flour and cook for 1 minute. Remove the pan from the heat and gradually stir in the stock and wine. Return the pan to the heat and bring to a boil.

3 Remove the pan from the heat once again and stir in the light cream, mixed herbs, lemon juice,

and zest. Season with salt and pepper to taste. Pour the sauce over the beans, mixing well. Serve at once.

COOK'S TIP

Use a wide variety of herbs for flavor, such as rosemary, thyme, tarragon, and sage.

VARIATION

Use lime rind and juice instead of lemon for an alternative citrus flavor. Replace the light cream with plain yogurt for a healthier version of this dish.

Curried Cauliflower & Spinach

Serves 4

INGREDIENTS

1 medium cauliflower	1 teaspoon turmeric	6 tablespoons vegetable stock
6 tablespoons vegetable oil	2 garlic cloves, crushed	1 tablespoon chopped cilantro
1 teaspoon mustard seeds	1 onion, halved and sliced	salt and pepper
1 teaspoon ground cumin	1 green chili, sliced	cilantro sprigs, to garnish
1 teaspoon garam masala	1 pound spinach	

1 Break the cauliflower into small florets.

2 Heat the oil in a deep flameproof casserole. Add the mustard seeds and cook until they begin to pop.

3 Stir in the remaining spices, the garlic, onion, and chili and cook for 2–3 minutes, stirring.

4 Add the cauliflower, spinach, vegetable stock, cilantro, and seasoning and cook over gentle heat for 15 minutes, or until the cauliflower is tender. Uncover the dish and boil for 1 minute to thicken the juices. Garnish and serve at once.

COOK'S TIP

Mustard seeds are used throughout India and are particularly popular in southern vegetarian cooking. They are fried in oil first to bring out their flavor before the other ingredients are added.

Eggplant & Zucchini Galette

Serves 4

INGREDIENTS
---

2 large eggplants, sliced

4 zucchini

2 x 14 ounce cans chopped
tomatoes, drained

2 tablespoons tomato paste

2 garlic cloves, crushed

4 tablespoons olive oil

1 teaspoon sugar

2 tablespoons chopped basil

olive oil, for frying

8 ounces Mozzarella cheese, sliced

salt and pepper

fresh basil leaves, to garnish

---

1 Put the eggplant slices in a colander and sprinkle with salt. Set aside to stand for about 30 minutes, then rinse well under cold water, and drain. Thinly slice the zucchini.

2 Meanwhile, put the tomatoes, tomato paste, garlic, olive oil, sugar, and chopped basil into a pan and simmer over low heat for about 20 minutes, or until reduced by half. Season well.

3 Heat 2 tablespoons of olive oil in a large, heavy-based skillet and cook the eggplant slices for about 2–3 minutes, until just beginning to brown. Remove from the skillet.

4 Add a further 2 tablespoons of oil to the skillet and fry the zucchini slices until browned.

5 Place half of the eggplant slices in the base of an ovenproof dish. Top with half of the tomato sauce and the zucchini and then half of the mozzarella.

6 Repeat the layers and bake in a preheated oven at 350°F for 45–50 minutes, or until the vegetables are tender. Garnish with basil leaves and serve.

Baked Celery with Cream & Pecans

Serves 4

INGREDIENTS

1 head of celery	½ cup pecan nut halves	¼ cup freshly grated
½ teaspoon ground cumin	⅔ cup vegetable stock	Parmesan cheese
½ teaspoon ground coriander	⅔ cup light cream	salt and pepper
1 garlic clove, crushed	1 cup fresh whole wheat	celery leaves, to garnish
1 red onion, thinly sliced	bread crumbs	

1 Trim the celery and cut into matchsticks. Place the celery in an ovenproof dish with the ground cumin, coriander, garlic, onion, and pecan nuts.

2 Mix the stock and cream together and pour it over the vegetables. Season with salt and pepper to taste.

3 Mix the bread crumbs and grated cheese together and sprinkle over the top to cover the vegetables completely.

4 Cook in a preheated oven at 400°F for 40 minutes, or until the vegetables are tender and the top crispy. Garnish with celery leaves and serve at once.

VARIATION

You could use carrots or zucchini instead of the celery, if you desired.

COOK'S TIP

Once grated, Parmesan cheese quickly loses its "bite" so it is best to grate only the amount you need for the recipe. Wrap the rest tightly in foil and it will keep for several months in the refrigerator.

Pepperonata

Serves 4

INGREDIENTS

4 tablespoons olive oil

1 onion, halved and finely sliced

2 red bell peppers, cut into strips

2 green bell peppers, cut into strips

2 yellow bell peppers, cut into strips

2 garlic cloves, crushed

2 x 14 ounce cans chopped
tomatoes, drained

2 tablespoons chopped cilantro

2 tablespoons chopped pitted
black olives

salt and pepper

1 Heat the oil in a large skillet. Add the onion and sauté for 5 minutes, stirring, until just beginning to color.

2 Add the bell peppers and garlic to the skillet and cook for a further 3–4 minutes.

3 Stir in the tomatoes and cilantro and season with salt and pepper. Cover the skillet and cook the vegetables gently for about 30 minutes, or until the mixture is dry.

4 Stir in the pitted black olives and serve the pepperonata at once.

VARIATION

If you don't like the distinctive flavor of fresh cilantro, you can replace it with 2 tablespoons chopped fresh flat leaf parsley. Use green olives instead of black ones, if desired.

COOK'S TIP

Stir the vegetables occasionally during the 30 minutes cooking time to prevent them from sticking to the bottom of the skillet. If the liquid has not evaporated by the end of the cooking time, remove the lid and boil rapidly until the dish is dry.

Souffléd Cheese Potatoes

Serves 4

INGREDIENTS
---

2 pounds potatoes, cut into chunks	pinch of cayenne pepper	salt and pepper
$^2/_3$ cup heavy cream	2 egg whites	chopped flat leaf parsley and grated
$^3/_4$ cup grated Swiss cheese	oil, for deep-frying	vegetarian cheese, to garnish

1 Cook the potatoes in a saucepan of boiling salted water for 10 minutes. Drain well and pat dry with absorbent paper towels. Set aside until required.

2 Mix together the heavy cream and Swiss cheese in a large bowl. Stir in the cayenne pepper and season with salt and pepper to taste.

3 Whisk the egg whites until stiff peaks form. Fold into the cheese mixture until fully incorporated.

4 Add the cooked potatoes, turning to coat thoroughly in the mixture.

5 Heat the oil for deep-frying to 350°F or until a cube of bread browns in 30 seconds. Remove the potatoes from the cheese mixture with a slotted spoon and cook in the oil, in batches, for 3–4 minutes, or until golden brown.

6 Transfer the potatoes to a serving dish and garnish with parsley and grated cheese. Serve.

VARIATION

Add other flavorings, such as grated nutmeg or curry powder, to the cream and cheese.

Bulgur Pilau

Serves 4

INGREDIENTS

6 tablespoons butter or
   vegetarian margarine
1 red onion, halved and sliced
2 garlic cloves, crushed
2 cups bulgur wheat
6 ounces tomatoes, seeded
   and chopped

$1^3/_4$ ounces baby corn,
   halved lengthwise
$2^3/_4$ ounces small broccoli florets
$3^3/_4$ cups vegetable stock
2 tablespoons honey
$^1/_3$ cup golden raisins

$^1/_2$ cup pine nuts
$^1/_2$ teaspoon ground cinnamon
$^1/_2$ teaspoon ground cumin
salt and pepper
sliced scallions,
   to garnish

1 Melt the butter or vegetarian margarine in a large flameproof casserole.

2 Add the onion and garlic and sauté for 2–3 minutes, stirring occasionally.

3 Add the bulgur wheat, tomatoes, corn, broccoli florets, and stock and bring to a boil. Reduce the heat, cover, and simmer for 15–20 minutes, stirring occasionally.

4 Stir in the honey, golden raisins, pine nuts, ground cinnamon, cumin, and salt and pepper to taste, mixing well. Remove the casserole from the heat, cover, and set aside for 10 minutes.

5 Spoon the bulgur pilau into a warm serving dish.

6 Garnish the bulgur pilau with sliced scallions and serve at once.

COOK'S TIP

The dish is left to stand for 10 minutes in order for the bulgur to finish cooking and the flavors to mingle.

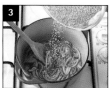

Carrot, Orange, & Poppy Seed Bake

Serves 4

INGREDIENTS

1½ pounds carrots, cut
   into thin strips
1 leek, sliced
1¼ cups fresh
   orange juice

2 tablespoons honey
1 garlic clove, crushed
1 teaspoon pumpkin pie spice
2 teaspoons chopped thyme
1 tablespoon poppy seeds

salt and pepper
fresh thyme sprigs and orange
   rind, to garnish

1 Cook the carrots and leek in a large saucepan of boiling lightly salted water for 5–6 minutes. Drain well and transfer to a shallow ovenproof dish until required.

2 Mix together the orange juice, honey, garlic, pumpkin pie spice, and thyme and pour the mixture over the vegetables. Add salt and pepper to taste.

3 Cover the ovenproof dish and cook in a preheated oven at 350°F for 30 minutes, or until the vegetables are tender.

4 Remove the lid and sprinkle with poppy seeds. Garnish with fresh thyme sprigs and orange rind and serve.

COOK'S TIP

Lemon or lime juice could be used instead of the orange juice if desired. Garnish with lemon or lime rind.

VARIATION

If desired, use 2 teaspoons cumin instead of the pumpkin pie spice and omit the thyme, as cumin works particularly well with carrots.

Greek Green Beans

Serves 4

INGREDIENTS

14 ounces can navy beans, drained	1 bay leaf	1 small red onion, chopped
1 tablespoon olive oil	2 sprigs oregano	1/4 cup pitted black olives, halved
3 garlic cloves, crushed	1 tablespoon tomato paste	salt and pepper
2 cups vegetable stock	juice of 1 lemon	

1 Put the navy beans in a large flameproof casserole.

2 Add the olive oil and crushed garlic and cook over gentle heat, stirring occasionally, for 4–5 minutes, until soft and translucent.

3 Add the vegetable stock, bay leaf, oregano, tomato paste, lemon juice and red onion, cover, and simmer, stirring occasionally for about 1 hour, or until the sauce has thickened.

4 Stir in the olives, season with salt and pepper to taste, and serve.

COOK'S TIP

This dish may be made in advance and served cold with crusty bread, if desired.

VARIATION

You can substitute other canned beans for the navy beans—try cannellini or black-eyed peas, or garbanzo beans instead. Remember to drain and rinse them thoroughly before use, as canned beans often have sugar or salt added.

Sweet & Sour Eggplant

Serves 4

INGREDIENTS
---

2 large eggplants
6 tablespoons olive oil
4 garlic cloves, crushed
1 onion, cut into eight

4 large tomatoes,
   seeded and chopped
3 tablespoons chopped mint
²/₃ cup vegetable stock
4 teaspoons brown sugar

2 tablespoons red
   wine vinegar
1 teaspoon chili flakes
salt and pepper
fresh mint sprigs, to garnish

---

1 Using a sharp knife, cut the eggplants into cubes. Put them in a colander, sprinkle with salt, and let stand for 30 minutes. Rinse thoroughly under cold running water and drain well. This process removes all the bitter juices from the eggplants. Pat thoroughly dry with absorbent paper towels.

2 Heat the oil in a large skillet and sauté the eggplant cubes, stirring constantly, for about 1–2 minutes.

3 Stir in the garlic and onion and cook for a further 2–3 minutes.

4 Stir in the tomatoes, mint, and stock, cover, and cook for 15–20 minutes, or until the vegetables are tender.

5 Stir in the brown sugar, red wine vinegar, and chili flakes, season with salt and pepper to taste, and cook for 2–3 minutes. Garnish the eggplant with fresh mint sprigs and serve.

COOK'S TIP

Mint is a popular herb in Middle Eastern cooking. It is a useful herb to grow yourself, as it can be added to a variety of dishes, particularly salads and vegetable dishes. It can be grown easily in a garden or window box.

Mini Vegetable Puff Pastries

Serves 4

INGREDIENTS

1 pound puff pastry
1 egg, beaten

FILLING:
8 ounces sweet potato, cubed

3½ ounces baby asparagus spears
2 tablespoons butter or vegetarian margarine
1 leek, sliced
2 small mushrooms, sliced

1 teaspoon lime juice
1 teaspoon chopped thyme
pinch of dried mustard
salt and pepper

1 Cut the pastry into 4 equal pieces. Roll each piece out on a lightly floured counter to form a 5-inch square. Place on dampened cookie sheets and score a smaller 2½-inch square inside with the point of a sharp knife.

2 Brush with beaten egg to glaze and cook in a preheated oven at 400°F for 20 minutes, or until the pastry has risen and is golden brown.

3 Remove the pastry squares from the oven, then carefully cut out the central square of pastry, lift it out, and reserve.

4 To make the filling, cook the sweet potato in a saucepan of boiling water for 15 minutes, then drain well. Blanch the asparagus in a saucepan of boiling water for 10 minutes, or until tender. Drain and reserve.

5 Melt the butter or margarine in a saucepan and sauté the leek and mushrooms for 2–3 minutes. Add the lime juice, thyme, and mustard, season well, and stir in the sweet potatoes and asparagus. Spoon into the pastry cases, top with the reserved pastry squares, and serve at once.

COOK'S TIP

Use a colorful selection of any vegetables you have at hand for this recipe.

Main Meals

This chapter contains a wide selection of delicious main-meal dishes which are more substantial than the snacks and light meal section and generally require more preparation and cooking. The potato is the main ingredient in many of the recipes in this chapter, but it also includes ideas for cooking with vegetables and for vegetarian dishes—so that there is sure to be something for everyone.

Some of the recipes included here contain meat, but many are purely vegetarian. There are recipes from all over the world as well as many traditional hearty bakes and roasts. They all make exciting eating at any time of the year and on any occasion. There are ideas for mid-week meals and for entertaining. There is no reason why you cannot experiment by substituting ingredients or adding your own imaginative touches to these meals.

Potato, Beef, & Peanut Pot

Serves 4

INGREDIENTS

1 tbsp vegetable oil	2 garlic cloves, crushed	1/4 cup unsalted peanuts
1/4 cup butter	2 large waxy potatoes, cubed	2 tsp light soy sauce
1 pound lean beef steak, cut into thin strips	1/2 tsp paprika	1 3/4 oz sugar snap peas
1 onion, halved and sliced	4 tbsp crunchy peanut butter	1 red bell pepper, cut into strips
	2 1/2 cups beef stock	parsley sprigs, to garnish (optional)

1 Heat the oil and butter in a flameproof casserole dish.

2 Add the beef strips and sauté them gently for 3–4 minutes, stirring and turning the meat, until it is sealed on all sides.

3 Add the onion and garlic and cook for a further 2 minutes, stirring constantly.

4 Add the potato cubes and cook for 3–4 minutes, or until they begin to brown slightly.

5 Stir in the paprika and peanut butter, then gradually blend in the beef stock. Bring the mixture to a boil, stirring frequently.

6 Finally, add the peanuts, soy sauce, sugar snap peas, and red bell pepper.

7 Cover and cook over a low heat for 45 minutes, or until the beef is cooked through.

8 Garnish the dish with parsley sprigs, if desired, and serve.

COOK'S TIP

Serve this dish with plain boiled rice or noodles, if desired.

VARIATION

Add a chopped green chili to the sauce for extra spice, if you prefer.

Potato Ravioli

Serves 4

INGREDIENTS

FILLING:

1 tbsp vegetable oil

4¹/₂ ounces ground beef

1 shallot, diced

1 garlic clove, crushed

1 tbsp all-purpose flour

1 tbsp tomato paste

²/₃ cup beef stock

1 celery stalk, chopped

2 tomatoes, skinned and diced

2 tsp chopped fresh basil

salt and pepper

RAVIOLI:

1 pound mealy potatoes, diced

3 small egg yolks

3 tbsp olive oil

1¹/₂ cups all-purpose flour

¹/₄ cup butter, for frying

shredded basil leaves, to garnish

1 To make the filling, heat the oil in a pan and fry the beef for 3–4 minutes, breaking it up with a spoon. Add the shallot and garlic and cook for 2–3 minutes, until the shallot has softened.

2 Stir in the flour and tomato paste and cook for 1 minute. Stir in the beef stock, celery, tomatoes, and chopped fresh basil. Season to taste with salt and pepper.

3 Cook the mixture over a low heat for 20 minutes. Remove from the heat and let cool.

4 To make the ravioli, cook the potatoes in a pan of boiling water for 10 minutes, until tender.

5 Mash the potatoes and place them in a mixing bowl. Blend in the egg yolks and oil. Season with salt and pepper, then stir in the flour and mix to form a dough.

6 On a lightly floured surface, divide the dough into 24 pieces and shape into flat rounds. Spoon the filling onto half of each round and fold the dough over to encase the filling, pressing down to seal the edges.

7 Melt the butter in a skillet and cook the ravioli for 6–8 minutes, turning once, until golden. Serve hot, garnished with shredded basil leaves.

Veal Italienne

Serves 4

INGREDIENTS

¹/₄ cup butter	2 tbsp all-purpose flour	2 tbsp chopped fresh basil
1 tbsp olive oil	2 tbsp tomato paste	salt and pepper
1¹/₂ pounds potatoes, cubed	²/₃ cup red wine	fresh basil leaves, to garnish
4 veal escalopes, weighing about	1¹/₄ cups chicken stock	
6 ounces each	8 ripe tomatoes, skinned, seeded,	
1 onion, cut into 8 wedges	and diced	
2 garlic cloves, crushed	¹/₄ cup pitted black olives, halved	

1 Heat the butter and oil in a large skillet. Add the potato cubes and cook for 5–7 minutes, stirring frequently, until they begin to brown.

2 Remove the potatoes from the skillet with a slotted spoon and set aside.

3 Place the veal in the skillet and cook for 2–3 minutes on each side, until sealed. Remove from the pan and set aside.

4 Stir the onion and garlic into the skillet and cook for 2–3 minutes.

5 Add the flour and tomato paste and cook for 1 minute, stirring. Gradually blend in the red wine and chicken stock, stirring to make a smooth sauce.

6 Return the potatoes and veal to the skillet. Stir in the tomatoes, olives, and chopped basil and season with salt and pepper.

7 Transfer to a casserole dish and cook in a preheated oven at 350°F for 1 hour, or until the potatoes and veal are cooked through. Garnish with basil leaves and serve.

COOK'S TIP

For a quicker cooking time and really tender meat, pound the meat with a meat mallet to flatten it slightly before cooking.

Lamb Hotpot

Serves 4

INGREDIENTS

1½ pounds rack of lamb cutlets	1 large onion, sliced thinly	salt and pepper
2 lamb's kidneys	2 tbsp chopped fresh thyme	fresh thyme sprigs, to garnish
1½ pounds waxy potatoes, scrubbed and thinly sliced	⅔ cup lamb stock	
	2 tbsp butter, melted	

1 Remove any excess fat from the lamb. Skin and core the kidneys, and cut them into slices.

2 Arrange a layer of potatoes in the base of a 7½-cup ovenproof dish.

3 Arrange the lamb cutlets on top of the potatoes and cover with the sliced kidneys, onion, and chopped fresh thyme.

4 Pour the lamb stock over the meat and season to taste with salt and pepper.

5 Layer the remaining potato slices on top, overlapping to completely cover the meat and sliced onion.

6 Brush the potato slices with the butter, cover the dish and cook in a preheated oven at 350°F for 1½ hours.

7 Remove the lid and cook for a further 30 minutes, until golden brown on top.

8 Garnish with fresh thyme sprigs and serve hot.

COOK'S TIP

Although this is a classic recipe, extra ingredients of your choice, such as celery or carrots, can be added to the dish for variety and color.

VARIATION

Traditionally, oysters are also included in this tasty hot pot. Add them to the layers along with the kidneys, if desired.

Potato & Lamb Kofta

Serves 4

INGREDIENTS

1 pound mealy potatoes, diced	1/2 tsp ground coriander	SAUCE:
2 tbsp butter	2 eggs, beaten	2/3 cup unsweetened yogurt
8 ounces ground lamb	oil, for deep-frying	2 ounces cucumber, finely chopped
1 onion, chopped	mint sprigs, to garnish	1 tbsp chopped mint
2 garlic cloves, crushed		1 garlic clove, crushed

1 Cook the diced potatoes in a saucepan of boiling water for 10 minutes, until cooked through. Drain, mash until smooth, and transfer to a mixing bowl.

2 Melt the butter in a skillet, add the lamb, onion, garlic, and coriander and fry for 15 minutes, stirring.

3 Drain off the liquid from the skillet, then stir the meat mixture into the mashed potatoes. Stir in the eggs and season.

4 To make the sauce, combine the yogurt, cucumber, mint, and garlic in a bowl and set aside.

5 Heat the oil in a large saucepan or a deep-fryer to 350°F–375°F, or until a cube of bread browns in 30 seconds. Drop spoonfuls of the potato mixture into the hot oil and cook in batches for 4–5 minutes, or until golden brown.

6 Remove the kofta with a slotted spoon, drain thoroughly on paper towels, set aside, and keep warm. Garnish with fresh mint sprigs and serve with the sauce.

COOK'S TIP

These kofta can be made with any sort of ground meat, such as turkey, chicken, or pork, and flavored with appropriate fresh herbs, such as sage or cilantro.

Spanish Potato Bake

Serves 4

INGREDIENTS

1 1/2 pounds waxy potatoes, diced
3 tbsp olive oil
1 onion, halved and sliced
2 garlic cloves, crushed
14 ounce can plum tomatoes,

chopped
2 3/4 ounces chorizo sausage,
sliced
1 green bell pepper, cut into strips
1/2 tsp paprika

1/4 cup pitted black olives, halved
8 eggs
1 tbsp chopped fresh parsley
salt and pepper

1 Cook the diced potatoes in a saucepan of boiling water for 10 minutes, or until softened. Drain and set aside.

2 Heat the olive oil in a skillet, add the onion and garlic, and fry gently for 2–3 minutes, until the onion softens.

3 Add the chopped canned tomatoes and cook over a low heat for about 10 minutes, or until the mixture has reduced slightly.

4 Stir the potatoes into the skillet with the chorizo, bell pepper, paprika, and olives. Cook for 5 minutes, stirring. Transfer to a shallow ovenproof dish.

5 Make 8 small hollows in the top of the mixture and break an egg into each hollow.

6 Cook in a preheated oven at 425°F for 5–6 minutes, or until the eggs are just cooked. Sprinkle with parsley and serve with crusty bread.

VARIATION

Add a little spice to the dish by incorporating 1 tsp chili powder in step 4, if desired.

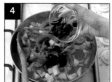

Potato & Pepperoni Pizza

Makes 1 large pizza

INGREDIENTS

2 pounds mealy potatoes, diced
1 tbsp butter
2 garlic cloves, crushed
2 tbsp mixed chopped fresh herbs
1 egg, beaten

¹/₃ cup sieved tomatoes
2 tbsp tomato paste
¹/₂ cup pepperoni slices
1 green bell pepper, cut into strips
1 yellow bell pepper, cut into strips

2 large open-cap mushrooms, sliced
¹/₄ cup pitted black olives, quartered
4¹/₂ ounces mozzarella cheese,
    sliced

1 Grease and flour a 9-inch pizza pan.

2 Cook the diced potatoes in a saucepan of boiling water for 10 minutes, or until cooked through. Drain and mash until smooth. Transfer the mashed potato to a mixing bowl and stir in the butter, garlic, herbs, and egg.

3 Spread the mixture into the prepared pizza pan. Cook in a preheated oven at 425°F for 7–10 minutes, or until the pizza base begins to set.

4 Mix the sieved tomatoes and tomato paste together and spoon it over the pizza base, to within ½ inch of the edge.

5 Arrange the pepperoni, bell peppers, mushrooms, and olives on top of the sieved tomatoes.

6 Scatter the mozzarella cheese on top of the pizza. Cook in the oven for 20 minutes, or until the base is cooked through and the cheese has melted on top. Serve hot with a mixed salad.

COOK'S TIP

This pizza base is softer in texture than a normal bread dough and is ideal served from the pan. Top with any of your favorite pizza ingredients that you have to hand.

Potato & Sausage Pan-Fry

Serves 4

INGREDIENTS

1½ pounds waxy potatoes, cubed	1 onion, quartered	1 tsp Worcestershire sauce
2 tbsp butter	1 zucchini, sliced	2 tbsp chopped mixed fresh herbs
8 large herbed sausages	⅔ cup dry white wine	salt and pepper
4 smoked bacon slices	1¼ cups vegetable stock	chopped fresh herbs, to garnish

1 Cook the cubed potatoes in a saucepan of boiling water for 10 minutes, or until softened. Drain thoroughly and set aside.

2 Meanwhile, melt the butter in a large skillet. Add the herbed sausages and cook for 5 minutes, turning them frequently to ensure that they brown on all sides.

3 Add the bacon slices, onion, zucchini, and potatoes to the skillet. Cook the mixture for a further 10 minutes, stirring the mixture and turning the sausages frequently.

4 Stir in the white wine, stock, Worcestershire sauce, and chopped mixed herbs. Season with salt and pepper to taste and cook the mixture over a gentle heat for 10 minutes. Season with a little more salt and pepper, if necessary.

5 Transfer the potato and sausage panfry to warm serving plates, garnish with chopped fresh herbs, and serve at once.

COOK'S TIP

Use different flavors of sausage to vary the dish—there are many different varieties available, such as leek and mustard.

VARIATION

For an attractive color, use a red onion cut into quarters rather than a white onion.

Potato, Tomato, & Sausage Pan-Fry

Serves 4

INGREDIENTS

2 large potatoes, sliced	²/₃ cup red wine	2 tbsp chopped fresh basil
1 tbsp vegetable oil	²/₃ cup sieved tomatoes	salt and pepper
8 flavored sausages	2 large tomatoes, each cut into 8	shredded fresh basil, to garnish
1 red onion, cut into 8	6 ounces broccoli florets,	
1 tbsp tomato paste	blanched	

1 Cook the sliced potatoes in a saucepan of boiling water for 7 minutes. Drain thoroughly and set aside.

2 Meanwhile, heat the oil in a large skillet. Add the sausages and cook for 5 minutes, turning the sausages frequently to ensure that they are browned on all sides.

3 Add the onion pieces to the pan and continue to cook for a further 5 minutes, stirring the mixture frequently.

4 Stir in the tomato paste, red wine, and the sieved tomatoes and mix together well. Add the tomato wedges, broccoli florets, and chopped basil to the pan-fry and mix carefully.

5 Add the parboiled potato slices to the pan. Cook the mixture for about 10 minutes, or until the sausages are completely cooked through. Season to taste with salt and pepper.

6 Garnish the panfry with fresh shredded basil and serve hot.

COOK'S TIP

Omit the sieved tomatoes from this recipe and use canned plum tomatoes or chopped tomatoes for convenience.

VARIATION

Broccoli is particularly good in this dish as it adds a splash of color, but other vegetables of your choice can be used instead, if preferred.

Potato, Chicken, & Banana Patties

Serves 4

INGREDIENTS

1 pound mealy potatoes, diced	1 onion, finely chopped	$^2/_3$ cup chicken stock
8 ounces ground chicken	2 tbsp chopped fresh sage	salt and pepper
1 large banana	2 tbsp butter	fresh sage leaves, to garnish
2 tbsp all-purpose flour	2 tbsp vegetable oil	
1 tsp lemon juice	$^2/_3$ cup light cream	

1 Cook the diced potatoes in a saucepan of boiling water for 10 minutes, until cooked through. Drain and mash the potatoes until smooth. Stir in the chicken.

2 Mash the banana and add it to the potato with the flour, lemon juice, onion, and half the chopped sage. Season well and stir the mixture together.

3 Divide the mixture into 8 equal portions. With lightly floured hands,

shape each portion into a round patty.

4 Heat the butter and oil in a skillet, add the potato patties and cook for 12–15 minutes, or until cooked through, turning once. Remove from the skillet and keep warm.

5 Stir the cream and stock into the skillet with the remaining chopped sage. Cook over a low heat for 2–3 minutes.

6 Arrange the potato patties on a serving plate, garnish with fresh sage leaves, and serve with the cream and sage sauce.

COOK'S TIP

Do not boil the sauce once the cream has been added, as it will curdle. Cook it gently over a very low heat.

Creamy Chicken & Potato Casserole

Serves 4

INGREDIENTS

2 tbsp vegetable oil	4 tbsp all-purpose flour	$^2/_3$ cup baby corn cobs, halved
$^1/_4$ cup butter	$3^3/_4$ cups chicken stock	lengthwise
4 chicken portions, about 8 ounces	$1^1/_4$ cups dry white wine	1 bouquet garni
each	$^2/_3$ cup baby carrots, halved	$^2/_3$ cup heavy cream
2 leeks, sliced	lengthwise	salt and pepper
1 garlic clove, crushed	1 pound small new potatoes	

1. Heat the oil in a large skillet. Cook the chicken for 10 minutes, turning until browned all over. Transfer the chicken to a casserole dish using a slotted spoon.

2. Add the leek and garlic to the skillet and cook for 2–3 minutes, stirring. Stir in the flour and cook for a further 1 minute. Remove the skillet from the heat and stir in the stock and wine. Season well.

3. Return the skillet to the heat and bring the mixture to a boil. Stir in the carrots, corn, potatoes, and bouquet garni.

4. Transfer the mixture to the casserole dish. Cover and cook in a preheated oven at 350°F for about 1 hour.

5. Remove the casserole from the oven and stir in the cream. Return the casserole to the oven, uncovered, and cook for a further 15 minutes. Remove the bouquet garni and discard. Taste and adjust the seasoning, if necessary. Serve the casserole with plain rice or fresh vegetables, such as broccoli or green beans.

COOK'S TIP

Use turkey fillets instead of the chicken, if desired, and vary the vegetables according to those you have to hand.

Potato-Topped Cod

Serves 4

INGREDIENTS

1/4 cup butter	1 tsp garam masala	4 cod fillets, about 6 ounces each
4 waxy potatoes, sliced	pinch of chili powder	1/2 cup grated Swiss cheese
1 large onion, finely chopped	1 tbsp chopped fresh dill	salt and pepper
1 tsp wholegrain mustard	1 1/4 cups fresh bread crumbs	fresh dill sprigs, to garnish

1 Melt half the butter in a skillet. Add the potatoes and fry for 5 minutes, turning until they are browned all over. Remove the potatoes from the skillet with a slotted spoon.

2 Add the remaining butter to the skillet and stir in the onion, mustard, garam masala, chili powder, chopped dill, and bread crumbs. Cook for 1–2 minutes, stirring well.

3 Layer half the potatoes in the base of an ovenproof dish and place the cod fillets on top. Cover the cod fillets with the rest of the potato slices. Season to taste with salt and pepper.

4 Spoon the spicy mixture from the skillet over the potatoes and sprinkle with the grated Swiss cheese.

5 Cook in a preheated oven at 400°F for 20–25 minutes, or until the topping is golden and crisp and the fish is cooked through. Garnish with fresh dill sprigs and serve at once.

COOK'S TIP

This dish is ideal served with baked vegetables which can be cooked in the oven at the same time.

VARIATION

You can use any fish for this recipe: for special occasions use salmon steaks or fillets.

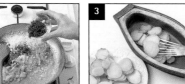

Potato Curry

Serves 4

INGREDIENTS

4 tbsp vegetable oil
1 1/2 pound waxy potatoes, cut into
    large chunks
2 onions, quartered
3 garlic cloves, crushed
1 tsp garam masala

1/2 tsp turmeric
1/2 tsp ground cumin
1/2 tsp ground coriander
1-inch piece fresh ginger root,
    grated
1 red chili, chopped
8 ounces cauliflower florets

4 tomatoes, peeled and quartered
3/4 cup frozen peas
2 tbsp chopped fresh cilantro
1 1/4 cups vegetable stock
shredded fresh cilantro, to garnish

1 Heat the vegetable oil in a large heavy-based saucepan or skillet. Add the potato chunks, onion, and garlic and fry gently for 2–3 minutes, stirring the mixture frequently.

2 Add the garam masala, turmeric, ground cumin, ground coriander, grated ginger, and chopped chili to the pan, mixing the spices into the vegetables. Fry for 1 minute, stirring constantly.

3 Add the cauliflower florets, tomatoes, peas, chopped cilantro, and vegetable stock to the curry mixture.

4 Cook the potato curry over a low heat for 30–40 minutes, or until the potatoes are completely cooked through.

5 Garnish the potato curry with fresh cilantro and serve with plain boiled rice or warm Indian bread.

COOK'S TIP

Use a large heavy-based saucepan or skillet for this recipe to ensure that the potatoes are cooked thoroughly.

Potato & Spinach Gnocchi

Serves 4

INGREDIENTS

10¹/₂ ounces mealy potatoes, diced	salt and pepper	SAUCE:
6 ounces spinach	spinach leaves, to garnish	1 tbsp olive oil
1 egg yolk		2 shallots, chopped
1 tsp olive oil		1 garlic clove, crushed
1 cup all-purpose flour		1¹/₄ cups sieved tomatoes
		2 tsp soft light brown sugar

1 Cook the diced potatoes in a saucepan of boiling water for 10 minutes, until cooked through. Drain and mash the potatoes.

2 Meanwhile, in a separate pan, blanch the spinach in a little boiling water for 1–2 minutes. Drain well and shred the leaves.

3 Transfer the mashed potato to a lightly floured chopping board and make a well in the center. Add the egg yolk, olive oil, spinach, and a little of the

flour and quickly mix the ingredients into the potato, adding more flour as you go, until you have a firm dough. Divide the mixture into very small dumplings.

4 Cook the gnocchi in batches in a saucepan of boiling salted water for about 5 minutes, or until they rise to the top of the pan.

5 Meanwhile, make the sauce. Put the oil, shallots, garlic, sieved tomatoes, and sugar into a saucepan and cook over a

low heat for 10–15 minutes, or until the sauce has thickened.

6 Drain the gnocchi using a slotted spoon and transfer to warm serving dishes. Spoon the sauce over the gnocchi and garnish with the fresh spinach leaves.

VARIATION

Add chopped fresh herbs and cheese to the gnocchi dough instead of the spinach, if desired.

Potato-Topped Vegetables in Wine

Serves 4

INGREDIENTS

1 carrot, diced
6 ounces cauliflower florets
6 ounces broccoli florets
1 fennel bulb, sliced
3/4 cup green beans, halved
2 tbsp butter
1/4 cup all-purpose flour

2/3 cup vegetable stock
1 2/3 cup dry white wine
2/3 cup milk
2 tbsp chopped fresh sage
2 1/4 cups quartered crimini
   mushrooms

TOPPING:
4 mealy potatoes, diced
2 tbsp butter
4 tbsp unsweetened yogurt
4 tbsp grated Parmesan cheese
1 tsp fennel seeds
salt and pepper

1 Cook the carrot, cauliflower, broccoli, fennel, and beans in a saucepan of boiling water for 10 minutes. Drain the vegetables thoroughly and set aside.

2 Melt the butter in a saucepan and stir in the flour. Cook for 1 minute, then remove from the heat. Stir in the stock, wine, and milk and bring to a boil, stirring until thickened. Stir in the reserved vegetables and mushrooms.

3 Meanwhile, make the topping. Cook the diced potatoes in a separate pan of boiling water for 10–15 minutes, or until cooked through. Drain the potatoes and mash with the butter, yogurt, and half the cheese. Stir in the fennel seeds.

4 Spoon the vegetable mixture into a 4-cup pie dish. Spoon or pipe the potato on top, covering the filling completely. Sprinkle the remaining cheese on top.

Cook in a preheated oven at 375°F for 30–35 minutes, or until the topping is golden. Serve hot.

COOK'S TIP

Any combination of vegetables may be used in this dish, and frozen mixed vegetables can be thawed and used for convenience and speed.

Potato & Three-Cheese Soufflé

Serves 4

INGREDIENTS

2 tbsp butter	8 eggs, separated	¼ cup grated sharp cheese
2 tsp all-purpose flour	¼ cup grated Swiss cheese	salt and pepper
2 pounds mealy potatoes	¼ cup crumbled blue cheese	

1 Grease a 10-cup soufflé dish with the butter and dust with the flour. Set aside.

2 Cook the potatoes in a saucepan of boiling water until cooked through. Mash until very smooth and transfer to a mixing bowl to cool.

3 Beat the egg yolks into the potato and stir in the 3 different cheeses. Season well with salt and pepper.

4 In a clean bowl, beat the egg whites until standing in peaks, then gently fold them into the potato mixture with a metal spoon until fully incorporated.

5 Spoon the potato mixture into the prepared soufflé dish.

6 Cook in a preheated oven at 425°F for 35–40 minutes, until risen and set. Serve immediately.

COOK'S TIP

Insert a toothpick into the center of the soufflé; it should come out clean when the soufflé is fully cooked through.

VARIATION

You can add chopped cooked bacon to the soufflé for extra flavor, if desired.

Nutty Harvest Loaf

Serves 4

INGREDIENTS

1 pound mealy potatoes, diced	1 egg, beaten	SAUCE:
2 tbsp butter	2 tbsp chopped fresh cilantro	$^2/_3$ cup crème fraîche
1 onion, chopped	$^2/_3$ cup vegetable stock	2 tsp tomato paste
2 garlic cloves, crushed	1 cup closed-cap mushrooms, sliced	2 tsp clear honey
$^3/_4$ cup unsalted peanuts	1 cup sliced sun-dried tomatoes	2 tbsp chopped fresh cilantro
$1^1/_4$ cups fresh white bread crumbs	salt and pepper	

1 Grease a 1-pound loaf pan. Cook the potatoes in a saucepan of boiling water for 10 minutes, until cooked through. Drain well, mash, and set aside.

2 Melt half the butter in a skillet. Add the onion and garlic and sauté gently for 2–3 minutes, until soft. Finely chop the nuts or blend them in a food processor for 30 seconds with the bread crumbs.

3 Mix the chopped nuts and bread crumbs into the potatoes with the egg, cilantro, and vegetable stock. Stir in the onion and garlic and mix well.

4 Melt the remaining butter in the skillet, add the sliced mushrooms, and cook for 2–3 minutes.

5 Press half the potato mixture into the base of the loaf pan. Spoon the mushrooms on top and sprinkle with the sun-dried tomatoes. Spoon the remaining potato mixture on top and smooth the surface. Cover with foil and bake in a preheated oven at 350°F for 1 hour, or until firm to the touch.

6 Meanwhile, mix the sauce ingredients together. Cut the nutty harvest loaf into slices and serve with the sauce.

Vegetable Cake

Serves 4

INGREDIENTS

BASE:	1 leek, chopped	8 ounces full-fat soft cheese
2 tbsp vegetable oil	1 zucchini, grated	1/4 cup grated sharp cheese
4 large waxy potatoes, sliced thinly	1 red bell pepper, diced	2 eggs, beaten
	1 green bell pepper, diced	salt and pepper
TOPPING:	1 carrot, grated	shredded cooked leek, to garnish
1 tbsp vegetable oil	2 tsp chopped fresh parsley	

1 Grease an 8-inch springform cake pan.

2 To make the base, heat the oil in a skillet. Cook the potato slices in batches over a medium heat until softened and browned. Drain thoroughly on paper towels and arrange the slices in the base of the pan.

3 To make the topping, heat the oil in a separate skillet and fry the leek over a low heat for 3–4 minutes, until softened.

4 Add the zucchini, bell peppers, carrot, and parsley to the skillet and cook over a low heat for 5–7 minutes, or until the vegetables have softened.

5 Meanwhile, beat the cheeses and eggs together in a bowl. Stir in the vegetables and season to taste with salt and pepper. Spoon the mixture on to the potato base.

6 Cook in a preheated oven at 375°F for 20–25 minutes, until the cake is set.

7 Remove the vegetable cake from the pan, garnish with shredded leek, and serve with a crisp salad.

COOK'S TIP

Add diced bean curd or diced meat, such as pork or chicken, to the topping, if desired. Cook the meat with the vegetables in step 4.

Bubble & Squeak

Serves 4

INGREDIENTS

1 pound mealy potatoes, diced	2 leeks, chopped	salt and pepper
8 ounces Savoy cabbage, shredded	1 garlic clove, crushed	shredded cooked leek, to garnish
5 tbsp vegetable oil	8 ounces smoked bean curd, cubed	

1 Cook the diced potatoes in a saucepan of boiling water for 10 minutes, until tender. Drain and mash the potatoes.

2 Meanwhile, in a separate saucepan, blanch the cabbage in boiling water for 5 minutes. Drain and add to the potato.

3 Heat the oil in a heavy-based skillet, add the leeks and garlic, and sauté gently for 2–3 minutes. Stir into the potato and cabbage mixture.

4 Add the smoked bean curd and season well with salt and pepper. Cook over a moderate heat for 10 minutes.

5 Carefully turn the whole mixture over and continue to cook over a moderate heat for a further 5–7 minutes, until crispy underneath. Serve immediately, garnished with shredded leek.

VARIATION

You can add cooked meats, such as beef or chicken, instead of the bean curd for a more traditional recipe. Any gravy from the cooked meats can also be added, but ensure that the mixture is not too wet.

COOK'S TIP

This vegetarian recipe is a perfect main meal, as the smoked bean curd cubes added to the basic bubble and squeak mixture make it very substantial.

Potato Hash

Serves 4

INGREDIENTS

2 tbsp butter	3 large waxy potatoes, diced	salt and pepper
1 red onion, halved and sliced	2 tbsp all-purpose flour	chopped fresh parsley, to garnish
1 carrot, diced	1^1/$_4$ cups vegetable stock	
^{1}/$_3$ cup green beans, halved	8 ounces bean curd, diced	

1 Melt the butter in a skillet. Add the onion, carrot, green beans, and potatoes and sauté gently, stirring, for 5–7 minutes, or until the vegetables begin to brown.

2 Add the flour to the skillet and cook for 1 minute, stirring constantly. Gradually pour in the stock.

3 Reduce the heat and leave the mixture to simmer for 15 minutes, or until the potatoes are tender.

4 Add the diced bean curd to the mixture and cook for a further 5 minutes. Season to taste with salt and pepper.

5 Sprinkle the chopped parsley over the top of the potato hash to garnish, then serve hot straight from the skillet.

COOK'S TIP

Hash is a cooking term meaning to chop food into small pieces. Therefore a traditional hash dish is made from chopped fresh ingredients, such as roast beef or corned beef, bell peppers, onion, and celery, often served with gravy.

VARIATION

Use cooked diced meat, such as beef or lamb, instead of the bean curd for a non-vegetarian dish.

Twice-Baked Potatoes with Pesto

Serves 4

INGREDIENTS

4 baking potatoes, about 8 ounces each	1 tbsp lemon juice	2 tbsp grated Parmesan cheese
⅔ cup heavy cream	2 garlic cloves, crushed	salt and pepper
⅓ cup vegetable stock	3 tbsp chopped fresh basil	
	2 tbsp pine nuts	

1 Scrub the potatoes and prick the skins with a fork. Rub a little salt into the skins and place on a cookie sheet.

2 Cook in a preheated oven at 375°F, for 1 hour or until the potatoes are cooked through and the skins crisp.

3 Remove the potatoes from the oven and cut them in half lengthwise. Using a spoon, scoop the potato flesh into a mixing bowl, leaving a thin shell of potato inside the skins.

Mash the potato flesh with a fork.

4 Meanwhile, mix the cream and stock in a saucepan and simmer for 8–10 minutes, or until reduced by half.

5 Stir in the lemon juice, garlic, and chopped basil and season to taste with salt and pepper. Stir the mixture into the potato flesh with the pine nuts.

6 Spoon the mixture back into the potato shells and sprinkle the Parmesan cheese on top. Return the potatoes to the oven for 10 minutes, or until the cheese has browned. Serve with salad.

VARIATION

Add full-fat soft cheese or thinly sliced mushrooms to the mashed potato flesh in step 5, if you prefer.

Baked Potatoes with Guacamole & Salsa

Serves 4

INGREDIENTS

4 baking potatoes, about 8 ounces each	1 tsp lemon juice	SALSA:
1 large ripe avocado	$4^1/_2$ ounces mixed salad greens	2 ripe tomatoes, seeded and diced
6 ounces bean curd diced	fresh cilantro sprigs, to garnish	1 tbsp chopped cilantro
2 garlic cloves, crushed		1 shallot, finely diced
1 onion, chopped finely		1 green chili, diced
1 tomato, chopped finely		1 tbsp lemon juice
		salt and pepper

1 Scrub the potatoes and prick the skins with a fork. Rub a little salt into the skins and place them on a cookie sheet.

2 Cook in a preheated oven at 375°F for 1 hour, or until cooked through and the skins are crisp.

3 Cut the potatoes in half lengthwise and scoop the flesh into a bowl, leaving a thin layer of potato inside the shells.

4 Halve and pit the avocado. Using a spoon, scoop out the avocado flesh and add to the bowl containing the potato. Stir in the lemon juice and mash the mixture together with a fork. Mix in the bean curd, garlic, onion, and tomato. Spoon the mixture into one half of the potato shells.

5 Arrange the salad greens on top of the guacamole mixture and place the other half of the potato shell on top.

6 To make the salsa, mix the tomatoes, cilantro, shallots, chili, lemon juice, and salt and pepper to taste in a bowl. Garnish the potatoes with sprigs of fresh cilantro and serve with the hot tomato salsa.

Pan Potato Cake

Serves 4

INGREDIENTS

1¹/₂ pounds waxy potatoes, unpeeled and sliced	¹/₄ cup butter	6 ounces bean curd, diced
1 carrot, diced	2 tbsp vegetable oil	2 tbsp chopped fresh sage
8 ounces small broccoli flowerets	1 red onion, quartered	³/₄ cup grated sharp cheese
	2 garlic cloves, crushed	

1 Cook the sliced potatoes in a saucepan of boiling water for 10 minutes. Drain thoroughly.

2 Meanwhile, cook the carrot and broccoli in a separate pan of boiling water for 5 minutes. Drain with a slotted spoon.

3 Heat the butter and oil in a 9-inch skillet, add the quartered red onion and crushed garlic, and sauté gently for 2–3 minutes. Add half the potatoes slices to the skillet, covering the base of the skillet.

4 Cover the potato slices with the carrot, broccoli, and bean curd. Sprinkle with half the sage and cover with the remaining potato slices. Sprinkle the grated cheese over the top.

5 Cook over a moderate heat for 8–10 minutes, then heat under a preheated broiler for 2–3 minutes, or until the cheese melts and browns.

6 Garnish with the remaining sage and serve straight from the skillet.

COOK'S TIP

Make sure that the mixture fills the whole width of your skillet so that all the layers remain intact.

Four-Cheese & Potato Layer Bake

Serves 4

INGREDIENTS

2 pounds unpeeled waxy potatoes, cut into wedges	14 ounce can artichoke hearts in brine, drained and halved	1 1/8 cup grated sharp cheese
2 tbsp butter	5 1/2 ounces frozen mixed	1/3 cup grated Parmesan cheese
1 red onion, halved and sliced	vegetables, thawed	8 ounces bean curd, sliced
2 garlic cloves, crushed	1 1/8 cup grated Swiss cheese	2 tbsp chopped fresh thyme
1/4 cup all-purpose flour	1/2 cup crumbled Gorgonzola	salt and pepper
2 1/2 cups milk	cheese	thyme sprigs, to garnish

1 Cook the potato wedges in a saucepan of boiling water for 10 minutes. Drain thoroughly.

2 Meanwhile, melt the butter in a saucepan. Add the sliced onion and garlic and sauté gently for 2–3 minutes.

3 Stir the flour into the pan and cook for 1 minute. Gradually add the milk and bring to a boil, stirring constantly.

4 Reduce the heat and add the artichoke hearts, mixed vegetables, half of each of the 4 cheeses, and the bean curd to the pan, mixing well. Stir in the chopped fresh thyme and season with salt and pepper to taste.

5 Arrange a layer of parboiled potato wedges in the base of a shallow ovenproof dish. Spoon the vegetable mixture over the top and cover with the

remaining potato wedges. Sprinkle the rest of the 4 cheeses over the top.

6 Cook in a preheated oven at 400°F for 30 minutes, or until the potatoes are cooked and the top is golden brown. Serve the bake garnished with fresh thyme sprigs.

Potato & Eggplant Gratin

Serves 4

INGREDIENTS

1 pound waxy potatoes, sliced	2 tbsp tomato paste	2 tbsp chopped fresh thyme
1 tbsp vegetable oil	2 tbsp all-purpose flour	1 pound unsweetened yogurt
1 onion, chopped	1¼ cups vegetable stock	2 eggs, beaten
2 garlic cloves, crushed	2 large tomatoes, sliced	salt and pepper
1 pound bean curd, diced	1 eggplant, sliced	

1 Cook the sliced potatoes in a saucepan of boiling water for 10 minutes, until tender but not breaking up. Drain and set aside.

2 Heat the oil in a pan and sauté the onion and garlic for 2–3 minutes.

3 Add the diced bean curd, tomato paste, and flour and cook for 1 minute. Gradually stir in the vegetable stock and bring to a boil, stirring constantly. Reduce the heat and simmer for 10 minutes.

4 Arrange a layer of the potato slices in the base of a deep ovenproof dish. Spoon the bean curd mixture on top.

5 Layer the tomatoes, then the eggplant, and then the remaining potato slices on top of the tofu mixture, making sure that it is completely covered.

6 Mix the yogurt and beaten eggs together in a bowl and season well with salt and pepper. Spoon the yogurt topping over the sliced potatoes.

7 Cook in a preheated oven at 375°F for 35–45 minutes, or until the topping is browned. Serve hot, with crisp salad greens.

VARIATION

You can use marinated or smoked bean curd for extra flavor, if you wish.

Spicy Potato & Nut Terrine

Serves 4

INGREDIENTS

8 ounces mealy potatoes, diced	2 tbsp chopped mixed herbs	SAUCE:
1¹/₂ cups pecans	1 tsp paprika	3 large tomatoes, skinned, seeded,
1¹/₂ cups unsalted cashews	1 tsp ground cumin	and chopped
1 onion, chopped finely	1 tsp ground coriander	2 tbsp tomato paste
2 garlic cloves, crushed	4 eggs, beaten	¹/₃ cup red wine
1¹/₂ cups diced open-cap	4¹/₂ ounces full-fat soft cheese	1 tbsp red wine vinegar
mushrooms	²/₃ cup grated Parmesan cheese	pinch of superfine sugar
2 tbsp butter	salt and pepper	

1 Lightly grease a 2-pound loaf pan and line with baking parchment.

2 Cook the potatoes in a pan of boiling water for 10 minutes, or until cooked through. Drain and mash the potatoes.

3 Finely chop the pecans and cashews or process in a food processor. Mix the nuts with the onion, garlic, and mushrooms. Melt the butter in a skillet and cook the nut mixture for 5–7 minutes. Add the herbs and spices to the pan. Stir in the eggs, cheeses, and potatoes and season.

4 Spoon the mixture into the prepared loaf pan, pressing down firmly. Cook in a preheated oven at 375°F, for 1 hour, or until set.

5 To make the sauce, mix the tomatoes, tomato paste, wine, wine vinegar, and sugar in a pan and bring to a boil, stirring. Cook for 10 minutes, or until the tomatoes have reduced. Pass the sauce through a strainer or blend in a food processor for 30 seconds. Turn the terrine out of the pan and cut into slices. Serve immediately with a little of the tomato sauce.

Mushroom & Spinach Puff Pastry

Serves 4

INGREDIENTS

2 tablespoons butter	6 ounces baby spinach	1 egg, beaten
1 red onion, halved and sliced	pinch of nutmeg	salt and pepper
2 garlic cloves, crushed	4 tablespoons heavy cream	2 teaspoons poppy seeds
3 cups button mushrooms, sliced	8 ounces prepared puff pastry	

1 Melt the butter in a skillet. Add the onion and garlic to the pan and sauté for 3–4 minutes, stirring well, until the onion is soft and translucent.

2 Add the mushrooms, spinach, and nutmeg and cook for a further 2–3 minutes.

3 Stir in the heavy cream, mixing well.

4 Season with salt and pepper to taste and remove the skillet from the heat.

5 Roll out the pastry on a lightly floured counter and cut into four neat 6-inch rounds.

6 Spoon a quarter of the filling onto one half of each round and fold the pastry over to encase the filling. Press down to seal the edges of the pastry and brush with the beaten egg. Sprinkle with the poppy seeds.

7 Place the packets on a dampened cookie sheet and cook in a preheated oven at 400°F for 20 minutes, until cooked through and the pastry has risen and is golden brown.

8 Transfer the mushroom and spinach puff pastry packets to warm serving plates and serve at once.

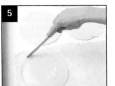

Garbanzo Bean Roast with Sherry Sauce

Serves 4

INGREDIENTS

1 pound can garbanzo beans, drained	2 garlic cloves, crushed	SAUCE:
1 teaspoon yeast extract	2 tablespoons dry sherry	1 tablespoon vegetable oil
1¼ cups chopped walnuts	2 tablespoons vegetable stock	1 leek, thinly sliced
1¼ cups fresh white bread crumbs	1 tablespoon chopped cilantro	4 tablespoons dry sherry
1 onion, finely chopped	8 ounces prepared puff pastry	²/₃ cup vegetable stock
1¼ cups sliced mushrooms	1 egg, beaten	
1¾ ounces canned corn, drained	2 tablespoons milk	
	salt and pepper	

1 Process the garbanzo beans, yeast extract, nuts, and bread crumbs in a food processor for 30 seconds. In a skillet sauté the onion and mushrooms in their own juices for 3–4 minutes. Stir in the garbanzo bean mixture, corn, and garlic. Add the sherry, stock, cilantro, and seasoning and bind the mixture together. Remove the skillet from the heat and set aside to cool completely.

2 Roll out the pastry on a lightly floured counter to form a rectangle 14 inches x 12 inches. Shape the garbanzo bean mixture into a loaf shape and wrap the pastry around it, sealing the edges. Place seam side down on a dampened cookie sheet and score the top in a criss-cross pattern. Mix the egg and milk and brush over the pastry. Cook in a preheated oven at 400°F for 25–30 minutes. Heat the oil for the sauce in a pan and sauté the leek for 5 minutes. Add the sherry and stock and bring to a boil. Simmer for 5 minutes and serve with the roast.

Kidney Bean Kiev

Serves 4

INGREDIENTS

GARLIC BUTTER:
8 tablespoons butter
3 garlic cloves, crushed
1 tablespoon chopped parsley

BEAN PATTIES:
1 pound 7 ounces canned red
   kidney beans
1¼ cups fresh white bread crumbs
2 tablespoons butter

1 leek, chopped
1 celery stalk, chopped
1 tablespoon chopped parsley
1 egg, beaten
salt and pepper
vegetable oil, for shallow frying

1 To make the garlic butter, put the butter, garlic, and parsley in a bowl and blend together with a wooden spoon. Place the garlic butter mixture on a sheet of waxed paper, roll into a cigar shape, and wrap in the baking parchment. Chill in the refrigerator until required.

2 Using a potato masher, mash the red kidney beans in a mixing bowl and stir in ¾ cup of the bread crumbs until the mixture is thoroughly blended.

3 Melt the butter in a skillet and sauté the leek and celery for 3–4 minutes, stirring.

4 Add the bean mixture to the skillet, together with the parsley, season with salt and pepper to taste and mix well. Remove from the heat and let cool slightly.

5 Shape the bean mixture into 4 equal-size ovals.

6 Slice the garlic butter into 4 and place a slice in the center of each bean patty. Mold the bean mixture around the garlic butter to encase it completely.

7 Dip each bean patty first into the beaten egg to coat and then roll them in the remaining bread crumbs.

8 Heat a little oil in a skillet and fry the patties, turning once, for 7–10 minutes, or until golden. Serve at once.

Cashew Nut Paella

Serves 4

INGREDIENTS

2 tablespoons olive oil

1 tablespoon butter

1 red onion, chopped

1 cup risotto rice

1 teaspoon ground turmeric

1 teaspoon ground cumin

$1/2$ teaspoon chili powder

3 garlic cloves, crushed

1 green chili, sliced

1 green bell pepper, diced

1 red bell pepper, diced

$2^3/4$ ounces baby corn,
    halved lengthwise

2 tablespoons pitted black olives

1 large tomato, seeded and diced

2 cups vegetable stock

$3/4$ cup unsalted cashews

$1/4$ cup frozen peas

2 tablespoons chopped parsley

pinch of cayenne pepper

salt and pepper

fresh herbs, to garnish

1 Heat together the olive oil and butter in a large, heavy-based skillet or paella pan until the butter has melted.

2 Add the chopped onion to the skillet and sauté for 2–3 minutes, stirring, until the onion has softened.

3 Stir in the rice, turmeric, cumin, chili powder, garlic, chili, bell peppers, corn cobs, olives, and tomato and cook over medium heat for 1–2 minutes, stirring occasionally.

4 Pour in the stock and bring the mixture to a boil. Reduce the heat and cook for 20 minutes, stirring constantly.

5 Add the cashew nuts and peas to the mixture in the skillet and cook for a further 5 minutes, stirring occasionally. Season to taste with salt and pepper and sprinkle with parsley and cayenne pepper. Transfer to warm serving plates, garnish, and serve at once.

COOK'S TIP

For authenticity and flavor, use a few saffron strands soaked in a little boiling water instead of the turmeric. Saffron has a lovely, nutty flavor.

Vegetable & Bean Curd Strudels

Serves 4

INGREDIENTS

FILLING:

2 tablespoons vegetable oil

2 tablespoons butter or vegetarian
   margarine

$1/3$ cup finely diced potatoes

1 leek, shredded

2 garlic cloves, crushed

1 teaspoon garam masala

$1/2$ teaspoon chili powder

$1/2$ teaspoon turmeric

$1^3/4$ ounces okra, sliced

$1^1/4$ cups sliced button mushrooms,

2 tomatoes, diced

8 ounces firm bean curd, diced

12 sheets phyllo pastry

2 tablespoons butter or vegetarian
   margarine, melted

salt and pepper

1 To make the filling, heat the oil and butter in a skillet. Add the potatoes and leek and cook for 2–3 minutes, stirring.

2 Add the garlic and spices, okra, mushrooms, tomatoes, bean curd, and seasoning and cook, stirring, for 5–7 minutes, or until tender.

3 Lay the pastry out on a chopping board and brush each individual sheet with butter. Place 3 sheets on top of one another. Repeat to make 4 stacks.

4 Spoon a quarter of the filling along the center of each stack and brush the edges with butter. Fold the short edges in and roll up lengthwise to form a cigar shape; and brush the outside with butter. Place the strudels on a greased cookie sheet.

5 Cook in a preheated oven at 375°F and cook the strudels for 20 minutes or until golden brown. Serve at once.

COOK'S TIP

Decorate the outside of the strudels with crumpled pastry trimmings before cooking for a really impressive effect.

Vegetable Lasagne

Serves 4

INGREDIENTS

1 eggplant, sliced	1 zucchini, diced	CHEESE SAUCE:
3 tablespoons olive oil	$1/2$ teaspoon chili powder	2 tablespoons butter or
2 garlic cloves, crushed	$1/2$ teaspoon ground cumin	vegetarian margarine
1 red onion, halved and sliced	2 tomatoes, chopped	1 tablespoon flour
1 green bell pepper, diced	$1^1/4$ cups sieved tomatoes	$2/3$ cup vegetable stock
1 red bell pepper, diced	2 tablespoons chopped basil	$1^1/4$ cups milk
1 yellow bell pepper, diced	8 lasagne noodles	$3/4$ cup grated vegetarian
3 cups sliced mixed mushrooms,	salt and pepper	Cheddar cheese
2 celery stalks, sliced		1 teaspoon Dijon mustard
		1 tablespoon chopped basil
		1 egg, beaten

1 Place the eggplant slices in a colander, sprinkle with salt, and set aside for 20 minutes. Rinse under cold water, drain, and reserve. Heat the oil in a pan and sauté the garlic and onion for 1–2 minutes. Add the bell peppers, mushrooms, celery, and zucchini and cook for about 3–4 minutes, stirring. Stir in the spices and cook for 1 minute. Mix the tomatoes,

sieved tomatoes, and basil together and season well.

2 For the sauce, melt the butter in a pan, add the flour, and cook, stirring constantly, for 1 minute. Remove from the heat and stir in the stock and milk. Return to the heat and add half of the cheese and the mustard. Boil, stirring, until thickened. Stir in the basil

and season to taste with salt and pepper. Remove from the heat and stir in the egg. Place half of the lasagne noodles in an ovenproof dish. Top with half of the vegetables, then half of the tomato sauce. Cover with half the eggplants. Repeat and spoon the cheese sauce on top. Sprinkle with cheese and cook in a preheated oven at 350°F for 40 minutes.

Lentil & Rice Casserole

Serves 4

INGREDIENTS

1¼ cups red split lentils	14 ounce can chopped tomatoes	8 baby corn, halved lengthwise
⅓ cup long-grain white rice	1 teaspoon ground cumin	1¾ ounces green beans, halved
5 cups vegetable stock	1 teaspoon chili powder	1 tablespoon fresh basil, shredded
⅔ cup dry white wine	1 teaspoon garam masala	salt and pepper
1 leek, cut into chunks	1 red bell pepper, sliced	fresh basil sprigs, to garnish
3 garlic cloves, crushed	3½ ounces small broccoli florets	

1 Place the lentils, rice, vegetable stock, and white wine in a flameproof casserole, bring to a boil, and simmer over gentle heat for about 20 minutes, stirring occasionally.

2 Add the leek, garlic, tomatoes, cumin, chili powder, garam masala, bell pepper, broccoli, baby corn, and green beans.

3 Bring the mixture to a boil, reduce the heat, cover the casserole, and simmer for a further 10–15 minutes, or until the vegetables are tender.

4 Add the shredded basil and season with salt and pepper to taste.

5 Garnish with fresh basil sprigs and serve at once.

VARIATION

You can vary the rice in this recipe—use brown or wild rice, if desired.

Vegetable Hot Pot

Serves 4

INGREDIENTS

2 large potatoes, thinly sliced	3$\frac{1}{2}$ ounces broccoli florets	1 eating apple, sliced
2 tablespoons vegetable oil	3$\frac{1}{2}$ ounces cauliflower florets	2 tablespoons chopped sage
1 red onion, halved and sliced	2 small turnips, quartered	pinch of cayenne pepper
1 leek, sliced	1 tablespoon all-purpose flour	$\frac{1}{2}$ cup grated vegetarian
2 garlic cloves, crushed	3$\frac{1}{2}$ cups vegetable stock	Cheddar cheese
1 carrot, cut into chunks	$\frac{2}{3}$ cup hard cider	salt and pepper

1 Cook the potato slices in a saucepan of boiling water for 10 minutes. Drain thoroughly and reserve.

2 Heat the oil in a flameproof casserole dish and sauté the onion, leek, and garlic for 2–3 minutes. Add the remaining vegetables and cook for a further 3–4 minutes, stirring.

3 Stir in the flour and cook for 1 minute. Gradually add the stock and cider and bring the mixture to a boil. Add the apple, sage, and cayenne pepper and season well. Remove the dish from the heat. Transfer the vegetables to an ovenproof dish.

4 Arrange the potato slices on top of the vegetable mixture to cover.

5 Sprinkle the cheese on top of the potato slices and cook in a preheated oven at 375°F for 30–35 minutes or until the potato is golden brown and beginning to crispen slightly around the edges. Serve at once.

COOK'S TIP

If the potato begins to brown too quickly, cover with foil for the last 10 minutes of cooking time to prevent the top from burning.

Vegetable Chop Suey

Serves 4

INGREDIENTS

2 tablespoons peanut oil	2³/₄ ounces broccoli florets	2 teaspoons light brown sugar
1 onion, chopped	1 zucchini, sliced	2 tablespoons light soy sauce
3 garlic cloves, chopped	1 ounce green beans	¹/₂ cup vegetable stock
1 green bell pepper, diced	1 carrot, cut into matchsticks	salt and pepper
1 red bell pepper, diced	3¹/₂ ounces bean sprouts	noodles, to serve

1 Heat the oil in a preheated wok until almost smoking. Add the onion and garlic and stir-fry for 30 seconds.

2 Stir in the bell peppers, broccoli, zucchini, beans, and carrot and stir-fry for a further 2–3 minutes.

3 Add the bean sprouts, light brown sugar, soy sauce, and vegetable stock. Season with salt and pepper to taste and cook for about 2 minutes.

4 Transfer the vegetables to serving plates and serve at once with noodles.

COOK'S TIP

The clever design of a wok, with its spherical base and high sloping sides, enables the food to be tossed so that it is cooked quickly and evenly. It is essential to heat the wok sufficiently before you add the ingredients to ensure quick and even cooking.

COOK'S TIP

Ensure that the vegetable pieces are all the same size in order that they all cook in the stated time.

VARIATION

Add 1 tablespoon chili oil for a hotter flavor and add cashew nuts for extra crunch.

Vegetable Toad-in-the-Hole

Serves 4

INGREDIENTS

BATTER:
³/₄ cup all-purpose flour
2 eggs, beaten
³/₄ cup milk
2 tablespoons whole-grain mustard
2 tablespoons vegetable oil

FILLING:
2 tablespoons butter
2 garlic cloves, crushed
1 onion, cut into eight
2³/₄ ounces baby carrots, halved
    lengthwise
1³/₄ ounces green beans

1³/₄ ounces canned corn, drained
2 tomatoes, seeded and cut
    into chunks
1 teaspoon whole-grain mustard
1 tablespoon chopped mixed herbs
salt and pepper

1 To make the batter, sift the flour and a pinch of salt into a large bowl. Make a well in the center and beat in the eggs and milk to make a batter. Stir in the mustard and let stand.

2 Pour the oil into a shallow ovenproof dish and heat in a preheated oven at 400°F for 10 minutes.

3 To make the filling, melt the butter in a skillet and sauté the garlic and onion for 2 minutes, stirring. Cook the carrots and beans in a saucepan of boiling water for 7 minutes, or until tender. Drain well.

4 Add the corn and tomato to the skillet, together with the mustard and herbs. Season well with salt and pepper and add the carrots and beans.

5 Remove the dish from the oven and pour in the batter. Spoon the vegetables into the center, return to the oven and cook for 30–35 minutes, until the batter has risen and set. Serve the vegetable toad-in-the-hole at once.

COOK'S TIP

It is important that the oil is hot before adding the batter, so that the batter begins to cook and rise at once.

Vegetable Jalousie

Serves 4

INGREDIENTS

1 pound prepared puff pastry	1 leek, shredded	2 tablespoons all-purpose flour
1 egg, beaten	2 garlic cloves, crushed	6 tablespoons vegetable stock
	1 red bell pepper, sliced	6 tablespoons milk
FILLING:	1 yellow bell pepper, sliced	4 tablespoons dry white wine
2 tablespoons butter or	³/₄ cups sliced mushrooms	1 tablespoon chopped oregano
vegetarian margarine	2³/₄ ounces small asparagus spears	salt and pepper

1 Melt the butter or margarine in a skillet and sauté the leek and garlic for 2 minutes, stirring. Add the remaining vegetables and stir for 3–4 minutes.

2 Add the flour and cook, stirring, for 1 minute. Remove from the heat and stir in the vegetable stock, milk, and white wine. Return to the heat and bring to a boil, stirring, until thickened. Stir in the oregano and season with salt and pepper to taste.

3 Roll half of the pastry out on a lightly floured counter to form a rectangle 15 inches x 6 inches.

4 Roll out the other half of the pastry to the same shape, but a little larger. Put the smaller rectangle on a cookie sheet lined with dampened baking parchment.

5 Spoon the filling evenly over the top of the smaller pastry rectangle, leaving a ½-inch clean edge.

6 Cut parallel slits across the larger rectangle at a slight angle to within 1 inch of each edge.

7 Brush the edge of the smaller rectangle with egg and place the larger rectangle on top, sealing the edges well.

8 Brush the whole jalousie with egg to glaze and cook in a preheated oven at 400°F for 30–35 minutes, until risen and golden. Serve at once.

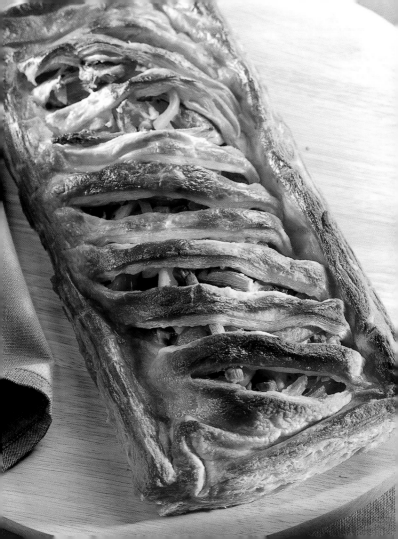

Cauliflower, Broccoli, & Cheese Flan

Serves 8

INGREDIENTS

PASTRY:

1¼ cups all-purpose flour

pinch of salt

½ teaspoon paprika

1 teaspoon dried thyme

6 tablespoons vegetarian margarine

3 tablespoons water

FILLING:

3½ ounces cauliflower florets

3½ ounces broccoli florets

1 onion, cut into eight

2 tablespoons butter or vegetarian margarine

1 tablespoon all-purpose flour

6 tablespoons vegetable stock

8 tablespoons milk

¾ cup grated vegetarian Cheddar cheese

salt and pepper

paprika and thyme, to garnish

1 To make the pastry, sift the flour and salt into a bowl. Add the paprika and thyme and rub in the margarine. Stir in the water and bind to form a dough.

2 Roll out the pastry on a floured counter and use to line a 7-inch loose-based flan pan. Prick the base with a fork and line with baking parchment. Fill with ceramic baking beans and bake in a preheated oven at 375°F for 15 minutes. Remove the parchment and beans and return the pastry case to the oven for a further 5 minutes.

3 To make the filling, cook the vegetables in a pan of boiling water for 10–12 minutes, until tender. Drain and reserve.

4 Melt the butter in a pan. Add the flour and cook, stirring, for 1 minute. Remove from the heat, stir in the stock and milk, and return to the heat. Bring to a boil, stirring, and add ½ cup of the grated cheese. Season to taste with salt and pepper.

5 Spoon the cauliflower, broccoli, and onion into the pastry case. Pour in the sauce and sprinkle with the cheese. Return to the oven for 10 minutes, until the cheese is bubbling. Dust with paprika, garnish and serve.

Roast Bell Pepper Tart

Serves 8

INGREDIENTS

PASTRY:

1¼ cups all-purpose flour

pinch of salt

6 tablespoons butter or
    vegetarian margarine

2 tablespoons green pitted olives,
    finely chopped

3 tablespoons cold water

FILLING:

1 red bell pepper

1 green bell pepper

1 yellow bell pepper

2 garlic cloves, crushed

2 tablespoons olive oil

1 cup grated mozzarella cheese

2 eggs

⅔ cup milk

1 tablespoon chopped basil

salt and pepper

1 To make the pastry, sift the flour and a pinch of salt into a bowl. Rub in the butter or margarine until the mixture resembles bread crumbs. Add the olives and cold water, bringing the mixture together to form a soft dough.

2 Roll out the dough on a floured counter and use to line an 8-inch-based flan pan. Prick the base with a fork and chill in the refrigerator.

3 Cut the bell peppers in half lengthwise and arrange in a single layer skin side uppermost on a cookie sheet. Mix the garlic and oil and brush over the bell peppers. Cook in a preheated oven at 400°F for 20 minutes, or until they are beginning to blister and char slightly. Let the bell peppers cool slightly and thinly slice. Arrange in the base of the pastry case, layering with the grated mozzarella cheese.

4 Beat the egg and milk and add the basil. Season and pour over the bell peppers. Put the tart on a cookie sheet and return to the oven for 20 minutes, or until set. Serve hot or cold.

Vegetable Biryani

Serves 4

INGREDIENTS

1 large potato, cubed	1 eggplant, halved and sliced	1 tablespoon curry powder
3¹/₂ ounces baby carrots	1¹/₄ cups plain yogurt	2 tablespoons butter
1³/₄ ounces okra, thickly sliced	1 tablespoon grated root ginger	2 onions, sliced
2 celery stalks, sliced	2 large onions, grated	1¹/₄ cups basmati rice
2³/₄ ounces baby button	4 garlic cloves, crushed	chopped cilantro, to garnish
mushrooms, halved	1 teaspoon turmeric	

1 Cook the potato cubes, carrots, and okra in a pan of boiling salted water for 7–8 minutes. Drain well and place in a large bowl. Mix with the celery, mushrooms, and eggplant.

2 Mix together the plain yogurt, ginger, grated onions, garlic, turmeric, and curry powder and spoon over the vegetables, tossing to coat thoroughly. Set aside to marinate for at least 2 hours.

3 Heat the butter in a skillet and cook the sliced onions for 5–6 minutes, until golden brown. Remove a few onions from the skillet and reserve for garnishing.

4 Cook the rice in a pan of boiling water for 7 minutes. Drain well.

5 Add the marinated vegetables to the onions in the skillet and cook, stirring occasionally, for 10 minutes.

6 Put half of the rice in a 9-cup casserole dish. Spoon the vegetables on top and cover with the remaining rice. Cover and cook in a preheated oven at 375°F for 20–25 minutes, or until the rice is tender.

7 Spoon the vegetable biryani onto a warm serving plate, garnish with the reserved fried onions and chopped cilantro, and serve at once.

Baked Cheese & Tomato Macaroni

Serves 4

INGREDIENTS

2 cups elbow macaroni

1½ cups grated vegetarian cheese

1 cup grated Parmesan cheese

4 tablespoons fresh white
    bread crumbs

1 tablespoon chopped basil

1 tablespoon butter or margarine

TOMATO SAUCE:

1 tablespoon olive oil

1 shallot, finely chopped

2 garlic cloves, crushed

1 pound canned chopped tomatoes

1 tablespoon chopped basil

salt and pepper

1 To make the tomato sauce, heat the oil in a saucepan and sauté the shallots and garlic for 1 minute. Add the tomatoes and basil, and salt and pepper to taste, and cook over a medium heat, stirring, for 10 minutes.

2 Meanwhile, cook the macaroni in a pan of boiling salted water for 8 minutes, or until almost tender. Drain.

3 Mix both of the cheeses together.

4 Grease a deep, oven-proof dish. Spoon a third of the tomato sauce into the base of the dish, top with a third of the macaroni, and then a third of the cheeses. Season with salt and pepper. Repeat the layers twice.

5 Combine the bread crumbs and basil and sprinkle over the top. Dot with the butter or margarine

and cook in a preheated oven at 375°F for 25 minutes, or until the dish is golden brown and bubbling. Serve at once.

COOK'S TIP

Use other pasta shapes, such as penne, if you have them at hand, instead of the macaroni.

Garbanzo Bean & Vegetable Casserole

Serves 4

INGREDIENTS

1 tablespoon olive oil
1 red onion, halved and sliced
3 garlic cloves, crushed
8 ounces spinach
1 fennel bulb, cut into eight
1 red bell pepper, diced

1 tablespoon all-purpose flour
3³/₄ cups vegetable stock
6 tablespoons dry white wine
14 ounce can garbanzo
    beans, drained
1 bay leaf

1 teaspoon ground coriander
¹/₂ teaspoons paprika
salt and pepper
fennel fronds, to garnish

1 Heat the olive oil in a large flameproof casserole and sauté the onion and garlic for 1 minute, stirring. Add the spinach and cook for 4 minutes, or until wilted.

2 Add the fennel and bell pepper and cook for 2 minutes, stirring.

3 Stir in the flour and cook, stirring, for 1 minute.

4 Add the stock, wine, garbanzo beans, bay leaf, coriander, and paprika, cover, and cook for 30 minutes. Season to taste, garnish with fennel fronds and serve at once.

VARIATION

Replace the coriander with nutmeg, if desired, as it works particularly well with spinach.

COOK'S TIP

Use other canned varieties or mixed beans instead of the garbanzo beans, if desired.

Sweet & Sour Vegetables & Bean Curd

Serves 4

INGREDIENTS

1 tablespoon peanut oil
2 garlic cloves, crushed
1 teaspoon grated ginger root
1¾ ounces baby corn
1¾ ounces snow peas
1 carrot, cut into matchsticks

1 green bell pepper, cut into matchsticks
8 scallions, trimmed
1¾ ounces canned bamboo shoots
8 ounces marinated firm bean curd, cubed

2 tablespoons dry sherry
2 tablespoons rice vinegar
2 tablespoons honey
1 tablespoon light soy sauce
⅔ cup vegetable stock
1 tablespoon cornstarch

1 Heat the oil in a preheated wok until almost smoking.

2 Add the garlic and grated ginger root and cook for 30 seconds, stirring frequently.

3 Add the baby corn, snow peas, carrot, and bell pepper and stir-fry for about 5 minutes or until the vegetables are tender.

4 Add the scallions, bamboo shoots, and bean curd and cook for a further 2 minutes.

5 Stir in the sherry, rice vinegar, honey, soy sauce, vegetable stock, and cornstarch and bring to a boil. Reduce the heat and simmer for 2 minutes. Transfer to serving dishes and serve at once.

VARIATION

You can replace any of the vegetables in this dish with others of your choice. For a colorful, attractive stir-fry, select vegetables with bright, contrasting colors.

Spicy Potato & Lemon Casserole

Serves 4

INGREDIENTS

1/2 cup olive oil	pinch of cayenne pepper	juice and rind of 2 large lemons
2 red onions, cut into eight	1 carrot, thickly sliced	1 1/4 cups vegetable stock
3 garlic cloves, crushed	2 small turnips, quartered	2 tablespoons chopped cilantro
2 teaspoons ground cumin	1 zucchini, sliced	salt and pepper
2 teaspoons ground coriander	1 pound potatoes, thickly sliced	

1 Heat the olive oil in a flameproof casserole.

2 Add the red onion and sauté for 3 minutes, stirring well.

3 Add the garlic and cook for 30 seconds. Mix in the spices and cook for 1 minute, stirring.

4 Add the carrot, turnips, zucchini, and potatoes and stir to coat in the oil.

5 Add the lemon juice, rind, stock, and salt and pepper to taste, cover, and cook over medium heat for 20–30 minutes, stirring occasionally.

6 Remove the lid, sprinkle in the cilantro, and stir well. Serve at once.

COOK'S TIP

Check the vegetables while cooking as they may begin to stick to the pan. Add a little more boiling water or stock if necessary.

COOK'S TIP

A selection of spices and herbs is important for adding variety to your cooking—add to your range each time you try a new recipe.

Vegetable Cannelloni

Serves 4

INGREDIENTS

1 eggplant	12 cannelloni tubes	2 garlic cloves, crushed
$^1/_2$ cup olive oil	salt and pepper	2 x 14 ounce cans chopped
8 ounces spinach		tomatoes
2 garlic cloves, crushed	TOMATO SAUCE:	1 teaspoon superfine sugar
1 teaspoon ground cumin	1 tablespoon olive oil	2 tablespoons chopped basil
1 cup chopped mushrooms	1 onion, chopped	$^1/_2$ cup sliced mozzarella

1 With a sharp knife, cut the eggplant into small dice.

2 Heat the oil in a skillet and cook the eggplant for 2–3 minutes.

3 Add the spinach, garlic, cumin, and mushrooms. Season and cook for 2–3 minutes, stirring. Spoon the mixture into the cannelloni tubes and arrange them in an ovenproof dish in a single layer.

4 To make the sauce, heat the olive oil in a saucepan and sauté the onion and garlic for 1 minute. Add the tomatoes, superfine sugar, and chopped basil and bring to a boil. Reduce the heat and simmer for about 5 minutes. Pour the sauce over the cannelloni tubes.

5 Arrange the sliced mozzarella on top of the sauce and cook in a preheated oven at 375°F for 30 minutes, or until the

cheese is bubbling and golden brown. Serve at once straight from the dish.

COOK'S TIP

You can prepare the tomato sauce in advance and store it in the refrigerator for up to 24 hours.

Cauliflower Bake

Serves 4

INGREDIENTS

1 pound cauliflower, broken
  into florets
2 large potatoes, cubed
3 1/2 ounces cherry tomatoes

SAUCE:
2 tablespoons butter or
  vegetarian margarine
1 leek, sliced
1 garlic clove, crushed
3 tablespoons all-purpose flour
1 1/4 cups milk

3/4 cup mixed grated cheese,
  such as vegetarian cheddar,
  parmesan, and swiss cheese
1/2 teaspoon paprika
2 tablespoons chopped flat
  leaf parsley
salt and pepper
chopped fresh parsley, to garnish

1 Cook the cauliflower in a saucepan of boiling water for 10 minutes. Drain well and reserve. Meanwhile, cook the potatoes in a pan of boiling water for 10 minutes, drain, and reserve.

2 To make the sauce, melt the butter or margarine in a saucepan and sauté the leek and garlic for 1 minute. Add the flour and cook, stirring constantly, for 1 minute. Remove the pan from the heat and gradually stir in the milk, 1/2 cup of the grated cheese, the paprika, and parsley. Return the pan to the heat and bring to a boil, stirring constantly. Season with salt and pepper to taste.

3 Spoon the cauliflower into a deep ovenproof dish. Add the cherry tomatoes and top with the potatoes. Pour the sauce over the potatoes and sprinkle on the remaining cheese.

4 Cook in a preheated oven at 350°F for 20 minutes, or until the vegetables are cooked through and the cheese is golden brown and bubbling. Garnish with parsley and serve at once.

VARIATION

This dish could also be made with broccoli instead of cauliflower.

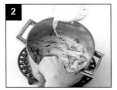

Leek & Herb Soufflé

Serves 4

INGREDIENTS

12 ounces baby leeks	½ cup walnuts	2 tablespoons plain yogurt
1 tablespoon olive oil	2 eggs, separated	salt and pepper
½ cup vegetable stock	2 tablespoons chopped mixed herbs	

1 Using a sharp knife, chop the leeks finely.

2 Heat the oil in a skillet and sauté the leeks, stirring, for 2–3 minutes.

3 Add the stock to the skillet and cook over gentle heat for a further 5 minutes.

4 Place the walnuts in a food processor and process until finely chopped.

5 Add the leek mixture to the nuts and process to form a purée. Transfer to a mixing bowl.

6 Combine the egg yolks, herbs, and yogurt and pour into the leek purée. Season with salt and pepper to taste and mix thoroughly.

7 In a separate mixing bowl, whisk the egg whites until firm peaks form.

8 Fold the egg whites into the leek mixture. Spoon the mixture into a lightly greased 3¾-cup soufflé dish and place on a warmed cookie sheet.

9 Cook in a preheated oven at 350°F for 35–40 minutes, or until just set and the top is golden brown. Serve the soufflé at once.

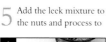

Artichoke & Cheese Tart

Serves 8

INGREDIENTS

1¼ cups whole wheat flour	FILLING:	½ cup crumbled gorgonzola cheese
2 garlic cloves, crushed	2 tablespoons olive oil	2 eggs, beaten
6 tablespoons butter or	1 red onion, halved and sliced	1 tablespoon chopped fresh
vegetarian margarine	10 canned or fresh artichoke hearts	rosemary
salt and pepper	1 cup grated vegetarian	⅔ cup milk
	Cheddar cheese	

1 Make the pastry. Sift the flour into a bowl, add a pinch of salt and the garlic. Rub in the butter or margarine until the mixture resembles bread crumbs. Stir in 3 tablespoons of water and mix to form a dough.

2 Roll out the pastry on a lightly floured counter to fit an 8-inch pie pan. Prick the pastry with a fork.

3 Heat the oil in a skillet and sauté the onion, stirring, for 3 minutes.

Add the artichoke hearts and cook for a further 2 minutes.

4 Mix the cheeses with the beaten eggs, rosemary, and milk. Stir in the drained artichoke mixture and season to taste.

5 Spoon the artichoke and cheese mixture into the pastry case and cook in a preheated oven at 400°F for 25 minutes, or until cooked and set. Serve the quiche hot or cold.

COOK'S TIP

Gently press the center of the quiche with your fingertip to test if it is cooked through. It should feel fairly firm, but not solid. If overcooked the quiche will begin to "weep."

Tagliatelle with Zucchini Sauce

Serves 4

INGREDIENTS

1 pound 7 ounces zucchini

6 tablespoons olive oil

3 garlic cloves, crushed

3 tablespoons chopped basil

2 red chilies, sliced

juice of 1 large lemon

5 tablespoons light cream

4 tablespoons freshly grated
Parmesan cheese

8 ounces tagliatelle

salt and pepper

salad greens and grated Parmesan
cheese, to serve (optional)

1 Using a vegetable peeler, slice the zucchini into very thin ribbons.

2 Heat the oil in a skillet and sauté the garlic for about 30 seconds.

3 Add the zucchini and cook over gentle heat, stirring, for 5–7 minutes.

4 Stir in the basil, chilies, lemon juice, light cream, and grated Parmesan

cheese and season with salt and pepper to taste.

5 Meanwhile, cook the tagliatelle in a large pan of lightly salted boiling water for 10 minutes, until "al dente." Drain the pasta thoroughly and transfer to a warm serving bowl.

6 Pile the zucchini mixture on top of the pasta. Serve at once with salad greens and extra Parmesan, if desired.

VARIATION

Lime juice and zest could be used instead of the lemon as an alternative.

Olive, Bell Pepper, & Cherry Tomato Pasta

Serves 4

INGREDIENTS
---

2 cups penne	1 yellow bell pepper, thinly sliced	2 tablespoons quartered, pitted
2 tablespoons olive oil	16 cherry tomatoes, halved	black olives
2 tablespoons butter	1 tablespoon chopped oregano	2³/₄ ounces arugula
2 garlic cloves, crushed	¹/₂ cup dry white wine	salt and pepper
1 green bell pepper, thinly sliced		fresh oregano sprigs, to garnish

1 Cook the pasta in a saucepan of boiling salted water for 8–10 minutes, or until "al dente." Drain thoroughly.

2 Heat the oil and butter in a pan until the butter melts. Sauté the garlic for 30 seconds. Add the bell peppers and cook for 3–4 minutes, stirring.

3 Stir in the cherry tomatoes, oregano, wine, and olives and cook for 3–4 minutes. Season well with salt and pepper and stir in the arugula until just wilted.

4 Transfer the pasta to a serving dish, spoon over the sauce, and mix well. Garnish and serve.

COOK'S TIP

Ensure that the saucepan is large enough to prevent the pasta from sticking together during cooking.

Spinach & Pine Nut Pasta

Serves 4

INGREDIENTS

8 ounces pasta shapes or spaghetti	1 onion, quartered and sliced	2 tablespoons pine nuts
1/2 cup olive oil	3 large flat mushrooms, sliced	6 tablespoons dry white wine
2 garlic cloves, crushed	8 ounces spinach	salt and pepper
		Parmesan shavings, to garnish

1 Cook the pasta in a saucepan of boiling salted water for 8–10 minutes, or until "al dente." Drain well.

2 Meanwhile, heat the oil in a large saucepan and sauté the garlic and onion for 1 minute.

3 Add the sliced mushrooms and cook for 2 minutes, stirring occasionally.

4 Add the spinach and cook for 4–5 minutes, or until the spinach has wilted.

5 Stir in the pine nuts and wine, season well with salt and pepper, and cook for 1 minute.

6 Transfer the pasta to a warm serving bowl and toss the sauce into it, mixing well. Garnish with shavings of Parmesan cheese and serve at once.

COOK'S TIP

Freshly grate a little nutmeg over the dish for extra flavor, as it is particularly good with spinach.

COOK'S TIP

"Al dente" means that the pasta should be tender but still have a bite to it.

Bean Curd & Vegetable Stir-Fry

Serves 4

INGREDIENTS

1¼ cups diced potatoes
1 tablespoon olive oil
1 red onion, sliced
8 ounces firm bean curd, diced

2 zucchini, diced
8 canned artichoke hearts, halved
²/₃ cup sieved tomatoes

1 teaspoon sugar
2 tablespoons chopped basil
salt and pepper

1 Cook the potatoes in a saucepan of boiling water for 10 minutes. Drain thoroughly and set aside until required.

2 Heat the oil in a large skillet and sauté the red onion for 2 minutes, until the onion has softened, stirring.

3 Stir in the bean curd and zucchini and cook for 3–4 minutes, until they begin to brown slightly. Add the potatoes, stirring to mix.

4 Stir in the artichoke hearts, sieved tomatoes, sugar, and basil, season with salt and pepper, and cook for a further 5 minutes, stirring well. Transfer the stir-fry to serving dishes and serve at once.

COOK'S TIP

Canned artichoke hearts should be drained thoroughly and rinsed before use because they often have salt added.

VARIATION

Eggplants could be used instead of the zucchini, if desired.

Cantonese Garden Vegetable Stir-Fry

Serves 4

INGREDIENTS

2 tablespoons peanut oil
1 teaspoon Chinese five-
   spice powder
2³/₄ ounces baby carrots, halved
2 celery stalks, sliced
2 baby leeks, sliced

1³/₄ ounces snow peas
4 baby zucchini, halved
   lengthwise
8 baby corn
8 ounces firm marinated
   bean curd, diced

4 tablespoons fresh orange juice
1 tablespoon honey
celery leaves and orange zest,
   to garnish
cooked rice or noodles, to serve

1 Heat the oil in a preheated wok until almost smoking. Add the Chinese five-spice powder, carrots, celery, leeks, snow peas, zucchini, and corn and stir-fry for 3–4 minutes over medium heat.

2 Add the bean curd and cook for a further 2 minutes, stirring constantly.

3 Stir in the orange juice and honey, reduce the heat, and cook for 1–2 minutes.

4 Transfer the stir-fry to a serving dish, garnish with celery leaves and orange zest, and serve with rice or noodles.

COOK'S TIP

Chinese five-spice powder is a mixture of fennel, star anise, cinnamon bark, cloves, and Szechuan pepper. It is very pungent, so should be used sparingly. If kept in an airtight container, it will keep indefinitely.

Risotto Verde

Serves 4

INGREDIENTS

7¹/₂ cups vegetable stock	1¹/₄ cups risotto (arborio) rice	3 tablespoons plain yogurt
2 tablespoons olive oil	1¹/₄ cups dry white wine	salt and pepper
2 garlic cloves, crushed	4 tablespoons chopped mixed herbs	shredded leek, to garnish
2 leeks, shredded	8 ounces baby spinach	

1 Pour the stock into a large saucepan and bring to a boil. Reduce the heat to a simmer.

2 Meanwhile, heat the oil in a separate pan and sauté the garlic and leeks for 2–3 minutes, until softened.

3 Stir in the rice and cook for 2 minutes, stirring, until well coated.

4 Pour in half of the wine and a little of the hot stock. Cook over a gentle heat until all of the liquid has been absorbed. Add the remaining stock and wine and cook over low heat for 25 minutes, or until the rice is creamy.

5 Stir in the chopped mixed herbs and baby spinach, season well with salt and pepper, and cook for 2 minutes.

6 Stir in the plain yogurt, transfer to a warm serving dish, garnish with the shredded leek and serve at once.

COOK'S TIP

Do not hurry the process of cooking the risotto, as the rice must absorb the liquid slowly in order for it to reach the correct consistency.

Baked Pasta in Tomato Sauce

Serves 8

INGREDIENTS

1 cup pasta shapes,
    such as penne or casareccia
1 tablespoon olive oil
1 leek, chopped
3 garlic cloves, crushed
1 green bell pepper, chopped
14 ounce can chopped tomatoes

2 tablespoons chopped, pitted
    black olives
2 eggs, beaten
1 tablespoon chopped basil

TOMATO SAUCE:
1 tablespoon olive oil

1 onion, chopped
8 ounce can chopped tomatoes
1 teaspoon sugar
2 tablespoons tomato paste
$^2/_3$ cup vegetable stock
salt and pepper

1 Cook the pasta in a saucepan of boiling salted water for 8 minutes. Drain thoroughly.

2 Meanwhile, heat the oil in a saucepan and sauté the leek and garlic for 2 minutes, stirring. Add the bell pepper, tomatoes, and olives and cook for a further 5 minutes.

3 Remove the pan from the heat and stir in the pasta, beaten eggs, and basil. Season well, and spoon into a lightly greased 4-cup ovenproof bowl.

4 Place the bowl in a roasting pan and half fill the pan with boiling water. Cover and cook in a preheated oven at 350°F for 40 minutes, until set.

5 To make the sauce, heat the oil in a pan and sauté the onion for 2 minutes. Add the remaining ingredients and cook for 10 minutes. Put the sauce in a food processor or blender and process until smooth. Return to a clean saucepan and heat until hot.

6 Turn the pasta out of the bowl onto a warm serving plate. Slice and serve at once with the tomato sauce.

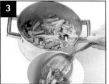

Spaghetti with Pear & Walnut Sauce

Serves 4

INGREDIENTS

8 ounces spaghetti	1 tablespoon olive oil	1 tablespoon lemon juice
2 small ripe pears, peeled and sliced	1 red onion, quartered and sliced	$^3/_4$ cup blue cheese
$^2/_3$ cup vegetable stock	1 garlic clove, crushed	salt and pepper
6 tablespoons dry white wine	$^1/_2$ cup walnut halves	fresh oregano sprigs, to garnish
2 tablespoons butter	2 tablespoons chopped oregano	

1 Cook the pasta in a saucepan of boiling salted water for 8–10 minutes, or until "al dente." Drain thoroughly and keep warm until required.

2 Meanwhile, place the pears in a pan and pour over the stock and wine. Poach the pears over gentle heat for 10 minutes. Drain and reserve the cooking liquid and pears.

3 Heat the butter and oil in a saucepan until the butter melts, then sauté the onion and garlic for 2–3 minutes, stirring.

4 Add the walnuts, oregano, and lemon juice, stirring.

5 Stir in the reserved pears with 4 tablespoons of the poaching liquid.

6 Crumble the dolcelatte cheese into the pan and cook over gentle heat, stirring occasionally, for 1–2 minutes, or until the cheese just begins to melt. Season the sauce with salt and pepper to taste.

7 Toss the pasta into the sauce, garnish and serve.

COOK'S TIP

You can use any good-flavored blue cheese for this dish. Varieties to try are Roquefort, which has a very strong flavor, gorgonzola, or Stilton.

Pies & Bakes

The following chapter includes a range of hearty
savory pies and bakes which are ideal for cold fall
and winter evenings. However, a few less robust
meals are also included which are more suitable
for a light spring or summer meal. Many of the
recipes are adaptable, and you may like to substitute
your favorite vegetables for the ones suggested
in the recipe, or vary them according to
seasonal availability.

There are both sweet and savory recipes in this
chapter, as the potato lends itself to sweeter dishes,
mixed with fruit and spices. Also included are a few
bread recipes, as the potato makes excellent bread;
an assortment of fabulous pies using different
pastries; and pastry bites. This chapter contains
something for every occasion, illustrating how well
potatoes and vegetables lend themselves to a
wide variety of dishes.

Potato, Beef, & Leek Turnovers

Makes 4

INGREDIENTS

8 ounces waxy potatoes, diced	1 leek, sliced	salt and pepper
1 small carrot, diced	8 ounces ready-made pie dough	1 egg, beaten
8 ounces beef steak, cubed	1 tbsp butter	

1 Lightly grease a cookie sheet with a little butter.

2 Mix the potatoes, carrots, beef, and leek in a large bowl. Season well with salt and pepper.

3 Divide the pie dough into 4 equal portions. On a lightly floured surface, roll each portion into an 8-inch round.

4 Spoon the potato mixture onto one half of each round, to within ½ inch of the edge. Top the potato mixture with the butter, dividing it equally between the 4 rounds.

Brush the pie dough edge with a little of the beaten egg.

5 Fold the pie dough over to encase the filling and crimp the edges together.

6 Transfer the turnovers to the prepared cookie sheet and brush them with the remaining beaten egg.

7 Cook in a preheated oven at 400°F for 20 minutes. Reduce the oven temperature to 325°F and cook the turnovers for a further 30 minutes until cooked and golden brown

8 Serve the pasties with a crisp salad or onion gravy.

COOK'S TIP

These turnovers can be made in advance and frozen.

VARIATION

Use other types of meat, such as pork or chicken, in the turnovers and add chunks of apple in step 2, if desired.

Potato & Tomato Calzone

Makes 4

INGREDIENTS

DOUGH:

4 cups white bread flour
1 tsp active dry yeast
1¼ cups vegetable stock
1 tbsp clear honey
1 tsp caraway seeds
milk, for glazing

FILLING:

8 ounces waxy potatoes, diced
1 tbsp vegetable oil
1 onion, halved and sliced
2 garlic cloves, crushed
²/₃ cup sun-dried tomatoes
2 tbsp chopped fresh basil

2 tbsp tomato paste
2 celery stalks, sliced
¹/₂ cup grated Mozzarella cheese

1 To make the dough, sift the flour into a large mixing bowl and stir in the yeast. Make a well in the center of the mixture.

2 Stir in the vegetable stock, honey, and caraway seeds and bring the mixture together to form a dough.

3 Turn the dough out onto a lightly floured surface and knead for 8 minutes, until smooth. Place the dough in a lightly oiled mixing bowl, cover, and leave to rise in a warm place for 1 hour, or until it has doubled in size.

4 Meanwhile, make the filling. Heat the oil in a skillet and add all the remaining ingredients, except for the cheese. Cook for about 5 minutes, stirring.

5 Divide the risen dough into 4 pieces. On a lightly floured surface, roll them out to form 7-inch rounds. Spoon equal amounts of the filling onto one half of each circle.

6 Sprinkle the cheese over the filling. Brush the edge of the dough with milk and fold the dough over to form 4 semicircles, pressing to seal the edges.

7 Place on a nonstick cookie sheet and brush with milk. Cook in a preheated oven at 425°F for 30 minutes, until golden.

Potato & Meat Phyllo Parcels

Serves 4

INGREDIENTS
---

8 ounces waxy potatoes, finely diced	1 small yellow bell pepper, finely diced	¹/₃ cup beef stock
1 tbsp vegetable oil	2 cups sliced button mushrooms	1 tbsp chopped fresh rosemary
4¹/₂ ounces ground beef	1 tbsp all-purpose flour	8 ounces phyllo pastry, thawed if frozen
1 leek, sliced	1 tbsp tomato paste	2 tbsp butter, melted
	¹/₃ cup red wine	salt and pepper

1 Cook the diced potatoes in a saucepan of boiling water for 5 minutes. Drain and set aside.

2 Meanwhile, heat the oil in a saucepan and sauté the ground beef, leek, yellow bell pepper, and mushrooms over a low heat for 5 minutes.

3 Stir in the flour and tomato paste and cook for 1 minute. Gradually add the red wine and beef stock, stirring to thicken. Add the rosemary, season to taste with salt and pepper, and leave to cool slightly.

4 Lay 4 sheets of phyllo pastry on a counter or board. Brush each sheet with butter and lay a second layer of phyllo on top. Trim the sheets to make four 8-inch squares.

5 Brush the edges of the pastry with a little butter. Spoon a quarter of the beef mixture into the center of each square. Bring up the corners and the sides of the squares to form a packet, scrunching the edges together. Make sure that the packets are well sealed by pressing the

pastry together, otherwise the filling will leak during baking.

6 Place the packets on a cookie sheet and brush with butter. Bake in a preheated oven at 350°F for 20 minutes. Serve hot.

Carrot-Topped Beef Pie

Serves 4

INGREDIENTS

1 pound ground beef	2 tbsp tomato paste	2 large carrots, diced
1 onion, chopped	1 celery stalk, chopped	2 tbsp butter
1 garlic clove, crushed	3 tbsp chopped fresh parsley	3 tbsp milk
1 tbsp all-purpose flour	1 tbsp Worcestershire sauce	salt and pepper
1 1/4 cups beef stock	1 1/2 pounds mealy potatoes, diced	

1 Dry-fry the beef in a large pan set over a high heat for 3–4 minutes, or until sealed. Add the onion and garlic and cook for a further 5 minutes, stirring.

2 Add the flour and cook for 1 minute. Gradually blend in the beef stock and tomato paste. Stir in the celery, 1 tbsp of the parsley, and the Worcestershire sauce. Season to taste with salt and pepper.

3 Bring the mixture to a boil, then reduce the heat, and simmer for 20–25 minutes. Spoon the beef mixture into a 5-cup pie dish.

4 Meanwhile, cook the potatoes and carrots in a saucepan of boiling water for 10 minutes. Drain and mash them together.

5 Stir the butter, milk, and the remaining parsley into the potato and carrot mixture and season. Spoon the potato on top of the beef mixture to cover it completely; alternatively, pipe the potato with a pastry bag.

6 Cook the pie in a preheated oven at 375°F for 45 minutes, or until cooked through and piping hot. Serve immediately.

VARIATION

You can use ground lamb, turkey, or pork instead of the beef, adding appropriate herbs, such as rosemary and sage, for added flavor.

Potato, Beef, & Kidney Pie

Serves 4

INGREDIENTS

8 ounces waxy potatoes, cubed	12 shallots	1 egg, beaten
2 tbsp butter	¼ cup all-purpose flour	salt and pepper
1 pound lean steak, cubed	⅔ cup beef stock	
5½ ounces ox kidney, cored and chopped	⅔ cup strong, dark beer	
	8 ounces ready-made puff pastry	

1 Cook the cubed potatoes in a saucepan of boiling water for 10 minutes. Drain thoroughly.

2 Meanwhile, melt the butter in a saucepan and add the steak cubes and the kidney. Cook for 5 minutes, stirring, until the meat is sealed on all sides.

3 Add the shallots and cook for a further 3–4 minutes. Stir in the flour and cook for 1 minute. Gradually stir in the beef stock and beer and bring to a boil, stirring constantly.

4 Stir the potatoes into the meat mixture and season with salt and pepper. Reduce the heat until the mixture is simmering. Cover the saucepan and cook for 1 hour, stirring occasionally.

5 Spoon the beef mixture into the base of a pie dish. Roll the pastry on a lightly floured surface until ½ inch larger than the top of the dish.

6 Cut a strip of pastry long enough and wide enough to fit around the

edge of the dish. Brush the edge of the dish with beaten egg and press the pastry strip around the edge. Brush with egg and place the pastry lid on top. Crimp to seal the edge and brush with beaten egg.

7 Cook in a preheated oven at 450°F for 20–25 minutes, or until the pastry has risen and is golden. Serve hot, straight from the dish.

Raised Potato, Pork, & Apple Pie

Serves 8

INGREDIENTS

FILLING:

2 pounds waxy potatoes, sliced

2 tbsp butter

2 tbsp vegetable oil

1 pound lean pork, cubed

2 onions, sliced

4 garlic cloves, crushed

4 tbsp tomato paste

2 1/2 cups stock

2 tbsp chopped fresh sage

2 eating apples, peeled and sliced

salt and pepper

PASTRY:

6 cups all-purpose flour

pinch of salt

10 tsp butter

1/2 cup shortening

1 1/4 cups water

1 egg, beaten

1 tsp gelatin

1 Cook the potatoes in boiling water for 10 minutes. Drain and set aside. Heat the butter and oil in a flameproof casserole dish and fry the pork until browned, turning. Add the onion and garlic and cook for 5 minutes. Stir in the rest of the filling ingredients, except for the potatoes and the apples. Reduce the heat, cover, and simmer for 1 1/2 hours. Drain the stock from the casserole dish and reserve. Let the pork cool.

2 To make the pastry, sift the flour into a bowl. Add the salt and make a well in the center. Melt the butter and shortening in a pan with the water; then bring to a boil. Pour into the flour and mix to form a dough. Turn the dough out onto a floured surface and knead until smooth. Reserve a quarter of the dough and use the rest to line the base and sides of a large pie pan or deep 8-inch loose-bottom cake pan.

3 Layer the pork, potatoes, and the apple in the base. Roll out the reserved pastry to make a lid. Dampen the edges and place the lid on top, sealing well. Brush with egg and make a hole in the top. Cook in a preheated oven at 400°F for 30 minutes, then at 325°F for 45 minutes. Dissolve the gelatin in the reserved stock and pour into the hole in the lid as the pie cools. Cool and chill. Serve the pie with a salad.

Potato, Sausage, & Onion Pie

Serves 4

INGREDIENTS

2 large waxy potatoes, unpeeled and sliced	2 garlic cloves, crushed	4 tbsp water
2 tbsp butter	$^2/_3$ cup vegetable stock	$^3/_4$ cup grated sharp cheese
4 thick pork and herb sausages	$1^2/_3$ cup hard cider or apple juice	salt and pepper
1 leek, sliced	2 tbsp chopped fresh sage	
	2 tbsp cornstarch	

1 Cook the sliced potatoes in a saucepan of boiling water for 10 minutes. Drain and set aside.

2 Meanwhile, melt the butter in a skillet and cook the sausages for 8–10 minutes, turning them frequently so that they brown on all sides. Remove the sausages from the skillet and cut them into thick slices.

3 Add the leek, garlic, and sausage slices to the skillet and cook for 2–3 minutes.

4 Add the vegetable stock, cider or apple juice, and chopped sage. Season with salt and pepper. Blend the cornstarch with the water. Stir it into the skillet and bring to a boil, stirring until the sauce is thick and clear. Spoon the mixture into the base of a deep pie dish.

5 Layer the potato slices on top of the sausage mixture to cover it completely. Season with salt and pepper and sprinkle the grated cheese over the top.

6 Cook in a preheated oven at 375°F for 25–30 minutes, or until the potatoes are cooked and the cheese is golden brown. Serve the pie hot.

VARIATION

Other vegetables, such as broccoli or cauliflower, can be added to the filling. You can use white wine instead of the cider or apple juice, if you prefer.

Potato & Broccoli Pie

Serves 4

INGREDIENTS
---

1 pound waxy potatoes, cut into chunks	¼ cup all-purpose flour	3 tbsp walnuts
2 tbsp butter	⅔ cup vegetable stock	8 ounces ready-made puff pastry
1 tbsp vegetable oil	⅔ cup milk	milk, for glazing
6 ounces lean pork, cubed	¾ cup crumbled dolcelatte or other creamy blue cheese	salt and pepper
1 red onion, cut into 8	6 ounces broccoli florets	

1 Cook the potato chunks in a saucepan of boiling water for 5 minutes. Drain and set aside.

2 Meanwhile, heat the butter and oil in a heavy-based pan. Add the pork cubes and cook for 5 minutes, turning until browned.

3 Add the onion and cook for a further 2 minutes. Stir in the flour and cook for 1 minute, then gradually stir in the vegetable stock and milk. Bring to a boil, stirring constantly.

4 Add the cheese, broccoli, potatoes, and walnuts to the pan and simmer for 5 minutes. Season with salt and pepper to taste, then spoon the mixture into a pie dish.

5 On a floured surface, roll out the pastry until 1 inch larger than the dish. Cut a 1-inch wide strip from the pastry. Dampen the edge of the dish and place the pastry strip around it. Brush the strip with milk and put the pastry lid on top.

6 Seal and crimp the edges and make 2 small slits in the center of the lid. Brush with milk to glaze and cook in a preheated oven at 400°F for 25 minutes, or until the pastry has risen and is golden.

COOK'S TIP

Use a hard cheese such as sharp cheese instead of the dolcelatte, if you prefer.

Potato & Ham Pie

Serves 4

INGREDIENTS

8 ounces waxy potatoes, cubed
2 tbsp butter
8 shallots, halved
1 1/3 cups diced smoked ham
1/4 cup all-purpose flour
1 1/4 cups milk

2 tbsp wholegrain mustard
1 3/4 ounces pineapple, cubed

PASTRY:
2 cups all-purpose flour
1/2 tsp dry mustard

pinch of salt
pinch of cayenne pepper
2/3 cup butter
1 cup grated sharp cheese
2 egg yolks, plus extra for brushing
4–6 tsp cold water

1 Cook the potato cubes in a saucepan of boiling water for 10 minutes. Drain and set aside.

2 Meanwhile, melt the butter in a pan, add the shallots, and sauté for 3–4 minutes, until they begin to color.

3 Add the ham and cook for 2–3 minutes. Stir in the flour and cook for 1 minute. Gradually stir in the milk. Add the mustard and pineapple and bring to a boil, stirring. Season well

with salt and pepper and add the potatoes.

4 Sift the flour for the pastry into a bowl with the mustard, salt, and cayenne. Rub the butter into the mixture until it resembles bread crumbs. Add the cheese and mix to form a dough with the egg yolks and water.

5 On a floured surface, roll out half the pastry and line a shallow pie dish. Trim the edges.

6 Spoon the filling into the pie dish. Brush the edges of the pastry with water.

7 Roll out the remaining pastry to make a lid and press it on top of the pie, sealing the edges. Decorate the top of the pie with the pastry trimmings. Brush the pie with egg yolk and cook in a preheated oven at 375°F for 40–45 minutes, or until the pastry is cooked and golden.

Potato & Turkey Pie

Serves 4

INGREDIENTS

10½ ounces waxy potatoes, diced	¼ cup all-purpose flour	3 tbsp walnut pieces
2 tbsp butter	1¼ cups milk	2 tbsp chopped fresh parsley
1 tbsp vegetable oil	⅔ cup heavy cream	salt and pepper
10½ ounces lean turkey meat, cubed	2 celery stalks, sliced	8 ounces ready made pie dough
1 red onion, halved and sliced	⅓ cup dried apricots, chopped	beaten egg, for brushing

1 Cook the diced potatoes in a saucepan of boiling water for 10 minutes, until tender. Drain and set aside.

2 Meanwhile, heat the butter and oil in a saucepan. Add the turkey and cook for 5 minutes, turning until browned.

3 Add the sliced onion and cook for 2–3 minutes. Stir in the flour and cook for 1 minute. Gradually stir in the milk and the heavy cream. Bring to a boil, stirring, then reduce the heat until the mixture is simmering.

4 Stir in the celery, apricots, walnut pieces, parsley, and potatoes. Season well with salt and pepper. Spoon the potato and turkey mixture into the base of a 5-cup pie dish.

5 On a lightly floured surface, roll out the pie dough until it is 1 inch larger than the dish. Trim a 1-inch wide strip from the pie dough and place the strip on the dampened rim of the dish. Brush the strip with water and cover with the pie dough lid, pressing to seal the edges.

6 Brush the top of the pie with beaten egg to glaze and cook in a preheated oven at 400°F for 25–30 minutes, or until the pie dough is cooked and golden brown. Serve at once.

Potato Crisp Pie

Serves 4

INGREDIENTS

2 large waxy potatoes, sliced	$^1/_4$ cup all-purpose flour	1 cup unsweetened yogurt
$^1/_4$ cup butter	$^2/_3$ cup dry white wine	$^1/_3$ cup rolled oats, toasted
1 skinless chicken breast fillet, about 6 oz	$^2/_3$ cup heavy cream	
2 garlic cloves, crushed	8 ounces broccoli florets	
4 scallions, sliced	4 large tomatoes, sliced	
	3 ounces Swiss cheese, sliced	

1 Cook the potatoes in a saucepan of boiling water for 10 minutes. Drain and set aside.

2 Meanwhile, melt the butter in a skillet. Cut the chicken into strips and cook for 5 minutes, turning. Add the garlic and scallions and cook for a further 2 minutes.

3 Stir in the flour and cook for 1 minute. Gradually add the wine and cream. Bring to a boil, stirring, then reduce the heat until the sauce is simmering, then cook for 5 minutes.

4 Meanwhile, blanch the broccoli in boiling water, drain, and rinse in cold water.

5 Place half the potatoes in the base of a pie dish and top with half the tomatoes and half the broccoli.

6 Spoon the chicken sauce on top and repeat the layers in the same order once more.

7 Arrange the slices of Swiss cheese on top and spoon over the yogurt. Sprinkle with the oats and cook in a preheated oven at 400°F for 25 minutes, until the top is golden brown. Serve the pie immediately.

COOK'S TIP

Add chopped nuts, such as pine nuts, to the topping for extra crunch, if desired.

Potato, Leek, & Chicken Pie

Serves 4

INGREDIENTS

8 ounces waxy potatoes, cubed	2½ cups sliced crimini or	2 tbsp chopped fresh sage
¼ cup butter	champignon marron	8 ounces phyllo pastry, thawed
1 skinless chicken breast fillet,	mushrooms	if frozen
about 6 oz, cubed	¼ cup all-purpose flour	3 tbsp butter, melted
1 leek, sliced	1¼ cups milk	salt and pepper
	1 tbsp Dijon mustard	

1 Cook the potato cubes in a saucepan of boiling water for 5 minutes. Drain and set aside.

2 Melt the butter in a skillet and cook the chicken cubes for 5 minutes, or until browned all over.

3 Add the leek and mushrooms and cook for 3 minutes, stirring. Stir in the flour and cook for 1 minute. Gradually add the milk and bring to a boil. Add the mustard, chopped sage, and potato cubes, lower the heat, and simmer for 10 minutes.

4 Meanwhile, line a deep pie dish with half of the sheets of phyllo pastry. Spoon the sauce into the dish and cover with one sheet of pastry. Brush the pastry with butter and lay another sheet on top. Brush this sheet with butter.

5 Cut the remaining phyllo pastry into strips and fold them on to the top of the pie to create a ruffled effect. Brush the strips with the melted butter and cook in a preheated oven 350°F for 45 minutes, or until golden brown and crisp. Serve hot.

COOK'S TIP

If the top of the pie starts to brown too quickly, cover it with foil halfway through the cooking time, to allow the pastry base to cook through without the top burning.

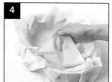

Layered Fish & Potato Pie

Serves 4

INGREDIENTS

2 pounds waxy potatoes, sliced
1/4 cup butter
1 red onion, halved and sliced
1/3 cup all-purpose flour

2 cups milk
2/3 cup heavy cream
8 ounces smoked haddock fillet, cubed
8 ounces cod fillet, cubed

1 red bell pepper, diced
4 1/2 ounces broccoli florets
2/3 cup grated Parmesan cheese
salt and pepper

1 Cook the sliced potatoes in a saucepan of boiling water for 10 minutes. Drain and set aside.

2 Meanwhile, melt the butter in a saucepan, add the onion and sauté gently for 3–4 minutes.

3 Add the flour and cook for 1 minute. Blend in the milk and cream and bring to a boil, stirring until thickened.

4 Arrange half the potato slices in the base of a shallow ovenproof dish.

5 Add the fish, diced bell pepper, and broccoli to the sauce and cook over a low heat for 10 minutes. Season with salt and pepper, then spoon the mixture on top of the potatoes in the dish.

6 Arrange the remaining potato slices in a layer on the fish mixture. Sprinkle the Parmesan cheese over the top.

7 Cook in a preheated oven at 350°F for 30 minutes, or until the potatoes are cooked and the top is golden.

COOK'S TIP

Choose your favorite combination of fish, adding salmon or various shellfish for special occasions.

Potato-Topped Smoked Fish Pie

Serves 4

INGREDIENTS

1 pound mealy potatoes, diced	$^1/_3$ cup all-purpose flour	few drops of Tabasco sauce
8 ounces rutabaga, diced	$1^1/_4$ cups milk	$4^1/_2$ ounces cooked peeled shrimp
$^1/_4$ cup butter	$^2/_3$ cup fish stock	2 tbsp chopped fresh parsley
1 leek, sliced	$^2/_3$ cup heavy cream	2 tbsp grated Parmesan cheese
$1^3/_4$ ounces baby corn cobs, sliced	1 pound smoked cod fillet, cut into	salt and pepper
1 zucchini, halved and sliced	cubes	

1 Cook the potatoes and rutabaga in a saucepan of boiling water for 20 minutes, until very tender. Drain and mash thoroughly until smooth.

2 Meanwhile, melt the butter in a saucepan, add the leeks, corn cobs, and zucchini, and sauté gently for 3–4 minutes, stirring.

3 Add the flour and cook for 1 minute. Gradually blend in the milk, fish stock, and cream and bring to a boil, stirring until the mixture begins to thicken.

4 Stir in the fish, reduce the heat, and cook for 5 minutes. Add the Tabasco sauce, shrimp, and half the parsley, and season. Spoon the mixture into the base of an ovenproof dish.

5 Mix the remaining parsley into the potato and rutabaga mixture, season, and spoon or pipe onto the fish mixture, covering it completely. Sprinkle with the grated cheese and cook in a preheated oven at 350°F for 20 minutes, until cooked through. Serve the pie immediately.

VARIATION

Add cooked mashed parsnip to the potato instead of the rutabaga.

Potato-Topped Lentil Bake

Serves 4

INGREDIENTS

TOPPING:

1$\frac{1}{2}$ pounds mealy potatoes, diced

2 tbsp butter

1 tbsp milk

$\frac{1}{2}$ cup chopped pecans

2 tbsp chopped fresh thyme

thyme sprigs, to garnish

FILLING:

1 cup red lentils

$\frac{1}{4}$ cup butter

1 leek, sliced

2 garlic cloves, crushed

1 celery stalk, chopped

4$\frac{1}{2}$ ounces broccoli florets

6 ounces smoked bean curd, cubed

2 tsp tomato paste

salt and pepper

1 To make the topping, cook the potatoes in a saucepan of boiling water for 10–15 minutes, or until tender. Drain well, add the butter and milk, and mash thoroughly. Stir in the pecans and chopped thyme and set aside.

2 Cook the lentils in boiling water for 20–30 minutes, or until tender. Drain and set aside.

3 Melt the butter in a pan, add the leek, garlic, celery, and broccoli.

Cook for 5 minutes, then add the bean curd cubes.

4 Stir the lentils into the bean curd and vegetable mixture together with the tomato paste. Season with salt and pepper to taste, then turn the mixture into the base of a shallow ovenproof dish.

5 Spoon the mashed potato on top of the lentil mixture to cover it completely.

6 Cook in a preheated oven at 400°F for 30–35 minutes, or until the topping is golden. Garnish with sprigs of fresh thyme and serve hot.

VARIATION

You can use any combination of vegetables in this dish. You can also add sliced cooked meat instead of the cubed bean curd for a non-vegetarian dish.

Potato & Eggplant Layer

Serves 4

INGREDIENTS

3 large waxy potatoes, sliced thinly	1 green bell pepper, diced	8 ounces bean curd, sliced
1 small eggplant, sliced thinly	1 tsp cumin seeds	1 cup fresh white bread crumbs
1 zucchini, sliced	7 ounce can chopped tomatoes	2 tbsp grated Parmesan cheese
2 tbsp vegetable oil	2 tbsp chopped fresh basil	salt and pepper
1 onion, diced	6 ounces Mozzarella cheese, sliced	fresh basil leaves, to garnish

1 Cook the sliced potatoes in a saucepan of boiling water for 5 minutes. Drain and set aside.

2 Lay the eggplant slices on a plate, sprinkle with salt, and leave for 20 minutes. Blanch the zucchini in boiling water for 2–3 minutes. Drain and set aside.

3 Meanwhile, heat 2 tbsp of the oil in a skillet, add the onion, and sauté gently for 2–3 minutes, until softened. Add the bell pepper, cumin seeds, basil,

and canned tomatoes. Season with salt and pepper. Reduce the heat and simmer for 30 minutes.

4 Rinse the eggplant slices and pat dry. Heat the remaining oil in a large skillet and fry the eggplant slices for 3–5 minutes, turning to brown both sides. Drain and set aside.

5 Arrange half the potato slices in the base of 4 small loose-bottomed flan pans. Cover with half the zucchini slices, half the eggplant slices, and half the

mozzarella slices. Lay the bean curd on top and spoon over the tomato sauce. Repeat the layers of potatoes, zucchini, eggplant, and mozzarella cheese.

6 Mix the bread crumbs and Parmesan cheese together and sprinkle over the top. Cook in a preheated oven at 375°F for 25–30 minutes, or until golden. Garnish with basil leaves and serve at once.

Sweet Potato Bread

Makes one loaf

INGREDIENTS

8 ounces sweet potatoes, diced	3 tbsp orange juice	1 tsp ground cinnamon
$^2/_3$ cup tepid water	$^1/_2$ cup semolina	grated rind of 1 orange
2 tbsp clear honey	2 cups white bread flour	1 cup butter
2 tbsp vegetable oil	1 packet active dry yeast	

1 Lightly grease a 1½-pound loaf pan.

2 Cook the sweet potatoes in a saucepan of boiling water for 10 minutes, or until soft. Drain well and mash until smooth.

3 Meanwhile, mix the water, honey, oil, and orange juice together in a large mixing bowl.

4 Add the mashed sweet potatoes, semolina, three-quarters of the flour, the yeast, cinnamon, and orange rind and mix well to form a dough. Let stand for about 10 minutes.

5 Cut the butter into small pieces and knead it into the dough with the remaining flour. Knead for about 5 minutes, until the dough is smooth.

6 Place the dough in the prepared loaf pan. Cover and leave in a warm place to rise for 1 hour or until doubled in size.

7 Cook the loaf in a preheated oven at 375°F for 45–60 minutes, or until the base sounds hollow when tapped with the knuckles. Serve the bread warm, cut into slices.

COOK'S TIP

If the baked loaf does not sound hollow on the base when it is tapped, remove it from the pan and return it to the oven for a few extra minutes, until thoroughly cooked.

Cheese & Potato Plait

Makes one loaf

INGREDIENTS

6 ounces mealy potatoes, diced	2 cups vegetable stock	1 cup grated Swiss cheese
2 packets active dry yeast	2 garlic cloves, crushed	1 tbsp vegetable oil
6 cups white bread flour	2 tbsp chopped fresh rosemary	1 tbsp salt

1 Lightly grease and flour a cookie sheet.

2 Cook the potatoes in a pan of boiling water for 10 minutes, or until soft. Drain and mash.

3 Transfer the mashed potatoes to a large mixing bowl, stir in the yeast, flour, and stock and mix to form a smooth dough.

4 Add the garlic, rosemary, and ¼ cup of the cheese and knead the dough for 5 minutes. Make a hollow in the dough, pour in the oil, and knead the dough.

5 Cover the dough and leave it to rise in a warm place for 1½ hours, or until doubled in size.

6 Knead the dough again and divide it into 3 equal portions. Roll each portion into a 14-inch sausage shape.

7 Pressing one end of each of the sausage shapes together, braid the dough and fold the remaining ends under.

8 Place the braid on the cookie sheet, cover, and leave to rise for 30 minutes.

9 Sprinkle the remaining cheese over the top of the braid and cook in a preheated oven at 375°F for 40 minutes, or until the base of the loaf sounds hollow when tapped. Cool slightly, then serve warm.

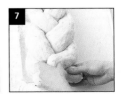

Potato & Nutmeg Scones

Makes 8

INGREDIENTS

8 ounces mealy potatoes, diced	½ tsp grated nutmeg	¼ cup heavy cream
1 cup all-purpose flour	⅓ cup golden raisins	2 tsp light brown sugar
1½ tsp baking powder	1 egg, beaten	

1 Line and grease a cookie sheet.

2 Cook the diced potatoes in a saucepan of boiling water for 10 minutes, or until soft. Drain well and mash the potatoes.

3 Transfer the mashed potatoes to a large mixing bowl and stir in the flour, baking powder, and nutmeg.

4 Stir in the golden raisins, egg, and cream and beat the mixture with a spoon until smooth.

5 Shape the mixture into 8 rounds ¾ inch thick and put on the cookie sheet.

6 Cook in a preheated oven at 400°F for about 15 minutes, or until the scones have risen and are golden. Sprinkle the scones with sugar and serve warm and spread with butter.

COOK'S TIP

For extra convenience, make a batch of scones in advance and open-freeze them. Thaw thoroughly and warm in a moderate oven when ready to serve.

VARIATION

This recipe may be used to make one large scone "cake" instead of the 8 small scones, if desired.

Potato Muffins

Serves 12

| INGREDIENTS |

6 ounces mealy potatoes, diced
3/4 cup self-rising flour

2 tbsp light brown sugar
1 tsp baking powder

3/4 cup raisins
4 eggs, separated

1 Lightly grease and flour 12 muffin pans.

2 Cook the diced potatoes in a saucepan of boiling water for 10 minutes, until cooked. Drain well and mash until smooth.

3 Transfer the mashed potatoes to a mixing bowl and add the flour, sugar, baking powder, raisins, and egg yolks. Stir well to mix thoroughly.

4 In a clean bowl, beat the egg whites until standing in peaks. Using a metal spoon, gently fold them into the potato mixture until fully incorporated.

5 Divide the mixture between the prepared pans.

6 Cook in a preheated oven at 400°F for 10 minutes. Reduce the oven temperature to 325°F and cook the muffins for 7–10 minutes, or until risen.

7 Remove the muffins from the pans and serve warm.

COOK'S TIP

Instead of spreading the muffins with plain butter, serve them with cinnamon butter made by blending ½ cup butter with a large pinch of ground cinnamon.

VARIATION

Other flavorings, such as cinnamon or nutmeg, can be added to the mixture, if desired.

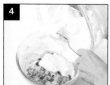

Fruity Potato Cake

Makes one cake

INGREDIENTS

1½ pounds sweet potatoes, diced	3 tbsp milk	9 cups chopped dried fruits, such as
1 tbsp butter, melted	1 tbsp lemon juice	apple, pear, or mango
¾ ounces raw brown crystal sugar	grated rind of 1 lemon	2 tsp baking powder
3 eggs	1 tsp caraway seeds	

1 Lightly grease a 7-inch square cake pan.

2 Cook the sweet potatoes in boiling water for 10 minutes, or until soft. Drain and mash the sweet potatoes until smooth.

3 Transfer the mashed sweet potatoes to a mixing bowl while still hot and add the butter and sugar, mixing to dissolve.

4 Beat in the eggs, lemon juice and rind, caraway seeds, and chopped dried fruit. Add the baking powder and mix well.

5 Pour the mixture into the prepared cake pan.

6 Cook in a preheated oven at 325°F for 1–1¼ hours or until cooked through. Remove the cake from the pan and transfer to a wire rack to cool. Cut into thick slices to serve.

COOK'S TIP

This cake is ideal as a special occasion dessert. It can be made in advance and frozen until required. Wrap the cake in plastic wrap and freeze. Thaw at room temperature for 24 hours and warm through in a moderate oven before serving.

Pumpkin Loaf

Serves 6-8

INGREDIENTS

3 1/2 cups chopped pumpkin flesh
1/2 cup butter, softened
3/4 cup superfine sugar
2 eggs, beaten
2 cups all-purpose flour, sifted

1 1/2 tsp baking powder
1/2 tsp salt

1 tsp ground apple pie spice
1/2 cup pumpkin seeds

1 Grease a 2-pound loaf pan with oil.

2 Wrap the pumpkin pieces in buttered foil. Cook in a preheated oven at 400°F for about 30–40 minutes, until they are cooked through and tender.

3 Let the pumpkin cool completely before mashing well to make a thick purée.

4 In a bowl, cream the butter and sugar together until light and fluffy. Add the eggs, a little at a time.

5 Stir in the pumpkin purée. Fold in the flour, baking powder, salt, and apple pie spice.

6 Fold the pumpkin seeds through the mixture. Spoon the mixture into the prepared loaf pan.

7 Bake in a preheated oven at 325°F for about 1 1/4–1 1/2 hours, or until a toothpick inserted into the center of the loaf comes out clean.

8 Let the loaf cool and serve buttered, if desired.

COOK'S TIP

To ensure that the pumpkin purée is dry, place it in a saucepan over a medium heat for a few minutes, stirring frequently, until it is thick.

Chili Corn Bread

Makes 12 bars

INGREDIENTS

1 cup all-purpose flour
1 cup cornmeal
1 tbsp baking powder
1/2 tsp salt

1 green chili, seeded and
  finely chopped
5 scallions, finely chopped
2 eggs
generous 1/2 cup sour cream

1/2 cup sunflower oil

1 Grease an 8-inch square cake pan and line the base with baking parchment.

2 In a large bowl, mix the flour, cornmeal, baking powder, and salt together.

3 Add the finely chopped green chili, and the scallions to the dry ingredients and mix until well combined.

4 In a large mixing bowl, beat the eggs, together with the sour cream and sunflower oil. Pour the mixture into the bowl of dry ingredients. Mix all of the ingredients together until well incorporated.

5 Pour the mixture into the prepared cake pan and level the surface with the back of a spoon.

6 Bake in a preheated oven at 400°F for 20–25 minutes, or until the loaf has risen and is lightly browned.

7 Let the bread cool slightly before turning out of the pan. Cut the bread into bars or squares to serve.

VARIATION

Add 3/4 cup of corn kernels to the mixture in step 3, if you prefer.

Cheese & Potato Bread

Serves 4

INGREDIENTS

2 cups all-purpose flour	1/2 tsp mustard powder	2 cups cooked, mashed potatoes
1 tsp salt	2 tsp baking powder	3/4 cup water
	1 cup grated Red Leicester cheese	1 tbsp oil

1 Lightly grease a cookie sheet.

2 Sift the flour, salt, mustard powder, and baking powder into a mixing bowl.

3 Reserve 2 tbsp of the grated cheese and stir the rest into the bowl with the mashed potatoes. Mix until well combined.

4 Pour in the water and the oil, and stir all the ingredients together (the mixture will be wet at this stage). Mix them all to make a soft dough.

5 Turn out the dough onto a floured surface and shape it into an 8-inch round loaf.

6 Place the loaf on the cookie sheet and mark it into 4 portions with a knife, without cutting through. Sprinkle with the reserved cheese.

7 Bake the loaf in a preheated oven at 425°F for approximately 25–30 minutes.

8 Transfer the bread to a wire rack and let cool. This bread should be served as fresh as possible.

COOK'S TIP

You can use instant potato mix for this bread, if you prefer.

VARIATION

Add 1/3 cup chopped ham to the mixture in step 3, if you prefer.

Mini Focaccia

Makes 4

INGREDIENTS

3 cups strong white flour
1/2 tsp salt
1 packet active dry yeast
2 tbsp olive oil

1 1/8 cups lukewarm water
1 cup pitted green or black
  olives, halved

TOPPING:
2 red onions, sliced
2 tbsp olive oil
1 tsp sea salt
1 tbsp thyme leaves

1 Lightly oil several cookie sheets. Sift the flour and salt into a large mixing bowl, then stir in the yeast. Pour in the olive oil and water and mix everything together to form a dough.

2 Turn the dough out onto a lightly floured surface and knead it for 10 minutes.

3 Place the dough in a greased bowl, cover, and leave in a warm place for about 1–1 1/2 hours, until it has doubled in size. Punch down the dough by kneading it again for 1–2 minutes.

4 Knead half of the olives into the dough. Divide the dough into quarters and then shape the quarters into rounds. Place them on the cookie sheets and push your fingers into the dough to achieve a dimpled effect.

5 To make the topping, sprinkle the red onions and remaining olives over the rounds. Drizzle the olive oil over the top and sprinkle with the sea salt and thyme. Cover and let the dough rise again for 30 minutes.

6 Bake in a preheated oven at 375°F for 20–25 minutes, or until the focaccia are well cooked and golden. Transfer to a wire rack and cool before serving.

Sun-Dried Tomato Rolls

Makes 8

INGREDIENTS

2 cups strong white
    bread flour
	$^1/_3$ cup butter, melted and
	    cooled slightly
		1 cup drained and finely
		    chopped sun-dried tomatoes

$^1/_2$ tsp salt	3 tbsp milk, warmed	milk, for brushing
1 packet active dry yeast	2 eggs, beaten	

1 Lightly grease a cookie sheet.

2 Sift the flour and salt into a large mixing bowl. Stir in the yeast, then pour in the butter, milk, and eggs. Mix together to form a dough.

3 Turn the dough onto a lightly floured surface and knead for about 5 minutes (alternatively, use an electric mixer with a dough hook).

4 Place the dough in a greased bowl, cover, and let rise in a warm place for 1–1½ hours, until the dough has doubled in size. Punch down the dough by kneading it lightly for a few minutes.

5 Knead the sun-dried tomatoes into the dough, sprinkling the counter with extra flour as the tomatoes are quite oily.

6 Divide the dough into 8 balls and place them on the prepared cookie sheet. Cover and let rise for about 30 minutes, until the rolls have doubled in size.

7 Lightly brush the rolls with a little milk and bake in a preheated oven, at 450°F for 10–15 minutes, until the rolls are golden brown.

8 Transfer the rolls to a wire rack and cool slightly before serving.

Cheese & Onion Pies

Makes 4

INGREDIENTS

3 tbsp vegetable oil
4 onions, peeled and finely sliced
4 garlic cloves, crushed
4 tbsp finely chopped fresh
    parsley

¾ cup grated sharp cheese
salt and pepper

PIE DOUGH:
1½ cups all-purpose flour
½ tsp salt
⅓ cup butter, cut into
    small pieces
3–4 tbsp water

1 Heat the oil in a skillet. Add the onions and garlic and sauté for 10–15 minutes, or until the onions are soft. Remove the pan from the heat and stir in the parsley and cheese, and season.

2 To make the pie dough, sift the flour and salt into a mixing bowl and rub in the butter with your fingertips until the mixture resembles breadcrumbs. Stir in the water and mix to a smooth dough.

3 On a lightly floured surface, roll out the dough and divide it into 8 portions.

4 Roll out each portion to a 4-inch round and use half of the rounds to line 4 individual tart pans.

5 Fill each round with a quarter of the onion mixture. Cover with the remaining 4 pie dough rounds. Make a slit in the top of each pie with the point of a knife and seal the edges with the back of a teaspoon.

6 Bake in a preheated oven at 425°F for about 20 minutes. The pies can be served hot or cold.

COOK'S TIP

You can prepare the onion filling in advance and store it in the refrigerator.

Red Onion Tart Tatin

Serves 4

INGREDIENTS

4 tbsp butter

2 tbsp sugar

1 pound 2 ounces red onions,
    peeled and quartered

3 tbsp red wine vinegar

2 tbsp fresh thyme leaves

8 ounces fresh ready-made puff
    pastry

salt and pepper

1 Place the butter and sugar in a 9-inch ovenproof skillet and cook over a medium heat until the butter has melted.

2 Add the red onion quarters and sweat them over a low heat for 10–15 minutes, until golden, stirring occasionally.

3 Add the red wine vinegar and fresh thyme leaves to the skillet. Season with salt and pepper to taste, then simmer over a medium heat until the liquid has reduced and the red onion pieces are coated in the buttery sauce.

4 On a lightly floured kitchen counter, roll out the pastry to a round slightly larger than the skillet.

5 Place the dough over the onion mixture and press down, tucking in the edges to seal the pie dough.

6 Bake in a preheated oven at 350°F for about 20–25 minutes. Let the tart stand for 10 minutes.

7 To turn out, place a serving plate over the skillet and carefully invert them both so that the dough crust becomes the base of the tart. Serve the tart warm.

VARIATION

Replace the red onions with shallots, leaving them whole, if you prefer.

Fresh Tomato Tarts

Serves 6

INGREDIENTS

9 ounces fresh ready-made puff
pastry
1 egg, beaten
2 tbsp pesto

6 plum tomatoes, sliced
salt and pepper

fresh thyme leaves, to garnish
(optional)

1 On a lightly floured kitchen counter, roll out the pastry dough to a rectangle measuring 12 × 10 inches.

2 Cut the rectangle in half and divide each half into 3 pieces to make 6 even-size rectangles. Chill in the refrigerator for 20 minutes.

3 Lightly score the edges of the dough rectangles and brush with the beaten egg.

4 Spread the pesto over the rectangles, dividing it equally between them, leaving a 1-inch border on each one.

5 Arrange the tomato slices in a line along the center of each rectangle on top of the pesto.

6 Season well with salt and pepper to taste and lightly sprinkle with fresh thyme leaves, if using.

7 Bake in a preheated oven at 400°F for 15–20 minutes, until well risen and a golden brown color.

8 Transfer the tomato tarts to warm serving plates straight from the oven and serve while they are still piping hot.

VARIATION

Instead of making individual tarts, roll the dough out to form 1 large rectangle. Spoon the pesto on and arrange the tomatoes over the top.

Provençal Tart

Serves 6-8

INGREDIENTS

9 ounces ready-made fresh puff
pastry
3 tbsp olive oil
2 red bell peppers, seeded and
diced

2 green bell peppers, seeded
and diced
²/₃ cup heavy cream

1 egg
2 zucchini, sliced
salt and pepper

1 Roll out the pastry on a lightly floured surface and line an 8-inch loose-bottomed quiche pan. Chill in the refrigerator for 20 minutes.

2 Meanwhile, heat 2 tbsp of the olive oil in a skillet and sauté the bell peppers for about 8 minutes, until softened, stirring frequently.

3 Whisk the heavy cream and egg together in a large mixing bowl and season to taste with salt and pepper. Stir in the cooked mixed bell peppers.

4 Heat the remaining oil in a pan and fry the zucchini slices for 4-5 minutes, until they are lightly browned.

5 Carefully pour the egg and bell pepper mixture into the pie shell.

6 Arrange the zucchini slices in a pattern around the edge of the tart.

7 Bake in a preheated oven at 350°F for 35-40 minutes, or until just set and golden brown. Serve hot or cold.

COOK'S TIP

This recipe could be used to make 6 individual tarts—use 6 × 4 inch pans and bake them for 20 minutes.

Celery & Onion Pies

Makes 12

INGREDIENTS

PIE DOUGH:
1 cup all-purpose flour
$\frac{1}{2}$ tsp salt
2 tbsp butter, cut into
    small pieces

$\frac{1}{4}$ cup grated sharp cheese
3–4 tbsp water

FILLING:
4 tbsp butter
1 cup finely chopped celery
2 garlic cloves, crushed
1 small onion, finely chopped

1 tbsp all-purpose flour
$\frac{1}{4}$ cup milk
salt
pinch of cayenne pepper

1 To make the filling, melt the butter, add the celery, garlic, and onion and sauté for 5 minutes, or until softened.

2 Remove from the heat and stir in the flour, then the milk. Heat gently until the mixture is thick, stirring frequently. Season with salt and cayenne pepper. Let cool.

3 To make the pastry, sift together the flour and salt into a mixing bowl and rub in the butter with your fingertips. Stir the cheese into the mixture, together with the cold water, and mix to form a dough.

4 Roll out three-quarters of the dough. Using a 2½-inch cookie cutter, cut out 12 rounds. Line a muffin pan with the rounds.

5 Divide the filling between the pie dough rounds. Roll out the remaining dough and, using a 2-inch cutter, cut out 12 rounds. Place the smaller rounds on top of the pie filling and seal well. Make a slit in each pie and chill for 30 minutes.

6 Bake in a preheated oven at 425°F for 15–20 minutes. Cool in the pan for about 10 minutes before turning out. Serve warm.

Asparagus & Goat Cheese Tart

Serves 6

INGREDIENTS

9 ounces fresh ready-made
   pie dough
9 ounces asparagus
1 tbsp vegetable oil
1 red onion, finely chopped

1/4 cup chopped hazelnuts
1 3/4 cups ounces goat cheese
2 eggs, beaten

4 tbsp light cream
salt and pepper

1 On a lightly floured surface, roll out the pie dough and line a 10-inch loose-bottomed quiche pan. Prick the base of the pie dough with a fork and chill in the refrigerator for about 30 minutes.

2 Line the pie shell with foil and dried beans and bake blind in a preheated oven at 375°F for about 15 minutes.

3 Remove the foil and beans from the pie shell, return the pie shell

to the oven and cook it for a further 15 minutes.

4 Cook the asparagus in boiling water for 2–3 minutes, drain, and cut into bite-size pieces.

5 Heat the oil in a small skillet and sauté the onion until soft. Spoon the asparagus, onion, and chopped hazelnuts into the prepared pie shell.

6 Beat together the cheese, eggs, and cream until smooth, or process in a blender until smooth.

Season well with salt and pepper, then pour the mixture over the asparagus, onion, and hazelnuts.

7 Bake in the oven for 15–20 minutes, or until the cheese filling is just set. Serve warm or cold.

VARIATION

Omit the hazelnuts and sprinkle Parmesan cheese over the top of the tart just before cooking in the oven, if you prefer.

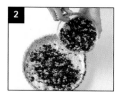

Onion Tart

Serves 6

INGREDIENTS
---

9 ounces fresh ready-made
   shortcrust pie dough
3 tbsp butter
1/2 cup diced bacon

1 pound 9 ounces onions, peeled
   and sliced thinly
2 eggs, beaten
2/3 cup grated Parmesan cheese
1 tsp dried sage

salt and pepper

---

1 Roll out the pie dough on a lightly floured counter and line a 10-inch loose-bottomed quiche pan.

2 Prick the base of the pie dough all over with a fork and chill for 30 minutes.

3 Heat the butter in a saucepan, add the diced bacon and sliced onions, and sweat them over a low heat for about 25 minutes, or until tender. If the onion slices start to turn brown, add a tablespoon of water to the saucepan.

4 Add the beaten eggs to the onion mixture and stir in the cheese, sage, and salt and pepper to taste. Mix until well combined.

5 Carefully spoon the onion mixture into the prepared pie shell, spreading the mixture to the edges of the shell.

6 Bake in a preheated oven at 350°F for 20–30 minutes, or until the tart has just set.

7 Leave the tart to cool slightly in the pan, then serve the onion tart warm or cold. Cut the tart into slices to serve.

VARIATION

For a vegetarian version, replace the bacon with the same quantity of chopped mushrooms.

Pissaladière

Serves 8

INGREDIENTS

4 tbsp olive oil	2 tbsp red wine vinegar	TOPPING:
1 pound 9 ounces red onions, thinly sliced	12 ounces fresh ready-made puff pastry	2 1³/₄ ounce cans anchovy fillets
2 garlic cloves, crushed	salt and pepper	12 pitted green olives
2 tsp superfine sugar		1 tsp dried marjoram

1 Lightly grease a jelly roll pan with butter. Heat the olive oil in a large saucepan. Add the onions and garlic and cook over a very low heat for about 30 minutes, stirring occasionally, until tender.

2 Add the sugar and vinegar to the pan and season with plenty of salt and pepper to taste. Stir until well combined.

3 On a lightly floured surface, roll out the pastry dough to a rectangle about 13 × 9 inches. Place the dough rectangle onto the prepared jelly roll pan, pushing the dough well into the corners of the pan.

4 Spread the onion mixture over the dough.

5 Top with the anchovy fillets and green olives, then sprinkle with the marjoram.

6 Bake in a preheated oven at 425°F for about 20–25 minutes, until the pissaladière is a light golden color. Serve piping hot, straight from the oven.

VARIATION

Cut the pissaladière into squares or triangles for easy finger food at a party or barbecue.

Mini Cheese & Onion Tarts

Serves 12

INGREDIENTS

PIE DOUGH:	FILLING:	salt
1 cup all-purpose flour	1 egg, beaten	cayenne pepper
$\frac{1}{4}$ tsp salt	generous $\frac{1}{3}$ cup light cream	
$\frac{1}{3}$ cup butter, cut into small pieces	$\frac{1}{2}$ cup grated Red Leicester cheese,	
1–2 tbsp water	3 scallions, finely chopped	

1 To make the pie dough, sift the flour and salt into a mixing bowl. Rub in the butter with your fingers until well combined and the mixture resembles fine breadcrumbs. Gradually stir in the water, adding little by little, and mix to form a smooth dough.

2 Roll out the pie dough on a lightly floured kitchen surface. Using a 3-inch cookie cutter, stamp out 12 rounds from the dough and line a muffin pan.

3 To make the filling, whisk together the beaten egg, light cream, grated Red Leicester cheese, and chopped scallions. Season with salt and cayenne.

4 Pour the filling mixture into the pie shells and bake in a preheated oven at 350°F for about 20–25 minutes, or until the filling is just set.

5 Serve the mini tarts warm or cold.

VARIATION

Top each mini tart with slices of fresh tomato before baking, if you prefer.

COOK'S TIP

If you use 6 ounces of ready-made pie dough instead of making it yourself, these tarts can be made in minutes.

Curry Turnovers

Serves 4

INGREDIENTS

1¾ cups plain whole-wheat flour

⅓ cup vegan margarine, cut into small pieces

4 tbsp water

2 tbsp oil

1¼ cups diced root vegetables (potatoes, carrots, and parsnips)

1 small onion, chopped

2 garlic cloves, finely chopped

½ tsp curry powder

½ tsp ground turmeric

½ tsp ground cumin

½ tsp wholegrain mustard

5 tbsp stock

soy milk, to glaze

1 Place the flour in a mixing bowl and rub in the vegan margarine with your fingertips until the mixture resembles breadcrumbs. Stir in the water and bring together to form a soft dough. Wrap and chill in the refrigerator for 30 minutes.

2 To make the filling, heat the oil in a large saucepan. Add the diced root vegetables, chopped onion, and garlic. Sauté for 2 minutes, then stir in all of the spices, turning the vegetables to coat them with the spices. Cook for a further 1 minute.

3 Add the stock to the pan and bring to a boil. Cover and simmer for about 20 minutes, stirring occasionally, until the vegetables are tender and the liquid has been absorbed. Let cool.

4 Divide the pie dough into 4 portions. Roll each portion into a 6-inch round. Place the filling equally on one half of each round.

5 Brush the edges of each round with soy milk, then fold over and press the edges together to seal. Place on a cookie sheet. Bake in a preheated oven at 400°F for 25-30 minutes, until the pastry is a light golden brown color.

Brazil Nut & Mushroom Pie

Serves 4-6

INGREDIENTS

PIE DOUGH:
1¾ cups plain whole-wheat
    flour
⅓ cup vegan margarine, cut into
    small pieces
4 tbsp water
soy milk, to glaze

FILLING:
2 tbsp vegan margarine
1 onion, chopped
1 garlic clove, finely chopped
2 cups sliced button mushrooms
1 tbsp all-purpose flour
⅔ cup vegetable stock
1 tbsp tomato paste
1½ cups chopped Brazil nuts

1⅓ cups fresh whole-wheat
    breadcrumbs
2 tbsp chopped fresh parsley
½ tsp pepper

1 To make the pie dough, rub the margarine into the flour until it resembles fine breadcrumbs. Stir in the water and bring together to form a dough. Wrap and chill for 30 minutes.

2 Melt the margarine for the filling in a skillet, add the onion, garlic, and mushrooms and sauté for 5 minutes, until softened. Add the flour and cook for

1 minute, stirring. Gradually add the stock, stirring until the sauce is smooth and beginning to thicken. Stir in the tomato paste, Brazil nuts, breadcrumbs, parsley, and pepper. Cool slightly.

3 On a lightly floured surface, roll out two-thirds of the pie dough and use to line an 8-inch loose-bottomed quiche pan or pie dish. Spread the filling in

the pie shell. Brush the edges of the pie dough with soy milk. Roll out the remaining pie dough to fit the top of the pie. Seal the edges, make a slit in the top of the pie dough, and brush with soy milk.

4 Bake in a preheated oven at 400°F for 30–40 minutes, until golden brown.

Lentil & Red Bell Pepper Flan

Serves 6-8

INGREDIENTS

PIE DOUGH:
1³/₄ cups plain whole-wheat
   flour
¹/₃ cup vegan margarine, cut into
   small pieces
4 tbsp water

FILLING:
³/₄ cup red lentils, rinsed
1¹/₄ cups vegetable stock
1 tbsp vegan margarine
1 onion, chopped
2 red bell peppers, cored, seeded,
   and diced
1 tsp yeast extract

1 tbsp tomato paste
3 tbsp chopped fresh parsley
pepper

1 To make the pie dough, place the flour in a mixing bowl and rub in the vegan margarine with your fingertips until the mixture resembles fine breadcrumbs. Stir in the water and bring together to form a dough. Wrap and chill in the refrigerator for 30 minutes.

2 Meanwhile, make the filling. Put the lentils in a saucepan with the stock, bring to a boil, and then simmer for 10 minutes, until the lentils are tender and can be mashed to a purée.

3 Melt the margarine in a small pan, add the chopped onion and diced red bell peppers and sauté until just soft.

4 Add the lentil purée, yeast extract, tomato paste, and parsley. Season with pepper. Mix until well combined.

5 On a lightly floured kitchen counter, roll out the dough and line a 10-inch loose-bottomed quiche pan. Prick the base of the pie dough with a fork and spoon the lentil purée mixture into the pie shell.

6 Bake in a preheated oven at 400°F for 30 minutes, until the filling is firm.

Index